Everyday People

Everyday People

Profiles from
the Garden State

AL SULLIVAN

Rutgers University Press
New Brunswick, New Jersey, and London

Library of Congress Cataloging-in-Publication data

Sullivan, Al, 1951–
    Everyday people : profiles from the Garden State / Al Sullivan.
        p.   cm.
    Includes bibliographical references and index.
    ISBN 0-8135-2950-6 (pbk. : alk. paper)
    1. New Jersey—Biography.   I. Title.

CT249.S85 2001
920.0749—dc21   00-45749

British Cataloging-in-Publication data for this book is available from the British Library.

Stories and photographs reprinted by permission of the Hudson Reporter Associates and Worrall Community Newspapers, Inc.

Manufactured in the United States of America

To Michael Richardson, the editor who made it all work

Contents

List of Illustrations — *xi*
Preface — *xiii*
Acknowledgments — *xvii*

PART ONE **Memories of War and Peace**

Helping Our Own — 3
Walking in the Name of Jesus — 7
They Call Him Mr. Sam — 10
A Man of Spirit — 12
One Hundred and Four Years Young — 16
Not Just a Caregiver — 19
Ten Velde's World — 24
An Amazing Moment in Time — 26
A Letter from the Past — 29
A Big Part of Secaucus — 31
What a Lucky Man — 34
A Model World — 36
Toy Soldiers March On — 40
High-Seas Romance — 43
A Taste of Ireland — 47
A Brief Stopover — 49
Call It Kismet — 51
Sweeping Hudson's Chimneys — 53
Haunted No More — 56
A Sense of Style — 60
Listen to the Music — 65

PART TWO   The Nature of Things

On Call   —   71
Protecting the Protectors   —   74
Saying Good-Bye   —   76
Three Faces of a Cop   —   78
A Sense of Integrity   —   80
Facing the Outside   —   84
Down and Out in Hoboken   —   88
Hero in the Emergency Room   —   91
Mistress of Modern Gothic   —   93
Images of Lisa   —   96
The Seduction of Howard Stern   —   101
A Summit of Hope   —   105
Buzzing about Bees   —   108
In Search of Skunk   —   110
A Little Tender, Loving Care   —   114
See Ya Later, Alligator   —   117
Beeping   —   121
One for the Record Books   —   123
A Natural Haven in the Heart of Bloomfield   —   125
The Hackensack Gets a Keeper   —   128
An Organized Man   —   132
From Out of Obscurity   —   137
A Matter Bigger Than Books   —   142
Not a Taxing Job   —   147
The Human Side of Legislation   —   151

PART THREE   The Arts and Sciences

Blast from the Past   —   157
Stretching Out the Walls of Education   —   158
Rocket Man   —   162
More Than Numbers   —   164
A Twist of Fate   —   167
Moving On   —   170
A Global Perspective   —   176
The End of a Double Life   —   180
Metaphors of Life   —   183

Building Community   —   187

A Walk through Hell   —   191

A Breakfast to Remember   —   194

Shooting for the Moon   —   197

Granting a Wish   —   200

A Drive through Secaucus's Past   —   203

Not Just Luck   —   207

Behind the Veil   —   209

A Dual Identity   —   212

All the World Loves Ollie   —   214

A Familiar Setting   —   218

Chapter and Verse   —   221

Poetry in the Woods   —   225

Final Chapter   —   229

By the Time I Got to Woodstock . . .   —   233

Index   —   239

Illustrations

Social worker Erin Jones — 20
Louis Markisello — 27
Harmon Kaplan — 37
Bill Miller — 44
Ron Simpson and his son, Ron Jr. — 54
The Reverend Mark Lewis — 61
Diane Rolnick — 97
Al McClure — 111
Dr. Richard Brady — 115
Bill Knox — 118
Richard Koeppen — 124
Captain Bill Sheehan — 129
Former Secaucus mayor Paul Amico — 133
Fran Holland — 138
Margaret Grazioli — 143
Jim Terhune — 148
Anthony Impreveduto — 152
William Koenig — 159
Michael Gehm — 168
Anthony D'Elia — 171
Dennis Pope — 181
Doug Depice — 184
Jon Van Kouwenhoven — 188
Anthony Iacono and his son, Paul — 201
Former mayor Anthony Just — 204
Oliver Garfunkel — 215
Joel Lewis — 222
Danny Shot, Laura Boss, and Hershel Silverman — 226
BlackWater Books — 230
Woodstock Monument — 234

Preface

Herb Jackson, a by-the-book journalist who eventually became a journalism professor at William Paterson University, was one of those men young students suffered through in order to get their degrees, his wisdom largely lost until later in their careers. He was a tough man, whose respect for the journalism profession made him want to weed out inept journalists early so that the rest of us could gain something from his experience.

Students had numerous nasty names for him because he stressed fundamentals. He was not against innovation, but he hated when students used technology to avoid learning basic skills. When the school installed computers in his classrooms for the first time in the 1980s, he ordered the technicians to remove the spell-check option from the word processing—then insisted that students compose their work in class.

"A journalist needs to know how to spell," he said, and though he privately admitted the virtues of a dictionary, he did not allow that in the class either.

In imparting his wisdom, Jackson seemed to sense which students had potential, and sometimes he gave them something extra, taking them aside to give them advice. As part of his lessons, he constantly boasted about writers who had worked their way to success and advised each student to follow their lead.

I took Jackson's classes very late in both our lives, after I had already started working as a reporter. I had heard rumor of his lessons while I was an undergraduate, and he had heard rumor of me—the somewhat radical undergraduate who had edited the college literary magazine and, disapproving of the college newspaper, had joined a faction of students to start our own. He had even heard of my off-campus efforts to bring an underground newspaper back to northern New Jersey after I had left school.

His eyes glinted a little when I walked into his class again in 1989. Other students claimed he got this look when he was faced with a particularly difficult challenge and intended to give someone hell.

I was in my late thirties and suddenly thrust into what might be called "the legitimate press." Having been raised on the *East Village Other* and the *Los Angeles Free Press,* I knew I needed to learn the rules, and I sought out the one man I thought could give me them.

If I was a challenge to Jackson, it was not in the way he expected. My hunger for his knowledge was so great that I rapidly drew his attention and his confidence, and later, for a brief time, I became a receptacle for his wisdom.

Of all these wisdoms, I remember one best.

"Find out what makes people tick and put that in your newspaper," Jackson told me.

It is a lesson that has guided my writing ever since, and one that is central to the pieces that appear in this book. Over the next decade, I would write more than three thousand stories, covering everything from school board meetings to the opening of a new beer distributor, and though I did not always live up to this expectation, in most cases I tried, and I am still trying. It is an ongoing process.

Although many formulas exist for writing profiles, few teach students how to search for a person's soul, the one unique element in a character that makes that person an individual, or how this element makes the person larger than life.

In this respect, journalism is like detective work, struggling through clues to a deeper meaning. It is an eternal struggle, with some subjects more willing to give up their secrets than others—and the story that later finds its way to paper becomes the testimony to a journalist's skills.

In this struggle, I have failed as often as I have succeeded, and yet sorting through a decade's worth of work, I came up with many more stories than I've had room to print here, and many more still that partially capture the essence of the person I interviewed. For me, however, this was not a matter of literature but a day-to-day job, subject to the grind of daily and weekly deadlines and the unnerving eye of sometimes disapproving editors, who did not like my deviations from the traditional 5W leads of standard journalism: who, what, where, when, and why. Some of my editors, however, glimpsed a bit of what I was trying to do and helped shape my work. This was particularly true for Michael Richardson, a longtime editor at The Hudson Reporter Associates, and Anthony Buccino at the Worrall Community Newspapers—although Michael, a graduate of the Columbia School of Journalism, would sometimes shake his head and firmly tell me when my copy didn't work.

This book would not exist if not for Dorothy Alexander, a friend and colleague with whom I briefly worked at the *Paterson News* in the early 1980s. She read through a number of the printed profiles and said they were more than just common pieces of journalism. I didn't believe her and still don't. What appears here is the stuff journalism should be built on, the search for deeper meaning in the people and situations we encounter in our reporting.

Perhaps, working on a weekly newspaper, I was granted freedoms most journalists don't have, space to create larger-than-life works, taking snapshots of people's lives that somehow symbolize the community in which they live. The Reporter chain and the Worrall group of newspapers were particularly generous in this regard, indulging me in my insistence upon blurring the boundary between what is normally considered "soft" and "hard" news.

News, to me, means people, what they do, what they say, what they think, how they are affected. In these pieces and in the many less timely pieces of the week-to-week grind, I have tried to reshape the 5Ws lead to reflect this.

Andy Newman—a former colleague from the *Reporter*—seemed to think I had what Jackson called "a nose for news."

"It is something you either have or you don't, and you have it," Dorothy Alexander agreed.

It is not me. It is the people I meet and interview and write about. Each one broadcasts his or her own story, and I have simply managed to tune into the right frequency at the right time to pick up their signal. Perhaps it is only a matter of allowing these people to open up and then, picking through the threads of their talk, find the ones that define their fundamental natures. I hardly think of these things at the time. Each story—to me—is a jigsaw puzzle, and I am so busy grabbing up the pieces, looking how this shape fits into that piece, that I hardly think in universal terms. Later, when the pieces fit together, when a person's personality somehow manages to peek through the print, I see the pattern.

Because these are snapshots of people at a particular time and place, their lives have evolved beyond the narrow frame of each story. A well-loved social worker moved on to a new job, a veteran with the sound of Pearl Harbor airplanes in his head silenced that memory by dying in his sleep. Some of the people—particularly those involved in public life—I continue to see, refreshing their portraits with weekly news accounts. Others, such as the woman walking in the name of Jesus, wandered into and out of my life, never to be seen again. Most stories, however, tend to repeat themselves, people popping up in other venues, doing other things. Yet for me, the moments captured in these stories reveal something essential and unchanging in their lives, and in my reporting on them, left me changed.

In selecting pieces for this book, I had a most difficult time, partly because of the volume of work to choose from, partly because news stories tend to lose significance after a very short period of time. But more importantly, structure in a book like this becomes extremely unwieldy, because no obvious natural structure exists. It took me months of sorting through the pieces to realize that the pattern emerging from a collection like this had to be one of a community of strangers and how each individual fit into the social mosaic. To maintain this rather arbitrary theme, I was forced to reject some pieces that meant the most to me and some I believed were very well written.

In choosing this collection, I tried to pick professions you might find typically in any community, and I hoped each piece once read would show how distinct that person is. Space restrictions forced me to eliminate duplications, even though the stories might be of equal merit. Over the years, I've interviewed everyone from movie stars to environmentalists, and generally more than one of each. I was hard pressed to choose between them. All of the people in all of the stories, here or discarded (for space or other considerations), are special to me, I have delved into their lives and secrets in a special way, making them all—in my head anyway—part of my individual community.

While the word count has always been my curse, as it is for all prolific journalists, it has the side benefit of helping pare down something that might go on forever. In the end, I find great truth in the tag line to the old television series *Naked City*. There is indeed a story inside each person you meet, and one starkly different from everyone else's, even though the superficial trappings of profession and age may be the same.

In putting together this book, I am hoping that the pieces manage to provide a snapshot of a larger society in the same way that the individual stories manage to provide snapshots of the people.

Acknowledgments

The list of people who provided me with inspiration, support, and guidance for the material in this book is almost endless, reaching back to a time decades ago when I first decided to become a journalist. The people most immediately responsible for shaping me as a writer and my work itself are my editors, especially in the Hudson Reporter Associates and the Worrall Community Newspapers. By far the most influential is Michael Richardson under whom I worked for nearly six years. His sensitivity to language and his own superb writing ability allowed him to shape my work while leaving the essence of my ideas intact.

Even his abilities would not have been enough had Lucha Mulato and David Unger, the publishers and owners of the Hudson Reporter Associates, not provided an atmosphere that allowed editors David Cruz and Caren Lissner to follow in Richardson's footsteps. Reporter Andy Newman, who worked with me during my first two years at the *Hudson Reporter* and who later moved on to the *New York Times*, was so remarkable a writer that he unwittingly inspired me by stirring up in me pangs of jealousy and the desire to improve my own work. Arts editor David Cogswell also encouraged me.

For a year, I worked for the Worrall Community Newspapers and discovered a similar creative atmosphere, although the Worrall newspaper tradition demanded hard-hitting stories, forcing me to relearn my craft. While working for those papers I met some tough and talented newspaper people, including Editor and Chief Tom Canavan and Regional Editor Anthony Puglise. Publisher David Worrall treated me with dignity and respect. In meeting Associate Editor Paul O'Keefe I learned how journalism could make a difference in a small town; his blood-and-guts kind of reporting made me reexamine my own skills as a writer. While at the Worrall papers I got to work under three very supportive editors, Anthony Buccino, Melinda Nerber, and Travis Cunningham. I want to thank in particular Willa Speiser, whose editing of this manuscript helped make it more understandable to a contemporary reader.

Work in this book was built on a solid foundation of underground journalism during the 1980s, when I wrote and published *Scrap Paper Review*. People like Jim Fruend, Michael Alexander, John Crowley, Mary Kay Klim, Joel Lewis, and others showed remarkable confidence in me as writer, editor, and publisher. Dorothy Alexander, a colleague on the *Paterson News* in 1985, pushed me to put this volume together and thus deserves the most credit for its becoming a reality.

Last, but not at all least, four people deserve my thanks, partly because they have known me longest and put up with the most as I worked toward this moment: my loving wife, Sharon Griffiths; James Garland; Rocky Molinari; and Frank Quackenbush.

PART ONE

Memories of
War and Peace

Helping Our Own

In a nagging cold rain that might well have reminded them of Eastern Europe, two Bosnian refugees stared at the door of their new home, shaking off the unusual May chill as they tried to smile. After having had to flee their home in Sarajevo, after months of wandering through the confusion of exploding bombs, retreating armies, and refugee camps, the mother and her fifteen-year-old daughter, along with donated furniture, were not now awaiting a United Nations rescue team, but the landlord with a key.

Although they were victims of the most atrocious European conflict since World War Two, the mother and her daughter didn't see Secaucus as an alien landscape. Before the war these two had lived in houses much the same as they found here, a middle-class family with father, mother, and daughter, living ordinary lives, living in an ordinary home, with father working an ordinary job. But as rumor of war grew with the rising volume of distant guns, and shells began to fall, father fled, leaving mother and daughter to fend for themselves, and when the bombs started exploding even nearer to home, mother and daughter fled, too.

"They feared for their lives," said Maryann McEnroe, the Secaucus teacher who was responsible for helping the daughter learn English. "They took their possessions and their savings and fled."

Over the following months, mother and daughter found themselves part of a mass movement of people seeking shelter from the war, a host of refugees who eventually crossed over the border into Croatia, where they were free from the shooting and rape, but largely without a way to earn money.

"There were so many refugees and not enough work," McEnroe said. "As a result, they went through their savings."

Unlike many of the others living under wretched conditions, the mother had a brother living in the United States, and when the brother heard of their situation, he offered to bring them here.

"She was thrilled," said McEnroe. "She loves it here and said she never wants to go back."

But when she got here, she found conditions less than normal. Her brother drank, and often went into fits of rage that resulted in throwing furniture against the walls. While he never attacked the woman or her daughter, they lived in dread of his mood swings, which turned him from Dr. Jekyll

3

into Mr. Hyde. Often they didn't know which one would walk through the door. He made mother and daughter sleep in the hall. He would not let them watch TV or enjoy any of the other comforts of middle-class life, although the mother cooked for him and cleaned his house.

One night, he got so drunk, he came home and told them he wanted them both out of his house. When the woman offered to make him supper, he told her he didn't want her to cook for him anymore. The next day, he came in sober, and when the woman did not cook his supper, he went into a rage demanding to know why not.

"She tried to tell him that he had told her not to, but he couldn't remember," McEnroe said. "That's why he said they had three days to get someplace else to live."

With no place else to turn, the daughter came to McEnroe, trying to find some kind of answer. As the girl's teacher, McEnroe had become aware of the fifteen-year-old girl's ordeal in coming to the United States. This part, however, shocked her. She and the girl had bonded right away.

"I'm close with all my students," McEnroe said, noting that she teaches English as a Second Language to students like this girl, and this often calls for getting to know more about her students' private lives than most teachers would. Here was someone who had literally been through hell, had come to America seeking some kind of relief, and was being put through hell here as well; McEnroe was being asked to rescue them.

"At first I didn't know what to do," she said. "But I knew I would put them up in my family room before I'd let them go back."

But McEnroe was not totally without resources, and she called the one person she knew who could help, a friend named Karyn Rosenbaum, who just happened to be the town's social services director.

In a small town like Secaucus, the social services director knows almost all the key people in town, but resources are always limited. When Rosenbaum heard about this problem, however, she started making phone calls. First, she called a nonprofit agency in Newark, which offered some help, but only temporary arrangements and only if the mother and daughter relocated to Newark.

"As soon as another refugee came, this woman and her daughter would get bumped and would be out on the street again," Rosenbaum said.

She believed someone in a higher office might have the resources to help, so she called Hudson County, and after about a dozen calls, found the appropriate office. But the social worker on the other end said the county didn't have money to cover a situation like this. They could only provide cash to supply a temporary move, not find a new home. Rosenbaum and McEnroe both worried over the detrimental effect constant shifting would have on the daughter, who is a good student at the high school and making significant progress in learning English.

"I explained that if we didn't find them a place to live this family would be out on the street; when that didn't do anything, I asked to speak with the supervisor," Rosenbaum said.

The supervisor, when he answered, went into an extended anti-immigrant diatribe, saying that his agency shouldn't be expected to pay for everyone coming to America.

"He told me he couldn't get a house in Jersey City and he's an American, so why he should help some immigrant," Rosenbaum said.

She was shocked, and furious, and insulted by what the man said. These were professionals she'd called, people paid to help other people. So was Rachel Ceglie, the assistant director of the Secaucus Housing Authority (SHA), who soon stepped in to help.

"I can understand that he might have personal feelings about things, I have my own feelings about things sometimes. But we're professionals, we're paid to do our job, and while we're doing our job we're supposed to put aside our personal feelings," Ceglie said.

When Rosenbaum asked the man what she was to do with the mother and daughter, the man told her, "Put them in a shelter."

"I told him 'no thank you, we'll use our own resources,'" Rosenbaum said, and then called the Interfaith Council of Churches in Newark.

"The official there was kind and said she wasn't surprised about what happened," Rosenbaum said, who learned the supervisor's actions weren't simply professionally unethical but were illegal, too. "So she recommended me to Legal Aid and suggested that I find a politician willing to help."

Legal Aid took the name and number of the clerk and supervisor. But this did not solve the original problem. Time was running out. If Rosenbaum didn't find a place for these people, they would soon wind up on the street, and it was clear by this time that she was going to have to find her own network.

The problem is, how do you help a woman who speaks no English and a fifteen-year-old, neither of whom have money or a source of income? Rosenbaum called Assemblyman Anthony Impreveduto, then sent McEnroe to his office with the girl.

"These are legal immigrants," Impreveduto said. "And they needed help. So I spoke with our housing folks because I knew these people were entitled to Section 8 or vouchers. Since this was an emergency situation, they could be elevated to the top of the list. The problem is, the housing authority can help pay the rent, but where were we to get an apartment?"

Rosenbaum meanwhile put the mother and daughter up in a local hotel, selecting one that would allow the daughter to walk to school every day while the town went about finding them an apartment. William Snyder, director of the SHA, assigned Ceglie to the case. She, with suggestions from Impreveduto, began to look for a more permanent solution. But rental units in Secaucus are rare, and to find one affordable enough to house these two even rarer. Then Ceglie came up with a gem, a two-bedroom apartment near the center of town.

"When the woman was told she had an apartment, she started to cry," Rosenbaum said.

But the town's homeless fund had only nine hundred dollars, and the land-lord wanted the first month's rent as well as a month-and-a-half security. Although Ceglie managed to talk the landlord into taking a single month's rent as security, mother and daughter would be moving into an unfurnished apartment. While the town could scratch enough together for an apartment, someone else would have to furnish it.

In stepped the Reverend Mark Lewis, Catherine Murray, and McEnroe her-self. The Reverend Mr. Lewis, pastor of the Church of Our Saviour, served a dual purpose. As part of a cooperative effort with the town's social service department, he had lent the town space to store donated furniture, some of which was given over to this effort. The church had also conducted a special sale the previous Christmas to build up a small emergency fund. The money from this fund went toward paying for temporary lodging in the motel, as well as deposits on various utilities at the new apartment.

"It's amazing how all this has come together," Reverend Lewis said. "We had it all in place."

Catherine Murray, a parishioner at the church, had another resource. As a resident of Harmon Cove Towers, she had a storage room there where she kept donated goods destined for battered women's centers in the area.

"But a needy family is a needy family," she said. "When Karyn called I went down there, packed up ten boxes with bedding and kitchen stuff, and brought it over."

Even McEnroe, who had started it all, had something to donate. She'd lived in town since 1967, and had so many relatives, all she had to do was go around and see if they had anything to spare, and they did.

Department of public works chief Mike Gonnelli then sent the department's van around to gather up the goods and bring them to the apartment. The town is still looking for particular items, though. Rosenbaum asked people with donations to call her at her office in town hall.

Apparently under pressure from above, the county agency that had refused to help the family called back to say they had a house to offer in Jersey City. Rosenbaum told them Secaucus had taken care of it already.

"Someone once said that we here in Secaucus don't care about anybody else," Rosenbaum said. "I don't think that's true. When someone comes here, they're ours, and we try our best to make sure we help. If someone lives here and they need help, we're concerned about them."

From *The Secaucus Reporter*, Hudson Reporter Associates, 1997.

Walking in the Name of Jesus

Almost from the minute you first lay eyes on Willa Scott, you know there is something special about her. Her crystal blue eyes have a sense of clarity usually lacking in the pain-racked expressions of the homeless—although in every other aspect she seems straight off the street. Even as she drops her two backpacks on the floor of the office, her movements have deliberation, and her sharp smile a perception of purpose.

"I met your photographer outside," she says. "She said I should talk to you."

She immediately dispels the urge to dismiss her, her stance and expression insistent—a self-promoting bundle of issues that won't go away or be kept silent by a pocketful of spare change. Echoing scenes from the 1969 film *Easy Rider*, she broadcasts an uncomfortable sense of absolute freedom. She inherently reminds you of how enslaved you are to things like mortgage, car payments, and a weekly paycheck. Scott has none of those things. She is a walking, talking protest against our wasteful way of life. She wears jeans, a T-shirt, a sweatshirt, and a cap covered with a variety of slogans she has hand-printed there, and she looks like an aging hippie who, like Rip Van Winkle, has just woken from a long sleep to find herself standing—this time in the 1990s.

A self-proclaimed Christian, Scott travels throughout the country, relying on the goodness of strangers and God to give her necessities. She has spent most of the last five years bicycling and walking across forty-seven states with

7

a sleeping bag, tarp, and some extra clothing. She hardly ever handles money. She says money corrupts. She once found twenty dollars on the street and thought it might be handy for a meal. But the Lord told her to give it away. So she gave it to the first panhandler she met. Sometimes motels and hotels will "donate" a room to her. Sometimes people will cook her a meal. In the Midwest, a man gave her shelter just as a tornado bore down on the street where she was walking. She seems to walk without coming to harm, and follows where the Lord tells her to go; the Lord, she says, tells her if danger is near.

But she keeps a record of her travels folded up in a jogger's pouch around her waist. It bulges with press clippings from curious reporters who have caught her act along the road. Her face is a marvel of sun-chiseled lines, like a road map defining her trips over the years. She carries cardboard signs with messages dedicated to various events she happens upon. She's been at the Indianapolis 500, decrying effects of pollution on the earth's ozone layer. Her sign on that occasion said, "Drivers stop your engines."

Ozone was the initial cause for her to hit the road. She began traveling in October 1990, about the time of the now famous World Series earthquake in San Francisco, and she managed to bicycle over the bridge before it fell. The automobile has become for her one of the primary symbols of evil in the world, one that shows humanity's disregard for God and nature.

"I saw Jesus. He said cars are the problem. We will not get out of those cars unless we really care about one another," she says. "I think we have an illness in the United States."

Although she has made dozens of trips across the United States, her latest venture to Maine came because of recent [June 1994] laws requiring the catalytic converter on cars. She said these produce acid, which in turn creates acid rain.

"I'm trying to get people to focus on what we'll do for each other and for the children," she says.

But her message varies with the town and the issues. In May Scott was in Kennebunkport, Maine, addressing issues of homelessness, health care, and the environment. She circulated petitions supporting the homeless.

Reactions to Scott are mixed. Sometimes people greet her with warmth. She recalls children feeding her peanut butter and jelly sandwiches at the Indianapolis 500 raceway. A businessman on her journey through Hudson County early in July bought her a meal at a Jersey City restaurant.

Police are a problem—though, she says, many treat her well. She's been arrested three times: once in Tempe, Arizona, when she showed up at the National Women's Golf Tournament. Another time, police stopped her at the White House and asked what she wanted.

"I told him I wanted more informed police. He looked at me oddly, then said 'I'll buy that' and let me go," she says.

On this trip she tries to catch up with President Bill Clinton on the road. She came south from Maine because she heard the president had visited the area.

"I'm trying to catch up with the president, but keep missing him," she says.

Scott has run into many national figures during her trips—governors, senators, and other dignitaries—who happen to be on the road when she is.

"I take the side roads and stay in private homes a lot," she says. "I find out what's happening in their area."

She has stumbled into the swearing in of state supreme court justices, the opening of bridges, the high points of campaign rallies, and the kickoff of various sporting events. She took petitions on health care and homelessness to Ted Kennedy's office in Washington. When she ran into the Clinton-Gore campaign in Minneapolis, she presented campaign workers with her poncho bearing two hundred signatures and the slogan "Get electric trains and save the ozone." In the same year, she crossed paths with then President George Bush over the Mackinaw Bridge in Michigan and held up her sign to him, which said "Bush, just keep walking."

"And he did," she laughs.

In Mobile, Alabama, she showed up to lend support to the people whose naval base was scheduled to close, trying to interest them in the issue of homelessness. She did the same in Richmond, Virginia.

Outside the Darlington International Speedway in South Carolina, police caught her rummaging through a grocery store dumpster. But instead of jail she was given free room and board at the local hotel. In Buffalo, she was called the "Ozone Woman'" and was stopped by the police on Route 20 just outside Sliver Creek for riding her bicycle in the snow. She told the police she was riding for the ozone and going to the University of Buffalo to teach the students lessons on cars. A railroad worker rescued her and brought her home for a meal.

On this trip to New Jersey, she found herself at a shopping center off Route 440 in Jersey City. She had stopped in at a dry cleaner's looking for a restroom.

"A gentleman from Paine Webber bought me lunch," she says. "People around us kept stopping to ask the meaning of my signs."

Scott claims to have a degree in psychology and a master's in theology from the University of California in Berkeley. She taught therapy in 1970 and gave a lecture at the Jungian Institute in Switzerland in 1977. She didn't explain the motivation for this current five-year odyssey across the United States, but her religious and intellectual stimulus, she says, came as a result of a 1962 illness.

"I got a blood clot on my lung," she said. "The doctors told me I was going to die. I prayed to Jesus to save me and told Him if he did I would work for Him. I didn't think I was going to make it. I was in intensive care. I was twenty-six years old."

But she did recover, and says she started working with dying children.

"And in each of them I saw Jesus's face," she says, noting that she intends to continue her walking tours of America until people get her message. "It's Jesus's message. He's just using me."

From *The Secaucus Reporter,* Hudson Reporter Associates, 1994.

They Call Him Mr. Sam

Needy people from Paterson to Newark call him Mr. Sam.

They often keep an eye out for Sam Ciccone when he pulls up in his patched, blue Chevy van, which has become a sign of hope, carrying food and clothing donated by relatively better-off families in Bloomfield, Glen Ridge, Belleville, and other towns.

This Bloomfield resident has been making regular deliveries as long as most people around the homeless shelters and charity kitchens can remember, sometimes coming as often as five days a week.

"I volunteer a lot," he said, naming a list of churches, food pantries, shelters and orphanages he has helped over the last few decades—places where a hungry person can get a meal.

He is out in every kind of weather, either making deliveries or collecting donations from supermarkets or generous individuals. In a given week, he might get a call from Assemblywoman Marion Crecco, a Bloomfield Republican, or someone might knock on his door. One day he might be found in Newark, another day in East Orange or Belleville or Paterson. Sometimes he is delivering clothing, sometimes food. When he puts out dented cans of food, they are always taken. There is always a need, he said. Ciccone, with the help of his wife, Rocchina, pays for his own auto insurance, gas, and other expenses on the truck. He never takes money, not even as a donation. In the past, friends from restaurants in Newark gave him leftovers, but they have since stopped because they fear a lawsuit.

"There is enough thrown out into dumpsters to feed everyone who goes hungry," Ciccone said, noting that the restaurants still help, cooking turkeys he had received as donations.

At seventy-three, Ciccone has had several careers, one of which led him to his charity work.

"I started out selling bleach," he said, "and then later, when swimming pools started to come in, we sold chlorine. It was hard work and long hours and after a while I got tired of that and started to look around for something else I could do."

He became involved with the salvage business, bidding on damaged shipments of goods that came in on trucks or off ships. Some of it was good, some of it banged up.

"You could recoup your money by selling what wasn't damaged," he said.

As a result of this, Ciccone had numerous items he couldn't sell, things like dented cans of food.

"So I looked around and saw that some of the shelters could use them," Ciccone said. "People always need something, even if it is something like a can of pineapple. That's a real luxury to people, something they can have for dessert."

Ciccone knows what it means to be poor, and knows what it means to go hungry. When he was a child during the Great Depression, he and his family sometimes ate beans and stale bread. When he got a job on a milk truck, he earned a dollar a week and a bottle of milk. His brother made a similar arrangement with a local meat market.

Ciccone was born and raised in Newark and moved to Bloomfield when he got married fifty years ago.

In 1983, he was diagnosed with cancer. Although the disease went into remission, the event changed his life, allowing him more time to dedicate to his volunteer work.

"A lot of congressmen and senators push out their chests and brag about how much they've done," Ciccone said. "But it is the volunteer who does the most. Without people volunteering, the tax rate in towns like Bloomfield would be much higher."

Ciccone sees himself as a political conservative, but one who believes that people need to be fed, then taught how to feed themselves. Helping people changes them, he says, and later they learn the pride involved in making their own way in the world.

"A job makes a person independent," Ciccone said. "A person working for McDonald's or any place can go out and buy what they want when they want, even if it's only a candy bar. But before you can get a person to work, you have to make sure that person gets fed. If we don't help now, some year we'll pay for it as taxpayers."

Helping people has gotten him into dangerous situations.

Some people have criticized him as a white man going into black neighborhoods. And some people have called him a racist because he is a white man feeding people of color.

"That doesn't bother me," he said. "I'm here because I want to help. I just want to make sure people get enough to eat. I tell them to take the food and not be so critical. A week later, they often come back and apologize. We all say things we don't mean."

One of the highlights of Ciccone's volunteer work has been his meeting and working with the late Mother Teresa. She helped establish the Newark shelters where Ciccone does much of his work. He said he will always remember seeing her speak before the United Nations and described her as one of the world's great people.

From *The Independent Press of Bloomfield,* Worrall Community Newspapers, 1998.

A Man of Spirit

Ronald West Jr. didn't drive a big car. He didn't own a big house or have a huge bank account, or fit the typical model of what most people would call a successful life. And yet, when he fell into a coma in August 1995, people came through his front door in a procession of ones, twos, and threes, each carrying the burden of their own lives, each bringing back stories of how West had helped them bear that burden better.

"Ronnie helped everybody," his sister Tracy Rosenberg said.

In fact, she hadn't heard so many stories or realized he had touched so many peoples' lives until they started coming up to her, visiting when he was in a coma, then later, after his death at age thirty-seven on August 23, 1995, when they paid their respects at the funeral. West touched everybody's life in a special way, often going out of his way to help, even when he needed help himself. People used to call him, saying they were scared. When they found themselves HIV-positive and asked him what they should do, West told them. He often brought people out of hiding, telling them, "You're living with AIDS, not dying from it."

More than two hundred people came to the funeral of this unassuming man.

"I never really believed he would die," Rosenberg said. "He had such a powerful spirit. I knew he would never give up."

And West never did, as his brother-in-law and best friend Steve Rosenberg said, "He didn't give up; AIDS beat him."

But seeing those people and hearing their stories was the most moving experience in Tracy Rosenberg's life. All of them had been touched by this powerful spirit, all of them had come to give something back, if only their memories and their shared pain, if only their comfort for the family of the man who had proven to be a best friend for each of them, helping them cope with their own lives, helping them to learn to help themselves. West saved peoples' lives, by talking to them, by giving them back a hope the fear of AIDS had stolen.

"I wanted to hear every story," Tracy said.

She does not deny the events that led up to her brother's illness. West suffered from alcoholism and went through a period when he made a lot of mistakes, partying, hanging out, doing things he may later have regretted. But many people scratch their heads when Rosenberg tells them AIDS was a blessing to her brother, something he himself had said after he had been diagnosed HIV-positive in 1986.

AIDS changed West, giving his life a focus it had lacked before, bringing him into contact with a whole new group of people he would not otherwise have met. The disease made him take stock of his life and made him get sober.

"He started taking care of himself, once he heard he was HIV-positive, and he began to go out and talk with people," Rosenberg said.

And talk he did.

West became a champion of his cause, from helping others deal with their drinking problems, to helping people cope with their infection. Ill or not himself, he kept on visiting people, attending speaking engagements, talking to people wherever and whenever they needed him.

"He was a powerful and spiritual being," Rosenberg said.

Although West's family moved to Secaucus in the 1980s, he took a more circuitous route, via Florida and Pennsylvania. When he first contracted the disease, Rosenberg feared he would take off for California, in order not to be a bother to the family or make them suffer. He didn't seem to understand just how much they loved him or how proud he made them in the end, one of those people whose courage and situation pulled the family back together and made it into something solid and invincible.

West will be remembered most for what he did to help people. He was a member of the Secaucus-based Alcoholic Anonymous group and Living Positive, an AIDS support group that operated out of Saint Augustine's Church in Union City. And he often visited local Veterans Administration hospitals and prisons to talk with people struggling with alcoholism. He routinely volunteered at Meadowlands Hospital and talked about his life to a group at Integrity House on Meadowview campus, and he played Santa Claus every year at the annual party for AA members and their families.

"He wanted to do something to help," Tracy Rosenberg said. "Even in his last days, he thought of others."

West was so strong, for so long, for so many, that when AIDS finally struck, people didn't believe it. In fact, he was sick for most of 1995. He grew quiet, something that told Rosenberg that the end was near. For days, he would lie in the recliner outside his mother's house and wouldn't come inside, as if he needed to capture every last moment of sunshine. He refused to take down his Christmas lights from the year before, leaving them up as 1995 went on. He told his friends and family he would not live to see another Christmas. But other signs showed of his fading; he told people that Madonna had come to see him, that he was married, that he had a Harley Davidson motorcycle.

"All the things he wanted in life, he believed he had," Steve Rosenberg said.

"He used to be so powerful, and then he looked so different, I went to church and prayed for God to take him, and God did," Tracy Rosenberg said.

His passing left a phenomenal vacuum in peoples' lives; family and friends wondered what to do next. And people had regrets. A new regimen of AIDS treatments appeared. If he could have held on for one more year, a whole new regimen of drugs might have saved his life. For Rosenberg, who had dedicated herself to helping him cope with his disease, the vacuum was particularly large. She couldn't give him treatments anymore. She couldn't hold his hand. She couldn't tell him how much she loved him.

In December 1995—three months after her brother's death—Rosenberg went to Hoboken to attend the World AIDS Day ceremonies there. She was looking for something, and maybe she didn't even know what, just something to fill the empty space. She didn't even know how to react, except to cry. And coming to Hoboken, she found other people with similar feelings, people with whom she could talk and cry. Then, she asked herself, why she had to come to Hoboken. Why couldn't she find this kind of event in Secaucus?

"My brother lived here in Secaucus," she said. "And maybe other people were suffering in Secaucus, too."

So Rosenberg went to talk to the mayor, and that began a year-long effort to bring this ceremony home. She went to school board meetings, council meetings, and any other meeting she could think of, met with every local official seeking their help. She pleaded her case before each, and was amazed when they responded.

Health officer Richard Manney said Rosenberg called him late in 1995 and asked what the town of Secaucus was doing about AIDS and why the town wasn't having a ceremony for World AIDS Day. These questions touched a nerve. While the health department did all it could in providing referrals and information, maybe something more needed to be done.

"I was touched by her concern," Manney said. "And the figures show we do have AIDS in this community."

Secaucus has had more than 120 cases of HIV reported, with more than 50 deaths from the disease. These figures do not include those anonymously tested.

"This was a pretty high number," Manney said, noting that 75 percent of the cases came about through IV-drug transmission, though two children had received it through their parents at birth. Manney began to make telephone calls; so did Rosenberg, calling everyone from Hartz Mountain Industries to North Hudson Community Action Corporation, trying to find out what could be done for World AIDS Day in 1996. Manney talked to the town librarian and Meadowlands Hospital, and, slowly, he shaped plans for a series of events to be held on December 2. In the end, people came forward—business leaders, political leaders, people from the churches, the schools, even from Mill Creek Mall, all with the idea that they might help promote AIDS awareness and provide the community with an opportunity to focus on HIV infection and AIDS. Rosenberg even managed to get a piece of the AIDS quilt to display at the high school.

"I'm on every mailing list you can imagine," she said. "I only wish it was larger."

Rosenberg also started her own AIDS support group at Immaculate Conception Church, where people can get comfort more than once a year, something West had wanted to do.

"We have a strong AA program in Secaucus. I wanted a program just as strong to support the victims of AIDS and their families," Rosenberg said. "A place where people can come and share their feelings with others in a similar situation."

She said most people are altered by the disease. They suffer grief and anger and confusion.

"Few people fully understand the effect this disease has on everyone," she said. "And one reason for the group is to make sure people aren't alone."

On November 13, the mayor and council honored Rosenberg for her efforts, something that may have embarrassed her a little.

"When they did that, I just wanted to cry. I wasn't proud. It was something I needed to do, something that we need here in Secaucus to help people share the grief. I wanted this town to wake up."

Rosenberg is worried about turnout for the December 2 ceremonies. She is hoping and praying she has made a difference. [Secaucus, unfortunately, ceased holding the ceremony a year or two later.]

"I want people to come out and support this," she said. "I want this to help change the way people react to AIDS. I want them to help someone if they hear that a person has AIDS, not gossip. I want the schools in this town to have a regular curriculum that is taught to every student. I want Ronnie to be remembered, to have his picture on the top of the world, for everybody to know, and for all those people whose lives he touched. I want people to know he didn't die in vain."

From *The Secaucus Reporter,* Hudson Reporter Associates, 1996.

One Hundred and Four Years Young

At the age of 104, Ruth Austin minces no words, often saying exactly what she thinks about anything. It is one of the endearing features that has made her a popular resident at the Job Haines Home in Bloomfield—popular with the staff, other residents, and visitors.

"She is just a delightful person," one of the workers said of Austin.

Even the Bloomfield Police wave as they go by, recalling earlier this year [1998] when they watched the Super Bowl with her and shared her peanuts.

"I couldn't believe how much they ate," Austin said, laughing. "I remember one of the officers asking me if I wanted some. I told him: 'No, you eat what you want, I'll have some tomorrow—if there are any left.' "

Perhaps it is this wry humor that has kept Austin lively and alert for so many years.

As a sports fan, she loves the Dallas Cowboys but will also cheer the New York Giants because her grandson loves the team. She also likes the New York Mets, and she will never cheer on the Yankees because she says they win too much. This grudge she holds from the 1950s, when the Yankees routinely beat her beloved Brooklyn Dodgers.

Old friends from the Hospital Center at Orange, where she trained as a nurse, call Austin "Greeny," based on her maiden name. Now, seventy-two years after her marriage, she still likes to recall her maiden name of Green, although when pressed, she says her favorite color is pink, and she laughs over the fact that she would have dressed her only child in pink, boy or girl.

Austin has been a resident of the Job Haines Home since 1993. Before that, she lived at the Canfield Home in West Caldwell.

She was born on June 7, 1894. She was one of nine children and spent her childhood in Jackson, Mississippi, She sees herself as a resident of two places, New Jersey and Mississippi, though she has returned to her southern home only twice since leaving as a teenager—once in 1950 and again in 1978.

Austin came north with her brother when he was transferred to the New York area, and she lived with an aunt in Newark. When she chose to pursue a career in nursing, she trained at the Hospital Center at Orange, from which she graduated in 1916. In 1997 the hospital held a reunion of its former graduates, but Austin, apparently not comfortable with travel even for such a short distance, decided not to go. The president of the reunion, however, came to her, bringing flowers and mementos, unable to pass up meeting the school's oldest living graduate. The next-oldest graduated in 1920.

Austin keeps a picture of herself as a young nurse, one of the many items hanging on the wall of her room. The picture is one that was taken just after she earned her nursing cap. She is particularly proud of that accomplishment and still has her cap.

Austin came to medicine just as the United States got ready to enter World War I, and she witnessed the devastating effect it had on the young veterans returning from the war. She was also witness to the horrors of the great influenza epidemic of 1918, which killed 400,000 to 500,000 people across the nation.

Austin has vivid memories surrounding the sinking of the *Titanic*. She lived though the Great Depression. She watched the world change with the arrival of radio and later television. She says she admires such modern innovations as the washing machine.

"I can't talk about the good old days with these wonderful appliances," she said.

In 104 years, Austin has experienced many moments of pleasure, but she recalls being particularly pleased when she received her engagement ring.

"At the time I thought that was the best thing ever," she said, and grinned, pointing to her wedding picture on the same wall as her daughter's baby picture.

Austin married in 1925 and has one daughter, Claire, two grandchildren, Janet and Gracie, a great-granddaughter, Amanda, and a great-grandson, Matthew.

Her husband, Edward Austin, who was born in Orange, worked for Thomas Edison within a few feet of Edison's office in the West Orange factory. She remembers her husband telling her of Edison's huge map of operations and how infuriated Edison became when something didn't go the way he wanted. Edison would check the map, then go off to check on the department.

One day, she looked out the window of the hospital in which she worked and saw a huge, red glow on the horizon. Moments later, someone rushed in, saying that Edison's West Orange plant was up in flames.

Her husband, she later learned, along with another employee, rescued a globe that was a favorite of the inventor's, something that is now on display at the Edison Museum.

Austin is independent, and she likes to keep things close at hand to do things for herself, employees at the Job Haines Home said.

Since joining the Job Haines Home community five years ago, Austin has become a highly visible resident, involved in several arts and crafts projects for the home as well as for her local church. She is also a dedicated needlework artist who practices her craft daily, and whose afghans are always popular gifts among friends and family.

Austin says life has been good, although she is at the age where she wonders if she will live to see her next birthday.

"Last year I wondered if I would live to be 104," she said. "This year I wonder if I'll see 105."

From *The Independent Press of Bloomfield,* Worrall Community Newspapers, 1998.

Not Just a Caregiver

Erin Jones needs no sign in her office saying, "Bless this mess." There is no mess. Even pamphlets that fill her desk seem organized, all of them lined up in neat stacks, information on everything from Medicare to safety. Even her piles of mail are neat.

Yet Jones is no organizational nerd. Although she has proven she can do almost everything from organizing teams for the Secaucus Senior Summer Olympics to finding a home care worker, she seems more a friend to many of the seniors than someone hired to help them get on with their lives. Outside Kroll Heights this week, she kept score for their summer games, taking as deep an interest in the activity as the seniors themselves, fitting into their world despite her young age.

Residents have come to accept this energetic social worker as one of their own. While she says she gets a little scared when people tell her they love her, she feels comfortable around seniors—something she learned from her family, where grandparents played a big role.

Social workers like Jones bridge two worlds, the theoretical text world of social psychology and the practical world of everyday people. In Secaucus, where she has become a vital part of the Secaucus Housing Authority, Jones has learned to turn theory into practice—even though half of what she does only the seniors see.

When she first came to the Secaucus Housing Authority in 1994, many of the SHA staff didn't know what to make of her. Jones says a lot of people thought of her as some kind of "do-gooder," a label she has tried to avoid.

SHA director William Snyder knew she had something special, and handed her the reigns of Project Independence, a plan he'd been contemplating once he became the director.

"I gave her the ball and told her to run with it," he says.

After she started in February 1994, Jones did run with it, and by most accounts, made things better for a lot of seniors.

Jones has no illusions about her job. It is one of those difficult positions that demand more of her emotionally and administratively than she likes to admit. Although praised by some of her co-workers, the most she'll say is that she finally has her feet on the ground.

Social worker Erin Jones, who left a strong impression on nearly every senior citizen with whom she came into contact, is pictured here in her office in Secaucus in 1994. In June 2000, she moved on to another job in West Orange.

"It takes a lot of creativity," she says with an odd self-deprecating laugh. "After all, I'm not working with a lot of money."

Jones gathered a few loyal souls, volunteers to help make various programs work. High school students, college students, even housewives who liked to help out, collectively formed a support system.

Project Independence was Snyder's brainchild, a way of keeping aging, competent seniors from becoming institutionalized. By providing a variety of necessary services, Snyder hopes to keep many seniors from seeking nursing home care. This may mean bringing in nurses or doctors, or something as simple as having someone come to wash a senior's dishes.

"It is a vision to allow the elderly to remain independent as long as humanly possible, rather than have them admitted prematurely to a nursing home facility," Snyder says. "It came to me when I noticed that the people who still had all their mental faculties could be allowed to age in place, if some of their problems could be addressed. Maybe they needed someone to cook for them or clean or help them get to a doctor."

Snyder says many seniors fear going into nursing homes, perceiving them as places where people go to die.

"If we could keep them in place and provide for their needs, many of these people could live happy and productive lives," Snyder says.

Over the last several years, significant changes have occurred in Secaucus involving the senior population. Kroll Heights opened, increasing the number of the town's senior building units to 275. The average age of the residents also increased. Many of the residents in the Elms—the town's first senior building—are now in their eighties and nineties, creating a greater need for services. According to Snyder, residents may suffer from any number of physical or mental illnesses, many may feel lonely or bored, or may need the services of a variety of medical or social services. A senior may need a doctor or a means of getting across town to the store. Under Project Independence, the Secaucus Housing Authority will help seniors find almost anything they need, from homemakers to transportation, will help them fill out federal forms for Pharmaceutical Aid to the Aged and Disabled (PAAD) or find recreation such as arts and crafts.

Jones has been key to the program's success, meeting with tenants and talking to them about major life issues such as loss, financial problems, loneliness, anxiety, depression, and family concerns. She tries to keep track of her contacts with seniors, while making up bus schedules, schedules for community room use, even schedules for recreational events.

With Jones, Snyder's vision has become possible.

"We want to keep seniors where they are," Jones says. "A nursing home would cost them five thousand dollars a month; a hospital, six hundred a day. By keeping seniors in place, they save money and people have a higher quality of life."

But all this is a lot of work, following up with frail seniors on a daily or weekly basis. Jones has a list of about thirty-five seniors she checks up on regularly, just to make sure they are all right and that they have everything they need.

"It's a list of tenants that I think are at risk," she says. "I just want to let them know someone's around."

In this regard, the SHA has instituted what it calls the "good morning program," in which residents are given a doorknob sign. They put it outside their doors each morning. A floor captain comes around at noon looking for the signs, then slips them back under the door. If a sign is missing and the senior has not notified anyone in the office that he or she is away, the apartment is checked.

For Jones, it is more personal than just setting up programs. She remembers one of her first visits to a nursing home when she saw a tenant waving to her. She didn't know why, though later she found out that person needed Jones to wave back.

"She needed me to wave to her to let her know she was alive," Jones says. "They all need to know that. They need to know they've not been left out of life."

Yet as helpful as Jones has proven in her year and a half in Secaucus, she says she won't do everything for the seniors. Sometimes, it is a matter of helping them do for themselves.

"I try to show people how to handle their own problems," she says. "It is not a matter of doing for them, but letting them do things for themselves, something that gives them full lives. It would be wrong to wait on them hand and foot. Some of these people have run whole households. I'm like a midwife, bringing them back out into life."

All of this is part of a holistic approach, one in which those in the senior community bond together to help each other.

"We're taking a holistic approach, not just the frail but the whole community, trying to build a sense of community," Jones says. "I can't go around and do everything for everybody."

She says other people have to pick up where she leaves off, and that part of the program is designed around interaction. Are there personality problems? As with any other group of people, sure there are. Seniors are building conscious and don't always want people from other buildings around. Some even resent the bridge connecting Kroll Heights with Lincoln Towers, and some resent having to go from one building to another to meet with Jones.

"Tolerance is one of the lessons many people—even elderly people— have to learn," she says. "But I've become the ears for everyone, listening to complaints about everything, including complaints about each other."

These complaints are based on fear, Jones says. Those who suffer most from the frailties of age are often looked down upon—even by other elderly people, who would rather hide those frailties behind locked doors than to face the prospect that they themselves might some day be that helpless.

"People are afraid of growing old, of losing their faculties, of saying and doing things that might be perceived as foolish or inept," she says.

Jones battles these perceptions. She draws people out from behind closed doors, struggling to keep them active in the community, and to overcome prejudices that one faction of elderly might have against another.

"I don't want to see these people locked away. I want them out and around, involved with other people," she says.

Jones, although only in her mid twenties, has a full range of experience. She has worked with the mentally ill, drug abusers, and inner city kids.

"In my short career I've worked with every age bracket," she says. "I love my job and love people. I have respect for these people and what some of these people have gone through in their lives."

In her approach to seniors, she says she's flexible, and not afraid of trying new things. Indeed, her list of activities includes everything from bingo to gardening, though over the month of August she has been keeping score in the senior Olympics, and has been reading up on poker rules—one of the areas of competition.

Sometimes she feels as if she's getting too involved. Each of these people means something to her, a kind of extended family. She knows more about them than most of their families, and she has come to find these people are special to her. She pays a price for such intimate knowledge, feeling sometimes that she's losing a little of her own life.

"But that's my choice," she says. "What comes around goes around."

She lives with a certain sense of spirituality, and is giving so much because some time in the future, someone will give back. But she does have a life of her own. She plays guitar, bikes off-road, and hikes in the woods. She calls these private activities of hers "free space."

Snyder says it takes the right kind of personality to do this kind of work.

"It is very difficult to deal with dying or help people when a family member is dying," he says. "Erin has that kind of personality. She has the ability to listen to these people as they empty out their problems to her. I'm great at conceptualizing. But she has what it takes to make a system work."

Local officials are not the only ones who believe Jones has been doing a good job. In 1993 the program won the National Association of Housing and Redevelopment Authority's Award of Merit in Housing and Community Development for the second straight year. In 1994, the town won the award for the construction of the Kroll Heights senior building. This year, Secaucus won for Project Independence. Snyder credits Jones for making it possible, and hopes to expand the program further in the future.

"This is only phase one," he says. "With grant money we can provide more health-related services, mental health services, and some non-medical services as well."

He also believes the Secaucus Housing Authority can export this program to other communities, and offer it as a national model for future senior care—though other communities will have to find their own Erin Jones.

From *The Secaucus Reporter,* Hudson Reporter Associates, 1994.

Ten Velde's World

Nick ten Velde is a stickler for details, something he says he may have picked up as a result of his years in a Japanese concentration camp as a kid. As a matter of survival, he learned that small things can be of immense importance, and though many of the things he presses to find out from town officials aren't a matter of life and death, they matter to him. Meeting after meeting, ten Velde is there, hounding local officials, until he gets the answers he wants.

Born and raised in Indonesia where his Dutch father owned a rubber plantation, ten Velde lived in relative luxury, enjoying, depending upon the season, the family's mountainside cabin or a mansion loaded with multiple cars. He called it the good life, something that was shattered with the invasion by the Japanese at the beginning of World War II.

Thrust out of his comfortable life, ten Velde's father led the resistance movement until the Japanese sank his boat, killing him, a moment ten Velde still cries over when retelling it fifty years later.

His own internment by the Japanese left scars too, but also an unquenchable need to understand everything, and an insistence upon knowing the details that many town officials find annoying.

"Generally, I don't like things to be squandered," ten Velde says. "If I see abuse, misuse, or waste or dishonesty, I say something about it."

Sitting in his kitchen just before Christmas, ten Velde goes over the latest Department of Public Works (DPW) report, underlining details he doesn't find clear enough, searching for subtle discrepancies he'll always find, such as why the DPW and a private contractor seem to be engaged in the same project in one of the town's ballfields, or why the cost of work hasn't been included with the report.

These details matter to him because, he says, he and other older citizens can't afford the high cost of living in Glen Ridge anymore, and that every cent wasted in some governmental department is another cent a senior citizen has to pay in rising taxes.

While ten Velde claims he once knew how to speak five languages, he often struggles to find the right word in English, infuriating some people who don't understand his difficulty. He says he likes people to use simple words he can understand.

So caught up is he in seeking details, however, that ten Velde often confuses people who find it difficult to follow his train of thought as he shifts from one issue to another, and even through time, his complaints sometimes centering on politicians who are no longer in office, or a battle over an issue that has already been resolved. But for the most part, his questions seek to keep town officials on their toes.

Town officials are not the sole focus of his attentions: ten Velde will talk to anyone about any issue he believes unfair, from the CEO of AT&T to a supplier he believes has charged him too much. During an interview with him in late December, he still fumed over his eight phone calls to Comcast to resolve a complaint with them.

Plenty of people disagree with ten Velde, and he knows it. He just doesn't care. He says he likes a good fight, as long as people are willing to come out and stand up for what they believe. He sees the lack of interest in public affairs as the biggest danger facing both Glen Ridge and America. This uninterest, he says, engenders corruption.

Contrary to popular opinion, ten Velde does not prowl the town looking for trouble the way so-called gadflies in other towns do. He sees plenty just looking out his window, from neighbors who leave piles of leaves filling the gutters to cars parking on the wrong side of the street.

And ten Velde has some very controversial opinions, especially when it comes to paying for educating Glen Ridge kids, noting that while many people come to Glen Ridge for the schools, older residents are being asked to subsidize programs for other people's kids.

"I'm all for paying for their basic education," ten Velde says. "That I agree with. But when seniors are being asked to pay for extracurricular activities, I think that's too much. Parents of children in those programs should co-pay."

Although he now owns and operates a small food company whose main product line is hot sauce, ten Velde has an undergraduate degree and a master's in engineering, a field in which he says he's obtained thirteen U.S. patents. He earned his degrees over years and several continents, at schools in Indonesia, the Netherlands, England, and the United States.

Ten Velde came to America in 1957, sponsored initially by Rotary International, an organization to which his father once belonged, and then by members of the McGraw-Hill publishing company, who helped him find his home in Glen Ridge, where he's lived since 1965.

"I'd like to live the rest of my life here," he says. "But with the way taxes are going up and with all the waste I see, I'm being driven out, just like every other senior citizen."

From *The Glen Ridge Paper*, Worrall Community Newspapers, 1997.

An Amazing
Moment in Time

For many people there's one special moment they will remember forever. Sometimes it's love, sometimes it's fifteen minutes of fame, sometimes it's simply being in the wrong or right spot at an appropriate time. For Louis Markisello that time was Pearl Harbor when the Japanese attacked.

It is hard to say whether it is a sparkling moment he is glad to have witnessed. It was a national tragedy in which many people suffered and died. Yet it is a moment to which Markisello thinks back often, wondering how it is he survived when so many other men did not.

Now, nearly eighty years old, he lives with the irony of his first impression, the sound of airplanes roaring overhead as he and his buddies made their way from their barracks to the mess hall for breakfast. The sound echoes in his head, though hearing loss now has become another, more personal tragedy. Fifty-three years later, he can still hear the planes, but he can't afford to buy a hearing aid to hear anything else.

In 1990, on the fiftieth anniversary of Pearl Harbor, Markisello received a medal commemorating him as of one of nine men from Hudson County to have survived the Pearl Harbor bombing.

Born and raised in North Bergen, Markisello was drafted in June 1941 and trained at Fort Eustis, Virginia, after basic training at Fort Dix, New Jersey.

"They took us out of one mud hole and put us into another," he says with a wry grin that wrinkles his gray face. "In that place we had water right up to the bottom of the bunks, and we used to land in water when we got up for morning roll call."

He laughs over the whole memory, the way a high school quarterback recalls the circumstances leading to his one big victory back in the good old days, his hand waving in the air as if shaping it out of the past. He has a two-foot-wide photo of his whole unit up on his bedroom wall, yellowed with age, though remarkably intact for having survived fifty years.

"I don't think there's another one like it still around," he says. He preserved this one by rolling it up and keeping it out of harm's way—unlike the unit of men it shows, who flew into danger without even knowing it. The whole tour was a training mission not meant to last more than a year.

Louis Markisello carried the sights and sounds of Pearl Harbor in his head for more than half a century—even as his hearing failed him late in life. Pictured here in January 1994, Markisello died early in 2000—a well-liked man in his senior citizen complex.

Beneath the photo, a dresser top is strewn with bottles of prescription drugs, for heart, head, liver, and other ailments now too numerous to enumerate.

When the bombs fell at 7:28 A.M. on December 7, 1941, his unit was stationed just up the road from the harbor. It was Sunday morning, and he was on his way to the mess hall when all of a sudden he heard planes.

"I was out in the open with about eight other men and I knew right away it meant trouble," Markisello said. His unit had been called down from alert the day before and brought back from their gunnery posts to the barracks. But the commanders told them not to get comfortable.

"We weren't supposed to unpack our bags or take our bedrolls apart," he said. "We didn't even get to the mess hall. We were just talking and a slew of planes flew over us right out of the sun. It was so bright we couldn't see the markings on the planes. To me it looked like the Japanese were arriving and I was right. I told the sergeant in charge of the guards to get his binoculars and look at the markings, and sure enough they were Japanese."

Markisello says no one knew exactly what it meant, but they saw the machine guns firing from the planes and the bullets hitting the ground.

"They were only up from us about forty or fifty feet. At that range, how could they miss?" he says. Fortunately, they did and he survived, and he chuckles softly, saying, "They must have been bad shots."

In the following hours, everything went crazy, people rushed to their positions, trucks roared trying to move the big guns, searchlights seared the sky with beams of light.

To this day Markisello has his suspicions about what happened on that day and those days preceding the attack, saying that a Japanese spy ring had later been uncovered in the basement of a local bar—a bar frequented by American troops.

Many of the units had stepped down from their alert positions. Many of the ships in the harbor were under repair. Markisello believes the Japanese had to have known, and recalls seeing much of the damage firsthand while he drove a truck from one post to another, hauling ammunition.

"The officer in charge said none of us would be likely to be leaving after that," he says. "We were scheduled to have a Christmas party and leave."

During the months that followed, Markisello got a transfer to a motor pool unit as he watched his old unit break up and its members scatter to various parts of the war front.

In 1943, he got leave, the first since being sent to Hawaii.

"I had an opportunity to go to officer's candidate school. But I eventually decided not to go. I didn't really want to be an officer," he says. "I wanted to be out of the service. I'd been there two years already, and we were only supposed to be out there for a year total."

When he finally was discharged in 1945, he came home to cold weather, wearing Class A greens, the dark green dress-up uniform used for official functions such as parades and award ceremonies. The weather seemed particularly harsh after so many years in Hawaii. He spent a short time living in West New York after he got out of the service. His mother and family had moved to Upstate New York while he was away. Eventually, they came back to North Bergen, where they bought a house.

"I went down to the shipyards to look for work," Markisello said. He finally ended up as a painter for three dollars a day, and he remained a painter for most of his life, contracting himself out in the beginning; later he got a job in a hospital maintenance department, cleaning floors, emptying trash, and making minor repairs, where he worked for about twelve years.

Markisello currently lives in Lincoln Towers senior housing in Secaucus. His apartment is clean but sparsely furnished. A small black-and-white television rests on top of a larger set, which has apparently ceased operating. A small television cart shows signs of a recent meal. He says there were quite a few men who went to Hawaii with him from North Bergen but he doesn't know what happened to them. He considers himself lucky.

He says it was all brought back a few months ago when a friend mailed him the obituary of one friend who had been with him in Pearl Harbor. He slides the clipping out from a small collection of papers that have come to signify that part of his life, and as he looks up, a glint of something sad shows in his eyes, as if someone important had vanished or some important page that says something about his own life has been turned.

Markisello says he has arthritis, so he can't write to people he used to know or answer the friend who sent the clipping. His hearing is bad, and when he goes outside and looks up or around too quickly, he gets dizzy. He's spent money on various tests, but the doctor says he's just getting old and there isn't a lot anyone can do but give him medication. Even his liver is bad.

"They thought I was a drinker," he says with an ironic kind of laugh that is neither happy nor sad. "They wouldn't believe me when I told them I hated the stuff. One cold beer and I'm filled up. How the heck can you be a drinker like that?"

But it is his inability to hear that bothers him most. He says life would be a little better if he had a hearing aid, but he can't afford one. Medicare allows only one hundred dollars toward such devices.

"Hearing aids cost a lot more than that," he says.

He tried to get Medicaid when the Housing Authority still had a social worker to help him fill out the forms, but his income is slightly over the maximum.

From *The Secaucus Reporter,* Hudson Reporter Associates, 1993.

A Letter from the Past

When the letter arrived at Borough Hall in the spring of 1992, Midge Bourne was still mayor. It was simply addressed to "the mayor," and she might have thought nothing more about it, except for the postmark and the stamp, showing it had originated in the Netherlands.

Inside, she found a brief typewritten paragraph asking for information about the family of Lewis J. Dundon, a fighter pilot who was shot down over Germany in World War II and died.

The English in the letter was remarkably good, and it had come from a thirty-seven-year-old man who had adopted Dundon's grave as part of an effort to honor those who had helped liberate their country from the Nazis.

Lewis John Dundon was twenty years old when he died. He flew for the United States Air Force Ninth Tactical Wing and was assigned to support ground troops by attacking enemy tanks and planes. On March 21, 1945, his plane took a direct hit from enemy ground fire. No one saw his parachute open when his plane crashed in Germany.

Four days later and thousands of miles away, his son was born in Glen Ridge, but the infant's death of an intestinal disorder a few weeks later only added to the family's misery. Dundon's wife clung to the hope that her husband, who was then listed as missing in action, was still alive.

Unbeknownst to American authorities, Dundon's body was recovered by German civilians, who buried him in a cornfield near Schoenberg, Germany. After the war, the United States Quartermaster Corps followed the cold trail that led to his grave and found his remains on March 7, 1946.

Years later, the Rabudas family, who lived in Kerkrade, near the German border, responded to requests from their local newspaper to adopt the grave of those soldiers who appeared to have no visitors.

"Actually, my mother, a widow at the time of the war, and I had permission to visit the American cemetery in 1948 before it was officially opened, and made a permanent resting place for thousands of men who fell in the general area in the later days of the war," wrote Martha Furey, the airman's sister, in a 1996 letter anticipating a visit from the Dutch family. "Also, my husband and I made a trip to Maagraten in 1988 when we were in the Netherlands. However, we arrived on a Saturday afternoon after the cemetery office was closed, so there was no record of that visit either."

While the Dutch family had done a significant amount of research to learn about the man in the grave they had adopted, they knew almost nothing about his home town of Glen Ridge or about his family. In his 1992 letter, Frans Rabudas wrote in the hope that his words would reach some family members.

"Let them know that there is a family who visits the grave from time to time, puts some flowers in a vase, prays a few moments and is grateful that a young American officer has given his life for our freedom," Rabudas wrote.

Bourne, who read those words, felt the hope in them, reaching out into the dark from that Dutch family so many miles away.

"They did not know if it was a big city or a small town when they sent the letter," Bourne said. "They didn't even know if the letter would be received by anyone in Glen Ridge who actually knew the man or his family."

In a tale full of ironies, Bourne was struck by the biggest irony of them all.

In mailing the letter to the mayor of Glen Ridge, the Dutch family had made contact with one of the few people in Glen Ridge who indeed knew where the family of that airman had gone. Bourne had grown up with that family. She knew the soldier's mother, his sister, and other members of the family.

At some point in the past, the surviving sister had moved out of Glen Ridge to New Vernon, New Jersey. But by the time the letter arrived in Glen Ridge in 1992, Furey had moved again, retiring to Cape Cod, Massachusetts. By luck or fate, Bourne had kept in touch during both of those moves and passed on the letter to Furey.

Rabudas worked for the post office in Kerkrade, speaking and writing good English. He researched all that he could to know about the airman's military assignment, and later he helped the sister obtain more information about her brother that she had not been able to obtain previously.

On July 17, 1996, the young family from the Netherlands arrived at Boston's Logan International Airport, then traveled south to take a tour of Glen Ridge. They visited the monument to soldiers in front of Borough Hall, and took home a VCR tape about the history of the town in which the airman had grown up. Because of the different technology in Europe, they could not play the tape.

Last Christmas, the family purchased a VCR capable of playing the tape, and, at last, they learned a little more about the place where their adopted airman had grown up.

From *The Glen Ridge Paper,* Worrall Community Newspapers, 1998.

A Big Part of Secaucus

For forty-five years, Rocco Impreveduto didn't talk about the war. He wasn't utterly silent. His family knew he had served in the army with distinction during World War II, that he had fought with the 78th "Lightning" Division of the Third Army at Anzio and at four other major battles in Italy, Africa, and France. They knew he had been wounded and awarded the Purple Heart.

Impreveduto, the Secaucus political patriarch who died December 20 [1996] at the age of seventy-three, just didn't go into details about any of it.

He had come home whole and apparently didn't see the point. He didn't hide or show shame either. He was clearly proud to have served and respectfully filled his role as a member of the Secaucus Veterans of Foreign Wars Post 3776. He didn't talk about the drawer full of decorations he'd received either, and, in fact, hadn't wanted them.

Yet from time to time, Impreveduto noted some of the ironies surrounding his military career, how when he was drafted in Union City he didn't go to Fort Dix with the rest of his buddies, but to Fort Sill, Oklahoma, where he was trained as a forward observer for artillery. He laughed about how local Native Americans adopted him as "that kid from Hoboken."

"He had never seen a real Indian before," his son Anthony said.

Once, when looking up at the Jersey City Heights, Impreveduto recalled when his unit was pinned down on the beaches at Anzio, and later mentioned how lucky he felt when on his way to serve in the Pacific, he heard news of the Japanese surrender.

But Impreveduto never talked about those last moments in Germany, when in April 1945, he and his unit helped liberate the Nazi concentration camp at Dachau.

Then, forty-five years later, when rumors of a new invasion of video games reached him, he decided to talk. The games, an innovation of a West Coast manufacturer, allowed kids to become concentration camp commandants and the score was kept by how many Jews the player could kill. The state assembly was holding hearings to outlaw the machines in New Jersey, and Impreveduto's son, Anthony, then in his second term as an assemblyman, asked his father to speak.

"I knew he had been one of the first GIs to enter Dachau," Anthony Impreveduto said. "But he never said anything about it. I suppose he didn't want to recall those years. But I came home and asked if he would talk to the committee and tell them what he saw. Frankly, I was surprised when he said yes."

Then, sitting under the flood of television camera lights before an assembly committee in Trenton, the older Impreveduto spoke. He told them of the dead and the near dead he had seen during that April morning forty-five years earlier, of people dying as his boots crunched over the gravelly soil, of skeleton people still walking, of people falling to kiss the feet and hands of the American soldiers who arrived to liberate them.

He told the committee about the piles of human remains and the stench of death, about the ditches filled with rotting bodies and the oven chambers where the bones of former human beings could still be found among the ashes. He talked about the starving people staring at him, about the guard dogs roving like sentinels to hold these helpless people at bay.

"It was a moving experience to hear that from my father," Anthony Impreveduto said. "It was the first time I'd ever heard him talk about that part of his life."

But most of the people who joined the sixty-car funeral procession for Rocco Impreveduto on December 23 knew as little about that aspect of his life as his family once had. Impreveduto made more of a name for himself in Secaucus than he ever did in war, though the only public office he held was commissioner of the Secaucus Housing Authority, where he had served since the late 1980s.

Some people called him "Mr. Senior Citizen," for all the attention he gave to those living in the town's senior citizens' buildings.

Born in Hoboken, Rocco Impreveduto lived in Union City for many years before moving to Secaucus. He owned and operated Archway Catering in Secaucus; he previously co-owned a butcher shop in Hoboken, and, later, a supermarket which he sold in 1970 in order to build the Archway. In 1985, he converted the catering hall into an office building.

Impreveduto didn't have any hobbies. He spent most of his time at his business, running the restaurant, and when he retired, spent a great deal of time among the senior citizens.

"He got a great deal of pleasure from helping people," Anthony Impreveduto said. "He had a personal touch with the seniors. At the funeral, many of the residents came to say good-bye to him, and thank him for what he did in his capacity as commissioner."

"Things are not going to be the same in the senior buildings without Rocco," said Charlie Searle, a seventy-year-old resident of the Elms, among many who'd come to pay their respects at the passing of a man they believed helped them over the years.

Impreveduto, seniors claimed, understood their problems, and talked to them on a level they could understand.

"My father had a direct positive impact," Anthony Impreveduto said. "When someone needed something, he made sure that person got it."

Others say Impreveduto did a lot behind the scenes, giving money to people in need or finding answers to their pressing problems.

"He made people feel good," said his younger son, Patrick Impreveduto, principal of Secaucus Middle School. "He didn't just help seniors, but anybody in need. He helped people when he could. If someone needed food, my father found it for them. He was a big, big part of this town."

At the wake, thousands of people showed up, lining the sidewalk for a chance to pay their respects.

"Everyone has something to say about Rocky," said Robert Flanagan.

"Nobody took care of the seniors like he did. He cared about them, and they knew it. Though his political enemies thought it was all an act, it wasn't. Rocky's enemies just didn't understand him."

For those who came to say good-bye, Impreveduto was a close friend, someone who they would miss, a gruff piece of old Hoboken who adopted Secaucus and its people, and cared for them all like a father. Some admitted he was no saint. He was a man who got angry sometimes, and rarely allowed other people to cross him, particularly in politics.

While Impreveduto helped people, especially his children, making sure each received an education, he also expected his family to work. Anthony worked as a delivery boy for the family butcher shop in Hoboken when he was young, and helped build the Archway in Secaucus years later.

"But I think my father should be remembered for loving his children," Anthony Impreveduto said.

"Rocco was a very dedicated man, he loved this town and loved what he was doing," said Mayor Anthony Just. "He did wonderful things for the seniors of Secaucus and he proved his leadership. Whatever he did, he meant well, and he took a lot of pride in the job he did with the housing authority. He was a big plus for Secaucus."

From *The Secaucus Reporter,* Hudson Reporter Associates, 1997.

What a Lucky Man

To have lived life and then to discover you have not lived it to its fullest is a crime against nature, according to American philosopher Henry Thoreau. Each person is obligated to get the most from living.

For Richard LeRoy Deiner, who turned seventy a few days ago, this is not a problem. Life has been good and full of those memories of which Thoreau would have heartily approved, complete with the sense of where he fits in the world. Deiner and his wife, Jo Ann, have seen a good deal of the planet over the years and have managed to share in some of the great mysteries of their generation, from designing the atomic reactor for the USS *Enterprise* aircraft carrier to taking fifty-mile backpacking trips in New Mexico.

Richard and Jo Ann have been one of the more active couples in Glen Ridge over the last two decades, both socially and civically. Richard grew up near Reading, Pennsylvania, in a community called Stony Creek Mills. His father worked as a letter carrier during the Great Depression, raising Deiner and his five brothers and five sisters. When they lost their home, the family moved to his grandmother's home nearby.

Although Richard and Jo Ann attended the same regional high school, where Richard excelled in track and field as well as his studies, they did not meet socially until after high school when both worked for the same civil engineering firm, where Richard discovered a taste for surveying and engineering.

The Korean War interrupted his career yet gave him the means to seek a higher education under the GI Bill. After service, and after getting a degree thanks to the GI Bill, Denier pursued a career as an electrical engineer and was hired by Westinghouse. He was given the rare opportunity to join a brand-new field of engineering for which there was not yet a degree: atomic engineering.

"I found it interesting," Denier said, "and I learned a lot about design work. We didn't handle the hardware. Everything we did was on paper."

His paperwork led to the construction of the reactor for the USS *Enterprise* and, while he never got to stand on its deck, he did manage to stand on the deck of an atomic submarine.

This was 1959, the height of the Cold War, but he said he felt no pressure, saying he made power plants not bombs, and though ships might be considered weapons, his was the world of mathematical calculations, not political rhetoric.

"It was a remarkable experience," he said. "My work allowed me to go into new areas where we had to invent as we went along."

Later, because of his work in the field, Deiner got to participate in one of the most important experiments of the post-atomic age, the 1976–77 atomic fusion test reactor program in Princeton.

When Deiner came to live in Glen Ridge in 1972, he had no idea that he would stay. He was supposed to transfer to a company in Atlanta, Georgia, but when the transfer fell through, he looked around, found a house, and moved in, raising his eight kids here.

Both he and his wife have traveled extensively over the years. He did some traveling during college, but much more after he retired in August 1993, visiting places from Russia to the Antarctic. He and his wife visited their son when the boy served as a Peace Corps volunteer in West Samoa. Richard said the conditions were primitive; Jo Ann disagreed. Both paid their way when they didn't have to. Most of the time, they traded their time-share with others for the varied trips around the world.

To go to Russia, Richard had to give up his top-secret security clearance. While they made their visit during the most liberated period just before the breakup of the Soviet Union, the clearance would have created impossible barriers. The trip was one of the more memorable of Richard's life, and he recalled many of the scenes there, including the multiple lines, one to order an item, one to pay for it, and another to actually get it. He remembered the longest lines were generally for foreign-made shoes and alcohol. He also remembered a few dealers who grew their own food, selling their produce outside the confines of the collective, the first stirrings of western-style capitalism.

Although he doesn't get around as much as he once did, Deiner is an avid bird watcher and was once known to go anywhere to get a glimpse of a rare species. In Glen Ridge, he is known for his work with the Boy Scouts, working under three scoutmasters as treasurer and trip coordinator from 1980 to 1992. Currently, he serves as the Red Cross disaster chairman, touring the town as part of his duties to provide aid to anyone who has suffered anything from a house fire to a train wreck to flooding or even an airplane crash. In looking back at his life, Deiner sees himself as growing up in a time of opportunity and security.

"A lot of people in my time period started out poor in the Depression and managed to work their way up into good positions without fear of layoff," Deiner said. "Many worked for the same employer for most of their lives. This is very different from today. We were very fortunate."

From *The Glen Ridge Paper,* Worrall Community Newspapers, 1998.

A Model World

Who says grown-ups can't build models?

For award-winning Harmon Kaplan, the industry and art of model building is largely aimed at adults, who keep the spirit alive while learning a lot about history, too.

Kaplan, a resident and dentist in Secaucus, builds museum-quality models, issues a monthly newsletter for scale-model enthusiasts in Paramus, and is a member of the New Jersey Historical Miniature Association.

*Pictured here in 1993, Harmon Kaplan,
a model builder and dentist, expanded his
love of knowledge by sharing it with others
as a literacy volunteer later in the decade.*

Most adult modelists are shy about admitting what they do, thinking it looks funny to others, Kaplan says.

"They kid around about it, then go home and paint a tank, and other people don't think it's something to be done by adult men."

Yet it isn't a hobby exclusively for kids anymore, not when a metal model kit from Italy can cost as much as five hundred dollars, while the more common types run anywhere from four to forty dollars.

Like many of today's modelists, Kaplan started building models as a kid. He says he might even have caught something from his father, who built wooden trains, though it was largely on his own initiative that he got into the plastic replicas he does today. But he also started building trains, and trains are more acceptable today to the public. People have been building and collecting model trains since the nineteenth century, and such models are often found in hobby shop window displays, along with associated models for buildings and scenery.

Part of the attraction, he admits, is love of the technology. His is conservative politically, and yet he says he doesn't see machines as the answer to the world's problems. He says he loves machines, but not always what they represent.

"There are other ways of solving world conflicts besides going to war," he says. "Maybe it's a male thing, but many of the advances that come to the civilian society are a result of something out of the military."

Born and raised in Weehawken, Kaplan graduated from New York University, then the University of Medicine and Dentistry of New Jersey before going into the navy. Like modeling, the navy seemed to be in his blood. His mother was a navy nurse. His father served in the navy reserve. Kaplan himself caught the tale end of the Vietnam War, serving as the ship's dentist on the USS *Midway* during the war's closing months. Even then, he was attracted to machines, riding with the navy pilots every chance he got.

"It was something that got me away from teeth for a while," he says.

His mates called him the Flying Dentist or the Flying Tooth.

"I'm a bit gung-ho when it comes to the military," Kaplan says. "Especially the American military."

He says he likes to build models of machines from World War II as well as more imaginative and futuristic science fiction models.

"World War II machines offer a greater diversity," he says. "While modern machinery is more versatile, its design lacks distinctiveness."

But he avoids the cliché of military model building. He doesn't like tanks, preferring the soft-skinned variety of machines like jeeps and transports. At one competition in which World War I was the theme, most people built biplanes. He made a model of a machine gun and won a ribbon.

Another cliché he avoids is building anything German. It's a matter of principle. While he admits there is a great popularity among modelers for Axis machinery, he dislikes glorifying that era of German history. For the one all-German show he did enter, he created a totally fictional one-person helicopter.

"It was a goof," he says, holding up the model like a proud father. A small furnace is strapped to the back of a little man Kaplan calls the Baron. This little fellow is a goggled gnomelike figure, throwing hand grenades over the side of his craft, mocking the era and philosophy behind the Axis machinery.

"I wanted to be part of the show without glorifying its military culture," he says. "I tried to do something to make people laugh."

Kaplan says many people in modeling take it all too seriously, which is one reason he does science fiction models.

"No serious modelist does science fiction," he says.

Yet modeling isn't all fun and games for Kaplan either. Some of his best work is on display at the Intrepid Air and Sea Museum on the New York City side of the Hudson River. An amphibious tank Kaplan just completed is ready to enter the museum's Okinawa exhibit. A lot of what he does is on commission for private collectors or for companies that would like to see a professional rendition of their models before going to market with them. For the Chicago Toy Show Kaplan did an alien spacecraft, and he has done models for the New York Toy Show as well. Tamya, one of the larger modeling companies, is currently studying photographs of Kaplan's work for possible future commissions.

Kaplan, however, warns future professional modelists not to give up their day jobs. Modeling companies pay builders like him in modeling kits.

"There's very little profit in any of this," Kaplan says, waving a hand over the collection of models that he's kept for himself, only a handful since more are on display around the country. "For the hundreds of hours of research and construction, I wind up largely with kits. I do it for myself, because I like doing it."

It is work. Building the model is only one aspect. It is the research that is time consuming and sometimes nearly impossible. Modeling kits give only the basic designs, and there are variations and authentic color combinations.

"It is an obsession. You try for perfection. A syndrome to take history further," he says, noting how modelists demand a level of authenticity that is frustrating. Some research he does from books and magazines, though libraries are carrying fewer of them as the years pass. The local reserve on Route 17 in Lodi station helps in supplying him with pictures and information. Motor pool people are happy to help, letting him thumb through their repair manuals.

An individual piece can take as long as forty hours to build. Kaplan avoids buying the add-on kits, most often shaping his own small detailed parts out of an odd assortment of junk, like toothpaste containers, old TV or radio parts, and various bottle caps. His girlfriend sometimes stops her friends from tossing out things in order to give them to him. But he says he's not a fanatic about accuracy unless he's doing the work for a commission.

"Sometimes I go and do a science fiction model just to get away from their demands," he says. "Nobody can tell me I've painted one of those pieces the wrong color."

Kaplan does enter competitions. There are shows all over the country, starting with local competitions. Those that win locally go on to the regional level, and eventually the nationals. Kaplan has a wall full of ribbons from local and regional events. An international contest is planned for next year. Modeling has changed significantly since Kaplan was a kid. With new photo-edge detail parts, models have become literal miniatures of the original machines, complete with handgrips, mirrors, and seat belt covers. An airplane model, for instance, can vary in detail from the very simple kind that most kids built in the old days to an exact duplicate of what one might find on an airport runway. Whole companies have sprung up to supply these pieces to complement

basic modeling kits. These specialized companies are now a cottage industry, advertising their goods in hobby magazines and elsewhere.

Kaplan calls it a kind of fanaticism, but it is hardly one that is dying. The
industry has numerous ways of getting kids involved that it didn't have when
he was young, with computer programs designed to show the ins and outs of
model making as a by-product of flight simulation programs.

Modeling groups are popular, and the one he attends has a membership
of about 150, with 75 to 80 very active members. Meetings of such groups often
have professional speakers, like the helicopter pilot who talked about his experiences in Vietnam. Although the hobby is not dying, many people young and
old outside the club don't have hobbies the way he did when Kaplan was young.

"I ask my patients what they do to amuse their minds," he said. "None of
them seem to have hobbies anymore."

From *The Secaucus Reporter,* Hudson Reporter Associates, 1993.

Toy Soldiers March On

Toy soldiers aren't for kids any more, or so says James Delson, owner and
operator of the Toy Soldier Company in Jersey City. He is the largest seller
of toy soldiers in the United States. Although his customers are adults, his
business is good.

"The stress is on playing, not collecting," he said, "though we do tell
people they can rebuild the collection mother threw out when they went into
the army or college."

After nine years in the business of marketing toy soldiers, Delson has
learned that two things sell: something new or something people had as kids.

Toy soldiers are largely a thing of the past, one of the casualties of the Vietnam War, after which the whole industry took a nosedive. With the change
of national mentality, people seemed to frown upon anything remotely military. It caused most companies to stop manufacturing quality toy soldiers.

"It was Vietnam," Delson said. "But the nature of television also changed
the way children played. It wasn't given to historical subjects. They even stopped
making movies about history."

Even the legendary GI Joe had cleaned up his act, trading Green Beret and other military-oriented action accessories for those of hunter, mountain climber, and other less warlike roles. Although years later GI Joe's military aspect again became popular; toy soldiers remained off the mainstream manufacturers' lists.

Gauging from Delson's success, however, some people still want toy soldiers.

Delson never intended to sell toy soldiers for a living. He was a screenwriter, not a salesman.

"I got into it by accident," he said.

His interest in toy soldiers started like that of many of his adult customers, with play as a kid. In high school, he began to accumulate quality toy soldiers. He played poker with other boys and bought the soldiers with the winnings.

"I'm very lucky," he said, though he did think to put some money aside for college.

But in 1966, Britains—one of the world's largest toy soldier makers—offered its lead soldiers for sale.

"They were under an international edict to stop making lead soldiers," he said.

Delson took the five hundred dollars he had saved for college and bought as many lead soldiers as he could. But he was no collector. He played with those soldiers, re-creating authentic battle scenes out of history. In 1971, someone told him the lead soldiers were valuable.

"I never thought to sell them before," he said.

When he did, he was able to buy massive amounts of plastic soldiers with the profits. From this and continued collecting, he was able to re-create huge battle scenes that were historically accurate in numbers and space. These often took up the whole floor of a living room or someone's front lawn.

"This was big scale," he said.

During this time, he was a successful freelance writer, selling screenplays, critical film reviews, and other work to national publications. While none of his screenplays were ever produced, they sold, and he rented an apartment in Paris where he continued his search for toy soldiers, wandering the streets of the city with an eye out for toy stores.

Early in 1984, he began to review computer games and through that and role-playing games like Dungeons and Dragons, he discovered a different aspect of game playing. Instead of masses of nameless warriors, individual heroes like Indiana Jones or Harold Godwinson or Robin Hood emerged.

"Instead of massive battles with more and more soldiers, now we had a few heroes with battles of twenty or thirty characters," Delson said.

His collection of toy soldiers by this time was massive. Since he would never use them all, he began to supplement his income by selling the excess. He looked around and found magazines that wrote about toy soldiers. He had no real idea of the value of the pieces. He simply made them up based on his own likes and dislikes.

"What was near and dear to me went for a high price, what wasn't, I charged less for," Delson said.

Again, luck prevailed—or perhaps he had a good sense of quality. His prices seemed to match the current market value. He began to advertise. No one had marketed on this scale before. There were a couple of mail-order houses, but they had limited selections. With the number of soldiers he had, he could supply almost anything anybody wanted. Early sales netted him about $75 to $80 a week. By the end of 1984, he had sold about $4,000 worth of toy soldiers. By the next year, the figure was $30,000.

Delson hired a secretary to help him, but still did business out of his apartment. His first physical expansion was to rent a closet from an upstairs neighbor to store some of the soldiers. By early 1986, he realized he could make a living out of this.

He stopped writing for the magazines. As chic as freelancing seemed, it wasn't steady income. Often pay came late. With the soldiers, he had to put out an initial investment, but people still had to pay him up front if they wanted to buy from him.

Then he set up shop briefly in Brooklyn, but soon came across the river to Jersey City looking for more space.

Now, nine years after he started, he's into the business big time. He's listed in Dunn and Bradstreet. He has several full- and part-time employees. While he isn't making a killing, he's increased his space from 5,000 square feet to 7,500.

"I work eighty hours a week and make less money than my lowest employees. But it's a chance to get a lot of soldiers," he said.

Since most of the companies that had made toy soldiers in the past went out of business, restocking was precarious. Marx, the biggest American manufacturer, folded in 1976. Its molds were sold off. A company calling itself Marx has since started up in Florida, but it only owns a portion of the original molds. The rest are scattered all over the world. Delson said Marx products now come from places like Canada, the Philippines, Mexico, England, even the former Soviet Union.

Other manufacturers are even more difficult to track down, and getting big toy companies back into quality soldiers has been a task. Several, however, have been inspired by Delson's success; though they don't predict making a fortune from the product.

For one thing, dealers are rare.

"There are about three dealers who control 80 percent of the toy soldier market," Delson said.

One of these is a wholesaler and store with about ten lines of soldiers. Another is a retailer and toy soldier museum with about the same amount, and there is Delson's company, with 160 lines. He has about 4,500 names on his mailing list and now advertises in *Military Times* magazine, *Civil War Times*, *American History* magazine, *World War II* magazine, *Wild West* magazine, and others, including even *The New Yorker* and *TV Guide*. He also puts out a three-hundred-page catalogue, as well as the most comprehensive toy soldier guide in the world.

Yet even as business improves and the Toy Soldier Company dominates the market, Delson still plays. In one section of his warehouse, he has set up a complete French city street from the time of the French Revolution, complete with crowds, shops, buildings, and a guillotine. Business has taken a toll, however. He is married now with two kids and works eighty hours a week. This leaves him less and less time for play, and the success of the business is still not certain. The toy soldier market, like anything else these days, is hardly rock solid. Yet he consoles himself with one fact.

"If business fails," Delson said, "I'll have all the toy soldiers I'll ever need for the rest of my life."

From *The Weehawken Reporter,* Hudson Reporter Associates, 1993.

High-Seas Romance

If there was any doubt about how seriously Bill Miller takes ships, one short stroll through his Secaucus condominium would dispel it. Living in a third-floor apartment that overlooks Route 3, the Turnpike and the soft side of the Palisades, Miller still manages to shape his world into the texture of life at sea. The woodwork of the development exterior and the twisting stairs that lead to his door, all give the sense of climbing decks—or at least the sense that most wobbly-legged landlubbers have of ships.

But over the threshold where his world begins, every inch of space contains some bit of memorabilia. Not all of it comes by way of seafaring, his says

Bill Miller eventually retired from teaching in Hoboken, but he never gave up his interest in cruise ships. By the end of the decade he had authored several additional books and had provided his expertise to several national television specials.

with a charming smile and regretful tinge in his eye. The rugs weren't bought overseas, though they could have been, and he seems disappointed— the way old, honest sailors seem when every sea tale they tell is not one of high adventure.

But the walls are covered with paintings of ships, rare posters left from various cruises over the years, or ship-related images from various historic times. On one wall hang oil paintings of shipping scenes from old Hoboken or Jersey City, painted for him by a friend who knew just how nostalgic Miller is, with all the proper touches to make them seem authentic: smokestacks, background of rising steam, and scurrying dock workers.

Like someone who is used to every sort of quarters, Miller has the room filled with knickknacks, and memories. He says he had to cram things in a little coming to Secaucus from Jersey City's Heights—though before that he lived in Hoboken, in even more crowded lodgings.

Yet the room is not cluttered so much as full, as if you had stepped inside Miller's head, greeted by the images of his life. The ships are obvious. He has loved ships since listening for them as a kid from his family's Hoboken brownstone near Twelfth and Garden, when he used to hear the moan of the ships' horns in the morning, and he used to slip down to the docks to watch the ships coming and going. Saturday mornings were particularly fruitful for the boy with ships in his eyes and dreams of foreign places.

Even in its twilight years in the 1950s and early 1960s, Hoboken's port was busy. When Miller was a boy liners such as the *Constitution,* the *Independence,* the *Mauritania,* the *New Amsterdam,* the *Leviathan,* and others docked here. Hoboken's Pier B was also the home of the biggest German shipping companies in the world, the Hamburg-Amerika Line and the North German Lloyd line.

The world's biggest ships docked here. One of these was the *Imperator,* a 52,000-ton ship with an average of 5,000 passengers per voyage. Hoboken was also a shipyard city, with Bethlehem Steel and the world's largest marine-engine repair shop here as well.

A sea of accomplishments.

Bill Miller has been living in Secaucus for just over two years. He is considered one of the foremost authorities on ocean liners of the present and past. Miller wrote four of his thirty-five books at sea. His books deal with almost every aspect of cruise ships, from liners during the various wars to the lavish interiors of the most opulent ships. He has also written more than five hundred magazine articles on similar subjects.

He has been historian of the American Merchant Marine Academy Museum, chairman of the Port of New York branch of the World Ship Society, and the executive director of New York's annual Harbor Festival. Among his other accomplishments, Miller has been a board member of the Ocean Liner Museum project, taught a course on the history of cruise liners at the New School, and been contributing editor to the *Monthly Ocean & Cruise News* and a feature contributor to *VIA Port,* the journal of the Port Authority of New York and New Jersey.

Miller lectures on cruise ships throughout the world. In September, he was awarded the Bowditch Award, the national award for Maritime Scholarship and Research.

Miller got interested in luxury cruise liners in the late 1950s while still a student at Hoboken High School. Many of the great ships were already beginning to vanish, and he decided to write about them. He sent his first story to a prestigious magazine called the *British Ship Journal,* which didn't respond to him for months. Then, one day he found his story in the magazine, and a strange feeling came over him when he saw his name in print. He showed the story to his homeroom teacher, who escorted Miller down to see the principal.

"You didn't get to see the principal much in those days," Miller recalls. "He was God-like and seemed nine feet tall."

This exaggerated image made Miller's satisfaction that much greater when the principal congratulated him. "'Great going, young man,' he told me. 'You're a credit to the Hoboken school system.'"

This moment influenced Miller in several ways. Not only would he go on to become one of the most internationally recognized writers about cruise ships, but the moment also led him to a career as a teacher in the Hoboken school system.

"I wanted to travel and teach," Miller says. "That's what I wanted; that's what I did."

Now a classroom teacher at the Demarest Middle School, Miller has taught in Hoboken for more than twenty-five years. In that time he has also made more than two hundred voyages to almost every part of the world, returning with tales of distant lands and ocean-going adventures that enthrall his students.

"They have the perception that travel means going by car, airplane, or spaceship," he says. "But travel by sea is something new to them."

His anecdotes and nearly twenty-five thousand slides have become a vital part of his social studies classes, giving his students a firsthand account of the world, whether it is the Valley of the Kings in Egypt or the icy surface of the Arctic.

"It broadens their senses and gives them a tremendous window on how people live and how they are different from people living in New Jersey or the United States," Miller says. "I try to use my experiences to make them aware of the diversity of the world, whether it is the poverty and culture of Brazil, or the food shortages and decaying buildings of Russia."

His first book, a guide to cruises, came out in 1972, and during the 1980s he hit his high-water mark, publishing as many as three books year.

"I was an after-school book factory," he says.

His latest book is a sixty-eight-page soft cover book called *Voyages,* which deals with some of his trips over the years, including to Australia, Alaska, China, as well as several river trips, up the Mississippi, Amazon, and Danube Rivers. An upcoming book about New York shipping is due out any day now and will include a look at freight traffic in Hoboken and Jersey City.

Miller goes on cruises whenever he can, though he has slacked off the hectic pace that once took him on nine voyages in a year. Whenever he had a break from school, Miller went to sea. "Sometimes I only came home to wash my socks," he says.

Although he could make a good living at travel writing, Miller says he likes to teach, and likes the idea of having a land base to come home to.

"Travel can be too much of a good thing," he says. "You can get tired of it, as with anything else."

Miller is scheduled to go to Mexico during the upcoming Christmas break and says there are places his schedule has not allowed him to see, like India or the Antarctic. But he has been to the North Pole.

This was one of his most vivid and—in a way—disturbing memories. Arriving by ship, Miller says, he walked out onto a barren strip of ice.

"I was struck by the sound of its silence," he says. "There was nothing but the wind whipping at me. I seemed to be alone on the planet earth, far away from the human race. I felt I could walk forever and not meet another human being or see a street or road sign ever again."

From *The Secaucus Reporter,* Hudson Reporter Associates, 1994.

A Taste of Ireland

At ninety, Josephine Beere Ryan is hardly the oldest of her siblings. Of the eleven surviving members, Ryan comes in second—her older sister is ninety-four—although all of the siblings are now over eighty, a long-lived Irish family that bridges the Atlantic. When she talks about an extended family, Ryan in fact means geography as well as age, with hundreds of family members spread out from Ireland to California, many of whom stop in on her when they pass near Secaucus.

Oddly enough, for all her siblings and all her grandchildren, Ryan only became a great-grandmother in July, when her granddaughter-in-law in Secaucus gave birth to a baby girl.

It was one of those special moments, not just for Ryan, but also for the entire family, who have been chattering about it in expectation for months, though the Beere family, as they call themselves, tends to celebrate each important event, as if they all had a part in it. Relations coming east or west are always welcome and a reason for celebration. Most recently, one family member brought back from Ireland a chart of the family tree, trying to get it here in time for Ryan's ninetieth birthday. This cousin managed to trace the family line back as far as 1849 and intends to do more for Ryan's ninety-first birthday in 1998.

Ryan speaks highly of her father, amazed that the man managed to raise sixteen children in a small house in Ireland on the wages he earned working for the railroad. He also lived into his nineties. Ryan's ninetieth birthday has given her time to reflect. Her life has been full of small ironies and coincidences. Like the fact that a cousin immigrated to America on the same ship she did—the *America*—thirty years later or how when Ryan got to America in 1922 she met and fell in love with a man who had grown up nine miles from where she had grown up in Ireland.

"But we had to come all the way to America to meet," she said with a deep laugh.

Ryan, who has spent the last twenty-three years in Secaucus, lived forty-five years in Hoboken. She just got off the boat in 1922 and didn't leave until the whole family picked up for Secaucus. She loves Hoboken, loved the trains and little stores. She said she never needed a car, getting around just fine on her own. She is full of stories of old Hoboken from a time when the Irish and Italians didn't mix, and tells a tale of how she wouldn't let her daughter travel beyond Willow Avenue for fear she might fall for an Italian boy—which her daughter did.

For years, her husband worked on the docks, and though he wanted to marry her in 1934, she would not say yes until she made a trip back to Ireland. She's been back three times: once to meet her in-laws just before World War II, once to help bury her brother in 1962, and then, finally, in 1983. The last time she visited the house where she grew up, and the village where she had wandered as a girl.

"I won't be going back again," she said, and since her husband died in 1990, she has lived a quiet life with her son's family. But with all the family members coming and going from Ireland, she still gets a taste of the old country and can look forward to hearing the stories of the family with each visit, her family keeping the memory alive.

From *The Secaucus Reporter,* Hudson Reporter Associates, 1997.

A Brief Stopover

Few people noticed the black limousine when it drove slowly through the streets of Union City on August 31, or the license plates that said it was an official United Nations vehicle. No motorcade preceded it, no press release had been made about it, in fact, no local official was aware of who was in that car or why that car drove so slowly along such seemingly insignificant streets.

It was scorching hot, one of the last hot days of the summer, and the wheels of the car stirred up the dust even though it moved along very slowly.

Esko T. Hamilo, now fifty-one, sat in the back seat gazing out over sites he'd not seen since he'd spent a year here as an exchange student for the 1962–63 school year. He didn't have time to make a long formal stop in Union City; he had only a half-day to spend in New York, a stopover before going onto Australia with his family. In fact, his coming to Union City came as an unexpected surprise, resulting from a casual remark he made during an official luncheon with the Finnish ambassador to the United Nations. Hamilo just mentioned he would like to see Union City again, something he'd thought about, even pondered over since his last time here as a senior attending the town's two high schools. But over the years, his career in the diplomatic corps had kept him from returning, dragging him off to places like Paris or Brussels. He had come to New York once since then, but had no time to cross the Hudson. This time, when the UN ambassador heard, he had the embassy lend Hamilo a car and driver and insisted he make the trip, even if only for a drive through. It was unlikely Hamilo would get the chance again.

No one had thought to bring a camera, though for the most part, what he came to see no one could take a picture of, just reeling images from the past that he was now comparing with today.

"It was a very nostalgic moment," said Tom Sullivan, the former columnist for the Hudson *Dispatch* who had been responsible for bringing Hamilo to America in 1962. "All the memories just flooded back. He remembered where he lived, where he bought candy, and, of course, the two schools he attended."

Sullivan came up with the idea of bringing a student to Union City after meeting a slightly older man who had just come to visit America from Finland.

"I was blown away by how confident this man was, so young, so polite, so in control of himself, that I asked about his background and where he was from," Sullivan said. "Then when he told me I wondered what it would be like to bring a student from there to attend our high schools here."

The paper was willing to sponsor the program and conducted a campaign to help raise money for his room and board.

"Everybody contributed," Sullivan said. "People from all over town gave from five cents to ten dollars."

Hamilo attended a classical European school, where subjects like Latin were still part of the basic curriculum. He was a top student, and when the headmaster asked if he wanted to come to America for a year, he agreed.

"We made all the arrangements," Sullivan said, "and it was an awesome year."

In those days there were no satellite transmissions, no instant communication; a small town that far away was extremely isolated. And in 1963, at the peak of the Cold War, that part of the world was as mysterious as another planet. Hamilo's father was the composing room foreman for the town's newspaper, Keski Soumailen, which means Central Fin Lander. Jyvuaskyla, Hamilo's home town, was a regional market town in the lake region of Finland, where people from farming, fishing, and lumber industries came in from outer areas to sell and buy, and the newspaper was their main means of news. Here, Hamilo developed a hunger for news about the world and was intrigued by tales of America.

But Union City was a different place then. So was the world. While a few Cubans were sprinkled in this part of the county, Hudson County had a population of eastern and southern European (Polish, Czech, Italian, and Greek) immigrants, all of them gripped with the fear of the Cold War. This was the season of the Cuban Missile Crisis, when Soviet people and others in surrounding nations were mysterious and exotic.

"By and large, not many people had a chance here in those days to actually meet a foreigner from those countries," Sullivan said. "People loved him here."

The year left a great impression on Hamilo, and he apparently left a great impression on people at both high schools.

At seventeen, Hamilo spoke German, French, and English as well as Finnish. In fact, he spoke English so well he scored highest in his adopted class on Emerson's English vocabulary test.

"People kept saying he ought to get into the diplomatic corps, and that's what he did, and now, after all these years, he's become an ambassador," Sullivan said.

Indeed, that's what Hamilo did, taking up study in diplomacy and entering the diplomatic corps. He rapidly rose through the ranks to become the attaché or secretary consul for Finnish embassies in capitals throughout

Europe. Then, at the beginning of August 1996, he was called home to Finland, and told that he was being named Finnish ambassador to Australia, New Zealand, and New Guinea. On his way to take up his post, he stopped here, saying his thanks to Union City as he slowly drove through.

From *The Secaucus Reporter,* Hudson Reporter Associates, 1997.

Call It Kismet

Almost from the day Ester Chigrupati turned sixteen, she has been getting proposals for marriage, something she attributes to an older culture in which arranged marriages are accepted.

"I never thought I would consent to an arranged marriage," Chigrupati said. "But when the right man came along, I thought it would be crazy for me to say no."

Unlike many of the arranged marriages that are common between those of Indian heritage and spouses born in India, Chigrupati is not trying to reforge a connection with her Indian roots; she is simply marrying someone she loves.

"I'm a Jersey girl," she said, noting that she has lived in Glen Ridge, Montclair, and Bloomfield before moving on to Tufts University in Massachusetts.

Chigrupati said she never felt the pressure that many children of traditional Indian families feel to get married. Many families in the Old World see twenty-five or twenty-six as already too old for a girl to fit into a new family.

Chigrupati is twenty-two, but she said the choice was always hers; she is getting married because she wants to, not because it is expected.

While her father has lived and worked in the United States for more than thirty years, he makes frequent trips back to India, where he gets numerous requests for his daughter's hand in marriage. Chigrupati said she never took any of them seriously, and perhaps, for a long time, thought the idea a little old-fashioned. She thought herself too young to marry and had planned to get her master's degree, and perhaps even a law degree, before looking for a life partner.

"I thought I might get established on my own," she said.

Then, her father went back to India last January, where again he was approached by people asking about his daughter and whether or not she would consider marriage. Her father promised nothing except to say he would bring the pictures back and show them to his daughter.

One picture was of a man named Solomon Kuchipudi, a doctor in India who had never even visited the United States.

"When I saw the picture I thought he was cute," Chigrupati said. "My father suggested I give him a call and we talked on the phone. It was a little awkward at first, but I liked what I heard."

Fate—or as she called it Kismet—seemed to play a hand. Not until later did she realized that her first phone call had come on St. Valentine's Day.

A week later, they spoke again.

"During that time we both thought a lot about each other, about what we were looking for in a spouse, so when we spoke again, we both had some hard questions to ask," she said.

Both came up to the second phone call with something she called "a marriage checklist" with questions about how the other person felt about kids, religion, careers. Each answer seemed to match on both lists.

"I liked the way he sounded," Chigrupati said. "We were both looking for the same things."

So when Kuchipudi proposed marriage during the second phone call, Chigrupati said yes.

"I would have been pretty stupid to let him go," she said. "When you see something you're looking for, you have to take it. It might not be there later when you go looking for it again."

Her father, of course, insisted that she go to India and meet her future husband face-to-face, and meet with his family. While she was in India, Kuchipudi gave her a ring.

Oddly enough, both Chigrupati and Kuchipudi are Christian, not Hindu, removing one possible obstacle from their path to marriage. While Kuchipudi's mother was Hindu, she had converted. The Chigrupati family has been Christian for three generations.

"We are very much in love," she said. "I never thought something like this would happen to me in my life. I don't know how it happened. I suppose it is Kismet. It is very beautiful how it all fell into place. I have no explanation for it."

Since the second phone call, the two have been in nearly constant contact, resulting in a phone bill of fifteen thousand dollars. In some ways, she said, the distance had allowed them to know each other better, even more intimately, than they would have if they saw each other day-to-day. She said if she had met him in the United States, things might have been different; she might not have gotten the chance to learn about him the way she has now.

"This way we had to talk to each other and learn about each other from what each of us said," she said.

Chigrupati said she intends to take a year off before pursuing her master's degree. Her marriage is scheduled for August 23, with a reception at the Doubletree Somerset. The couple will live in Pittsburgh, where Kuchipudi will do part of his residency over the next year. After that, both will see where Kismet takes them.

From *The Glen Ridge Paper,* Worrall Community Newspapers, 1998.

Sweeping Hudson's Chimneys

No one in a million years would picture Ron Simpson dancing across the rooftops singing, or doing any of the mad antics from the 1966 film *Mary Poppins.* Yet for many Americans, the role played by Dick Van Dyke in that film typifies what they have come to expect from a chimney sweep, calling up images out of Charles Dickens, horse-and-buggy traffic, and weekly coal deliveries.

Ron Simpson does not sing or prance across the rooftops, although he was trained in England and retains a touch of it in his thick Australian accent. If he resembles anyone from the movies it would be Crocodile Dundee. He has the same leathery look of that movie character, but lacks the hat and the Bowie knife, though he claims his accent is deceptive.

"When I'm in Queensland, people tell me I talk with an English accent," he says with a laugh. "When I'm England they tell me I sound Australian. I guess I have a touch of both."

He smokes like a steam pipe, one cigarette after another, and insists on explaining things in detail. He won't have a misunderstanding over what he means, even when it comes to telling people what they don't want to hear.

Ron Simpson and his son, Ron Jr. — pictured here in 1996 — did so well in cornering the Hudson County chimneysweeping market that by the year 2000 they were investing in real estate.

"I always tell people what's what," he says. "That way there's no confusion later on."

Sweeping chimneys has evolved into a complex profession that few people this side of the Atlantic understand, more than just a once-a-month or -season brushing out of soot. Simpson, at the age of fifty-eight, has become a jack-of-all-trades out of necessity, a man, who after being born in England, trained in England, and emigrating to Australia, learned about heating systems and how to offer service with a smile.

"I'm a mason by trade," he said, noting that in England, sweeping chimneys was the first step in learning a mason's trade. For Simpson, that meant starting a career as an apprentice mason when he was fifteen years old, and learning not just about how chimneys were made but also how whole buildings were constructed around such heating systems. As an apprentice, Simpson earned the honor of becoming the Guild of Master Sweeps' apprentice of the year three times—a feat that started a friendly rivalry with his own son, who later repeated the feat as an automotive apprentice in Australia.

As a mason, Simpson learned the construction business from the ground up—not just how to sweep chimneys but how to build them, and how to build everything attached to them. Eventually, in Australia, where such businesses were regulated by the government, he started his own business and brought many of the skills he learned to Hudson County when he set up business here in 1992.

Along the way, Simpson's interests wandered, sending him into professions as similar to masonry as construction, as different as sailing the high seas.

"As a young man I went to sea a few times," he said, giving a leathery grin that is almost his trademark. He once thought to make his fortune by investing in the lucrative tourist trade surrounding the America's Cup sailboat races, buying a share in a 144-foot, 250-passenger boat, part of the spectator fleet.

Later, he decided maybe he would like to sail his own ship, went back to school to qualify for captain of an oceangoing ship. He bought several boats over the years, including one he still owns that is dry-docked in Florida.

But the sea never stole his heart, and he came back again and again to construction; for a while, he renovated apartments in Hudson County, part of the reconstruction boom that made fortunes for other contractors. Then, one day, looking out the window, he saw the chimneys of Hoboken, hundreds of chimneys stirred up memories of his past, yet created the odd sensation that he had stumbled into a graveyard where bricks fell out onto roofs and nobody noticed.

"People just weren't paying attention to their chimneys," he said.

While all modern buildings had chimneys of some sort to accommodate their heating systems, many of the chimneys Simpson saw came out of the classic period of chimney construction, a style predominant during his years as an apprentice.

"The technique for building chimneys is very similar here to what it was in England," he said, noting that many of the buildings in Hoboken use a turn-of-the-century technology. "The average building in Hudson County comes from the older era of construction in chimneys, when they used a lime mortar which was the sealant between the bricks used most often before the invention of concrete, which is the basic material used today."

The problem with lime mortar is that over time—especially over the hundred years since many of the Hudson County chimneys were built—the lime oozes out.

Chimneys have also suffered through numerous changes in fuel.

"People will just about burn anything in a fireplace, plastic, wood, treated wood, paper, oiled timber, even coal," he said.

When one woman in Secaucus put a match to a kerosene-treated log earlier this year, she had no idea that her chimney was clogged, or that soot from a dozen years hung down inside of it like a black spider's web, or that when she put the match to the log, a flame would shoot up the chimney and knock the top off—and nearly set her roof on fire.

Some of the wood people burn is dangerous, depending upon how the wood has been treated. Most of the pressurized woods have glue in them, which is less harmful, but some treated timber releases carbon monoxide gasses when it's burned.

"While you can burn almost anything, the best is untreated timber," Simpson said. "Coal is still good, but most people are looking for aesthetic appeal."

Simpson saw something dreadful in that vision of crumbling chimneys, and he wondered why no one here specialized in repairing them. Only later did he discover the trend of the late 1970s and early 1980s, when people seemed to think chimneys hideous and did many appalling things to disguise them, wrapping them up in aluminum or rubber, painting over them, or sealing them up.

"People did everything wrong you could think of," Simpson said, and decided right then to do something about it, like a man with a mission looking to make his fortune by doing what he was first trained to do. The renewed popularity of fireplaces helped. But even without this trend, many of the old chimneys were still in use, converted to vent hot water and heating systems, even as bricks fell out of them. Over the last two years, he's wandered from one end of Hudson County to the other, cleaning, unblocking, and repairing chimneys, just the way he did as a kid, many years ago in England.

From *The Hudson Current*, Hudson Reporter Associates, 1996.

Haunted No More

When Martha Wiecorneck saw the man hanging out in front her house and staring at the building across the street, she began to wonder. She didn't know who this man was, but knew the house near the corner of Raydol and Chestnut Court had always meant trouble, as if a cloud of bad luck hung over it. Like the time the original owner dragged people off the street to convert it from a barn to a house, slapping pieces of junk wood onto it until it stood three stories tall.

"[The original owner] was a strange kind of man who didn't get along with the neighbors well," Martha said. "He built a camper inside the garage and it was so big he couldn't get it out the door."

Many of the stories about the old house might have come from a Stephen King novel or a cheap detective thriller from late-night television.

"It was a real circus," she said with a glint in her eyes and a distant look, adding that she could recall every step up to the point when the house got taken over by drug dealers, junkies, and other strange folks coming and going at all hours of the day and night. She certainly recalled the day they left, when ten police cars pulled up to the curb and hauled them off—leaving the house to the rats and squirrels.

Then, after the house had been sitting vacant for a long time, Martha's mystery man came, stopping almost daily to stare up at the dilapidated structure, squinting at it as if he could see something there no one else could see.

"I didn't know who he was at the time," Martha said. "He just got out of his car and stared at the house, then after a few times doing this, he knocked on my door."

The man, Joe Fontana, was a local contractor who liked to fix up old houses, though she could tell from the way he stared at the house across the street that he thought this house was special.

"He told me he wanted to buy the house," she said. "The house was going up on auction. He said he was going to bid on it and asked me to wish him good luck."

Yet even in its deplorable condition and with its dark history, the house did not come cheaply. Other bidders must have seen something in the place, too—though its back wall comes within two feet of the barbed-wire-topped fence that separates the residential neighborhood from Meadowview County Hospital, where the Youth House and other drug and detention programs are located. Joe thought he was going to get a good deal, maybe buy the building and property for $50,000 or $60,000. The bidding war ended at $112,000—with much more to be spent later after the building's condition became evident.

In a little over a year, however, Joe managed to transform that eyesore into one of the most talked about construction projects in the town, a building more like a mansion than the madhouse it had been.

Don Papas, who travels frequently in the area, was stunned by the change.

"It's captivating," he said. "I saw the house when Joe first bought it and then later when the outside was done. Everybody called it an eyesore. I call this eyesore relief."

Indeed so marvelous a change came over the place in a single year that the editors of *Better Homes and Gardens* intend to feature it in their magazine when Joe finally finishes the interior—perhaps by December. [The *Better Homes and Gardens* story, unfortunately, never materialized.] The current building is only a shell with the basement and third floor still in need of massive reconstruction. But the outside has people—even strangers—stopping on the street to stare.

The red brick wall running along the front of the triangular-shaped property is all new; along its base, an extended flower box with red impatiens and green shrubs gives the house color, as Joe puts it, though it has a grander sense of eloquence which draws people to it, with lanterns running along the top of its wall, guarding the archway and gate that leads to the backyard.

But the most talked about aspect of the new construction is the ornamental rock garden on the south side of the house, complete with pond and pump-supported waterfall. A small park bench looks down from the top like a scene from a local park. A plastic duck floats in the water and there is a statue of a deer on a small grassy knoll.

Yet signs of the continuing battle with the past remain. Behind the row of evergreens that line the front yard like a fence, the inner workings of the year-long project show. Ladders, abandoned lawn chairs, green workshop shelves, trash cans, bags of concrete mix, even a road sign mingle with the wild wheat and fireweed. Stacks of lumber, a garden hose, a metal utility sink, the base an old-fashioned bathroom sink, shovels, rakes, bags of peat moss, even a wheelbarrow or two sprawl there.

Joe got title to the property on June 17, 1993—yet admits he'd been so anxious about what he could do with the property that he'd already started work inside the structure before the signing, trying to untangle the mess years of improper additions had created. Before he started, the building had slatted-style siding. The original barn door had been boarded up with plywood.

Joe said he had a vision in his head from the start. He passed the building, saw it, and says the work was a matter of turning the old place into what he saw. He admits, however, that he had second thoughts once he began to take the place apart and discovered how the previous owners had constructed it.

"If I knew then what I know now, I probably would have torn the building down and started from scratch," he said, although according to local zoning, he would not have been able to build a three-story house on this site.

The $112,000 purchase price was only the beginning. Doing much of the work himself, he has not kept close tabs on what he's spent, yet he sees the project as a creative challenge, and the cost has been substantially reduced by finding salvageable things to use—like the hot tub that he got at a discount.

The windows, which are top quality, he got as a result of a mansion being renovated. He said he's squirreled away other items, filling the basements with stones and tools that might come in handy later. Even among some of his competitors, there is a grudging respect for Joe's ability to find deals and collect useful items.

Yet Joe sings the praises of Home Depot, and he may be the local store's biggest customer, although he brags of having used other branches of the discount home repair superstore chain before the Secaucus store opened, traveling to Clifton and other locations just for the better prices.

Standing in front of his building with his hands on his hips, Joe looks like the classic image of an old-fashioned carpenter, wearing a tank-top shirt, his muscular arms tanned, the smell of sawdust around him. His features are classically Italian, very reflective of a county where men like him were the backbone of the mid-century construction industry. He grins often and constantly eyes the building, turning his head as if calculating a wood cut or a piece of something that needs to be nailed in place.

"The former residents let the place go to hell. Rats and squirrels took over," he said. "Neighbors used to see them walking their ferrets up and down the street the way other people walk dogs. Ferrets hunt rats, and this place had a lot of rats."

When he started work on the inside, Joe found rat and squirrel droppings everywhere, and part of the roof had been eaten away by gnawing squirrels. The smell of squirrel urine infested the place as well, since squirrels spray as part of their nest making.

"There were over fifty squirrels in the house when I started," he said, "and a few dead ones, too. I had problems for months after I closed up everything."

His tenant complained about hearing squirrels running up and down inside the walls, trying to get back into the house. He found they had gotten access into the space between the brick and the main wall.

The mason work is a story in itself, he said, noting that the building used six thousand bricks. At first Joe worried if he would be able to find someone to do the work. But the masons arrived, they took one look at the house and leaped out of their truck, no price discussed, they just went to work.

"They worked so fast that there are Dunkin' Donuts and pizza boxes still in the walls," Joe laughed.

Joe's gotten in under the town's tax-abatement program, which helps owners of aging houses rebuild, renovate, and restore such buildings. The town now offers people with houses more than twenty years old an opportunity to rebuild.

"It's a way of getting our housing stock modernized," said Councilman Mike Grecco.

"This is the kind of thing we had in mind when we voted to continue the rebate program," Mayor Anthony Just said. "Secaucus will never look like the South Bronx because of programs like this."

Although the exterior of Joe's house is a neighborhood work of art, the interior is still a major headache. Years of neglect, structural damage, and bad workmanship have left Joe shaking his head. One apartment in the building is livable, but work on the upper floor still involves installing a new internal framework, making up for the crazy, haphazard workmanship done during previous construction. But it's not an issue of money—it's one of pride. This is Joe's project, and in the end, Joe intends to live here. He credits the neighborhood, his family, and cooperation from with members of the department of public works and other town officials for helping make the whole thing work.

"Without them I couldn't have kept going," he said.

Although he is still a bachelor, Joe says he's looking to settle down. He has serious plans for the future. He wants to get married and move in here to raise a family.

"Yeah, I want kids," he said with an almost embarrassed grin. "At least three of them."

From *The Secaucus Reporter,* Hudson Reporter Associates, 1995.

A Sense of Style

Perhaps the oddest thing the Reverend Mark Lewis discovered when he took over as pastor of the Church of Our Saviour a year ago was its 1925 Sears, Roebuck–designed church building. It seemed to symbolize something about the parish, and he found himself intrigued by what kind of people he might find here. Something seemed to call out to him, making him feel wanted.

"When I came to Secaucus and saw this church a year ago, I felt that it had charisma about it. I'm not sure exactly what it was, but I knew I wanted to be a part of it. It felt very magnetic, a very real sense of the curious," he said.

After nearly two years without a permanent minister, the church and its small congregation seem to take to him, too—one more curious twist of fate

The Reverend Mark Lewis—pictured here in 1995—attracted enough parishioners to his congregation that they outgrew their 1925 Sears, Roebuck church and by the year 2000 had made plans for expansion.

for a man who once served a Washington, D.C., congregation that included President George Bush.

"It was strange to think that on any given Sunday I might be preaching to the president of United States," the Reverend Mr. Lewis said in a lively and excited pattern of speech that has made him popular with his Secaucus parishioners. "I wasn't anyone important there, and I'm not sure it even happened, but it could have happened."

Rev. Mark Lewis was born and raised in the South, and still speaks with an Arkansas accent so distinctive that you feel as if you're not in Secaucus at all when you listen to him. But the mind behind the voice is most startling, a mind educated in conflicting religious doctrine. His father was an extreme libertarian. His grandmother, a socialist, taught Marxist religious theory in the South during the 1940s. Caught between a fundamentalist Baptist doctrine on one side and the Marxist interpretation on the other, Lewis said he grew up confused.

"At the height of the 1960s when both sides were butting heads, I found myself standing in the breech, Baptists on one side, Marxists on the other, and I thought, both sides of Christianity can't be right."

Yet during that time, the Reverend Mr. Lewis said he discovered just how broad a range Christianity covers, so broad that it sometimes appears to conflict with itself, though it really doesn't.

"I stood in the breech for five or six years, and got a chance to look around," he said. "You have to understand [that]when I grew up I didn't even know a Catholic. All I saw were fundamental Baptists and muscular Marxists."

For a while, he worked in publishing as an editor. He got his degree as an undergraduate at the University of the South in Sewanee, Tennessee, then his master's in English at the University of Virginia. When he finally decided to become a minister, he attended the Virginia Theological Seminary in Alexandria.

The Episcopal faith introduced him to something he calls "the drama of liturgy" and made him realize there was much more to Christianity than the two extremes he knew. In fact, he said, he discovered a history of intellectual freedom in the Christian Church he'd not previously suspected. In the Episcopal Church, he found a channel in which he could develop a religious path and still have the eloquence of language and music.

"When I discovered all this, I said, this is for me; this has history and this has style," he said.

It is this sense of style the Reverend Mr. Lewis has brought to Secaucus, although he admits that he's had to reshape his thinking a little since arriving here a year ago.

"I came ready for things to happen fast and I learned the hard way," he said. "When dealing with groups or working with an institution, things happen slowly."

Although he knows more people have come to his church over the last year, the exact extent of that growth is still unclear to him. When he first arrived, the church had been without a regular minister for more than two years. Sunday service sometimes saw as few as twenty churchgoers. Since his coming, a Sunday service has brought as many as sixty. Part of this increase he attributes to the fact that the church finally has a full-time minister again.

"Any fool knows you'll get an increase in attendance once you have a regular minister," he said with a laugh.

Yet part of the increase may be an honest reaction to the kind of preaching Lewis has brought to the church, a style of rhetorical sermonizing one parishioner fondly called "a bundle of fire."

"There were more people at the Easter service this year than any time since the 1920s when the building was put up," the Reverend Mr. Lewis said.

Part of what he brings to the church is historical.

"The history of the Anglican Church always has centered around people who want to think about religion rather than react to it emotionally," Reverend Lewis said, calling this "a mind and heart" approach to faith, an approach without an insistence upon dogma or rules.

"Most Anglicans recoil from rules, cherish an individualistic approach to politics and religion," he said. "We've always insisted on people working through issues rather than relying on rules and regulations to build their faith."

In his effort to help his congregation think through their religion, Mr. Lewis said he is trying to move outside the walls of the building, outside the box of religion, and make faith function in the real world, trying to shatter people's preconception of the word *church*.

"I want to liven it up and make it contemporary. I want this community to face the outside world with people as people who know God and their faith," he said. "I want to bring people into this church who want to help us help others."

Catherine Murray, a resident of Harmon Cove Towers, discovered the Church of Our Saviour about a year ago, and has been attending ever since. She calls the Reverend Mr. Lewis "a bundle of fire," saying she'd never met a minister like him.

"He spoke my language and understood what it meant to be a working mom," she said. "He's tuned in."

Murray said she talks to Mr. Lewis several times a week, as well as attending Sunday service, and finds that he understands the needs of the more modern churchgoer.

"He's sort of taking the church, kicking and screaming into the 1990s," she said. "He's very bright and eloquent, and he turns a phrase in a very passionate way. After the sermon, he's all wound up."

Not only has she found his preaching style something special, but she also has observed that he pays attention to the small details that mean a lot to parishioners. Mr. Lewis set up a baby-sitting room at the church so that single mothers like Murray could attend services on Sunday.

"Kicking and screaming" may not be an exact description of Lewis's approach, although some of his new parishioners urge him on toward making more rapid changes and grow frustrated with him when he insists on taking things at a more leisurely pace.

"I need to tell them that's not how we work here. We may not be as efficient or quick as we ought to be, but I'm determined to have people here do things together, even if that means doing things slowly," he said.

This is especially important because his congregation is made up of a diverse mingling of old Secaucus and new, some from a working-class background, others from a background with a broader education.

"One family has been attending this church for four generations. Some of the kids coming to Sunday school are related to those who came here sixty-five years ago," Mr. Lewis said. "They've stuck with the place, for them, this place has worked for the last sixty-five years."

Indeed, some of the parents of current parishioners helped build the church here in 1920s, a prefabricated building purchased from Sears, Roebuck. Such kits were shipped in pieces and assembled by the buyer much the way bicycles or bookshelves might be today. The congregation itself began in the early 1920s when a number of English immigrants began moving into Secaucus. Church officials in Jersey City noted the influx when they received more and more calls for ministerial services.

In 1923 parishioners began regular services, meeting in a public building, a rented hall in the Plaza section of town. By 1925, they had enough money to purchase the prefab building and put it up along what was then Route 3. By 1953, they had enough money to purchase a piece of land across the street. At that time, they picked up the building, put in down on its current location, and built a house beside it.

"It has held up grandly," Lewis said. "That's because it has been cared for, loved, and cherished with no lapses in maintenance or care."

Parishioners added their own touches over the years, such as contemporary stained glass.

"It's not from Tiffany's, but it's beautiful just the same," Lewis said.

As with Murray, many of the church's newer parishioners come from Harmon Cove, partly because of the nearby location, partly because of the nature of the faith.

"Many people are looking for something spiritual without all the trappings of a more ritualistic based church," the Reverend Mr. Lewis said. "While we're a small church, we're intentionally open and accepting, more modern, inclusive and pragmatic."

Although slow, the changes are coming as new members join the church, bringing new ideas and energy with them.

"It is a radical thing, a sense of constant change, old members needing to adjust to the new ideas being brought in," Mr. Lewis said. "We've learned that the church changes whenever anybody new joins it."

Yet not all the new ideas are generated by the new parishioners. Earlier this year several of the top lay leaders asked if they could find more current hymns than the ones previously used. Many of those date back to Martin Luther.

"We've got no stick-in-the-muds here," Lewis said. "The fold is seeking to know and love God, but on the ground. These people have energy and the feeling is contagious. They're looking to know who God is. I'd quit here in a New York minute if what we had here did not work or wasn't enriching. I'd stay home and read the *Times*."

Among plans generated by the congregation is the conscious effort to reach out into the local community and help. While not thundering ahead, the church is moving slowly in that direction. With the help of some of its top lay leaders, such as Elanore Ruther and Edna Mondadori, the church has offered its help to the town, working closely with the office for social services to provide space to store furniture, clothing, and other items destined for needy families.

"We keep looking to give, even though we don't have a big bank account," Mr. Lewis said. "In fact, because we don't have a big bank account, we must be more creative. While you might see this church as poor and lean, I see it more as lean and muscular."

The rate of growth, while hardly what he expected when he started, is gratifying, and now after a year here, he said, he's calmer, and more rooted in Secaucus and the subcommunity of the church.

"It's a holistic feeling," he said. "I feel more complete, slower, calmer. The noise inside of me has harmonized in a great way here. I've never felt more at home in any place in my life."

From *The Secaucus Reporter,* Hudson Reporter Associates, 1996.

Listen to the Music

One of the first things Patricia Brady-Danzig teaches her students is how to breathe, a bit of yoga that helps a singer shape the sound.

Of course, the lessons she taught at the Secaucus Community School during two sessions in February weren't strictly the kind of voice instruction she has taught in the past, when she was the music director at Immaculate Conception Church for seventeen years.

A classically trained soprano, Brady-Danzig toured more than eleven countries to become an international singing star, after taking fifteen years off to raise a family. Her mother said Brady-Danzig could sing a whole song by age two. And over the course of the last twenty years, she has performed in venues from Carnegie Hall to equally impressive international stages in Germany and Romania. Her busy schedule was part of the reason she decided to retire from the church.

"I would get an offer to go somewhere, but I couldn't," she said.

In fact, since retiring from the church in 1997, Brady-Danzig has been busier than ever, with scheduled stops in Italy, Ireland, and Mexico. Over the last two years, she has also released two CDs, *A Woman's Life in Love* and *Romanian Melodies,* and has had a music resource center named after her at Caldwell College. During that time Brady-Danzig has also continued to teach throughout the tristate area.

Yet as eager as she was to leave, something here in Secaucus drew her back, feelings for the people with whom she spent so many years, singing and shaping music of praise at the Immaculate Conception Church. So last year, almost as a gesture to those people she left behind, Brady-Danzig returned to Secaucus to share her talents by teaching a two-week seminar at the Secaucus Adult School.

Adult School officials and her friends at the church had asked her to host a seminar on singing and music. How could she refuse?

Billed as "A Musical Potpourri—All the Things You Ever Wanted to Know about Music," the program covered everything from Broadway to the Beatles, opera to Frank Sinatra, with numerous stops along the way to study the history and social temperament surrounding various genres.

In some ways the people who come to Brady-Danzig's classes are as much friends as students, seeking out an excuse to continue the song-full relationship they have shared with her over the years. In fact, her classes seemed to come from the various parts of her life, half from Secaucus, half from the Essex County where she lives and sometimes performs. People breathe in and out at her instruction, then follow her through the scales in anticipation of singing anything from light opera pieces to old church hymns. Many of the people who share the class seem to have grown on Brady-Danzig, too, making her seek them out during the regular year. She calls one former student and associate in Secaucus just to keep her talking.

"She had a stroke, and though she is recovering well, I like to encourage her to speak," Brady-Danzig said.

During the last class of this year, seven people came, all of them seeming to know a lot about music already, and a lot about the teacher, following her lead through this and that, nodding their heads as she makes points about the music she is playing or they are reviewing over the tape deck.

"I attended the Sunday service for a few years," said Gus Wilke, a resident of Secaucus. "I was very impressed with her variety of musical knowledge."

Ruth Brown, another Secaucus resident, said she had missed Brady-Danzig when the latter left as the choir's leader, and felt the class was a good way to get back in touch with the woman and the music.

Other people in the class came from North Caldwell and Verona and seemed as comfortable here in the classroom as those who had sung with her for years.

But it's the music that's the central theme, and these people tap their feet and clap their hands to the familiar melodies played on the stereo or tinkled out by Brady-Danzig's able fingers on the piano. Brady-Danzig said she started the class for those who wish to familiarize themselves with various types of music and for those who want to improve their musical talents. Yet beyond the music, the class often deals with the behind-the-scene social forces that helped shape the sound and performance.

In a study of Nat King Cole, the class covered not only his rise from a brilliant jazz performer to one of the most recognizable vocalist in musical history but also his struggle with racism during a particularly volatile time in history, how he overcame not only the prejudices of a white society but also the criticisms of the black community.

Sitting in on one of her classes quickly makes clear that Brady-Danzig sees music as a means of communicating something ordinary words cannot, a way of shaping feelings about life, history, and human relations that cannot always be found in a textbook. Most importantly, song—in any of its forms— seems to brings out emotions in people, making them laugh, making them cry, making them happy, and sometimes making them sad. Yet, in some ways, the whole experience is a means of connecting with people she has come to love and people who have come to love her, a once-a-year trip back to her roots in Secaucus that those who attend her class appreciate.

"I love the music, and it makes me happy to be here," said Secaucus resident Dixie Pizzuti.

From *The Secaucus Reporter,* Hudson Reporter Associates, 1999.

PART TWO

The Nature of Things

On Call

It all starts with a sound they call "Star Wars," a kind of electronic hum that the dispatcher at the Glen Ridge police station uses to tell members of the emergency squad that they can expect a message momentarily, a sound emitted through a beeperlike speaker each carries on his or her belt.

It is a contact tone that the dispatcher sends when someone calls 911 asking for medical assistance, and it is an eerie sound that tells each member of the Glen Ridge Volunteer Ambulance Squad that someone could be in trouble, and that within a few minutes, the squad could be asked to help save someone's life.

A moment after the tone warns them, the dispatcher's voice comes on, telling them where to go and in general terms what they can expect to find when they get there.

In a small town like Glen Ridge they know all of the streets, how to weave through them to find the quickest way. But each person on the squad also knows they will likely be dealing with someone they know from town when they reach their destination. Each member of the squad learns cardiopulmonary resuscitation from the squad's own instructor. Most of the squad's members are EMTs or on their way to earning their certificates, and they can handle all but the most serious cases. When a situation involves a serious injury or a life-and-death situation, the squad calls in the paramedics who also reside in Glen Ridge at Mountainside Hospital.

Calls could be of any kind, from a child's falling to a man complaining of chest pains. About 20 percent of the cases involve motor vehicle accidents. Many more cases deal with chest pains or difficulty breathing. Squad members supply what is called "basic life support," first aid that will get a patient to the hospital to be treated. Paramedics, usually paid staff assigned to a hospital, perform advanced life support for people who are unconscious, suffer chest pains, have difficulty breathing, sustain strokes, fall from more than twenty feet, or get severely hurt in a traffic accident.

"An EMT cannot do anything invasive," said Captain Bob Hayes, "such as perform a medical procedure, give drugs, or install an IV."

But EMTs can stop bleeding, put a splint on a leg or arm, treat minor injuries such as a cut, and complete tasks that will prevent a person from additional injury, whether this involves a backboard or a collar.

"My philosophy has always been that we will get you to the hospital no worse than we find you," Hayes said, though he admitted there are situation in which the injuries are so pronounced no one could live up to that promise. "Stabilize and get the person to a doctor, that's what we do."

"It's a remarkably rewarding job," Ellen See said.

When pressed about the more gruesome aspects, she shrugged and said squad members get a kind of "tunnel vision" with so much attention spent on getting a person to safety that the blood is hardly noticeable.

Hayes agreed, saying that most of the time an EMT is too busy thinking about what comes next to think about what he or she is dealing with. It is part of the training, he said, something that keeps an EMT concentrating on helping people, going through the routines they have established for various situations.

EMTs and other squad members are there to help people who are scared and in pain and who need as much comfort as possible en route to the hospital.

Sam Argow, an EMT in training, laughed and said a kind of force takes over, making him focus on the specific needs of each patient. If a patient is conscious, the squad asks which hospital the patient wants; the unit will take the patient to any hospital within ten miles, provided the patient's life is not endangered. If so, the unit goes to Mountainside Hospital. The squad also provides nonemergency transportation for the disabled. Unlike many other services around the state, the Glen Ridge Volunteer Ambulance Squad does this for free.

"They couldn't pay me enough to do this," Hayes joked, noting that people who volunteer their time are those who want to help people in need. Some of the members of the squad are retired, some are students, many work day jobs, but all, Hayes said, are phenomenal people. A majority of the staff live in Glen Ridge, with a few from East Orange and Bloomfield.

The day crew on this warm winter day has already handled three calls. A crew of three is on duty day and night, seven days a week, though the day shift always presents some difficulties because most people only have time to volunteer at night. This is a common problem with volunteer squads up and down the state and has caused the demise of several squads or caused some squads to pay the daytime staff. Some towns have eliminated its volunteer corps entirely, at a significant cost to the taxpayers and a significant loss to the sense of community that volunteer squads provide.

The Glen Ridge squad is always seeking people to fill this slot. While Glen Ridge does have mutual aid agreements with Montclair and Bloomfield, it is generally Glen Ridge that supplies those towns with aid, not the other way around.

Each team, day or night, has at least two EMTs on duty, and the squad itself handles an average of one and a half calls a day. Last year, the squad responded to 673 calls.

Hayes, See, and Argow make up the day crew today, and their ages and reasons for volunteering vary.

See is in her mid-twenties and attends William Paterson College. She is pretty, smart, and dedicated. She said volunteering runs in the family. Her father is on the squad. When she first considered coming on board, she talked to him about what he did, and was inspired. She is currently studying medical science in a pre-med program. While she hasn't made a decision about a career, she believes this is the right place to be.

Hayes is one of the elder statesmen of the squad, someone so dedicated many residents of Glen Ridge see him and the squad as the same.

Argow is one of the younger members, someone who joined because he wanted to learn leadership and has an interest in the medical field. He said he owes the squad. When his brother got hurt, Hayes transported him to the hospital.

Hayes said the squad isn't looking for supermen, nor do volunteers have to be men. Ten of the forty-two members are women. Towns bordering Glen Ridge don't take on many women because those squads feel most women aren't capable of lifting victims. The Glen Ridge squad doesn't make those distinctions. Police, who are always on the scene, are more than willing to help. But, more importantly, an extra set of hands on an emergency scene is always a benefit.

Anyone seventeen years of age or older in reasonably good physical shape with a valid driver's license is welcome. While non-EMTs can ride, everyone who volunteers is expected to train for an EMT certificate at a Bergen County facility. This involves 120 hours of classroom course study. Argow said the course is worth four college credits. Of the forty-two members of the Glen Ridge squad, thirty-three are EMTs. The oldest member is Lou Hahler, who joined the squad in 1956.

Glen Ridge has two ambulances, a full-size emergency unit, and a van. Both are fully equipped to handle most medical emergencies, carrying most of what an EMT might need.

"The borough is generous," Hayes says, noting that the cost of registration and insurance is picked up by the borough, which also does the maintenance while the squad pays for the parts. The borough also allows the squad to use the old firehouse for storing the ambulances as well as use of the meeting room. The community is generous, too, giving the squad about twenty thousand dollars a year in operating funds.

From *The Glen Ridge Paper,* Worrall Community Newspapers, 1998.

Protecting the Protectors

"Even on what people might call routine calls, firefighters are at risk," says Councilman John Reilly, steering his car through traffic along Paterson Plank Road from the North End in response to a report of a house fire. The blue firefighter light flashes from dozens of other vehicles in Secaucus as other volunteers scurry out from their usual Sunday morning activities to answer the call.

Reilly, one of the sixty volunteers who make up the volunteer fire department, had been on his way to the North End on another matter when the call came in, forcing him to turn around and follow a route that—coincidentally—was the same route fellow firefighter Joe Tagliani followed last June when a sudden heart attack ended his life.

The thirty-four-year-old Tagliani had been driving the rig out of the North End Firehouse when he complained of chest pains and had the good sense to pull the vehicle to the side of the road before collapsing. Although trained in CPR and First Responder techniques, his fellow firefighters, who immediately began and maintained cardiopulmonary resuscitation until an ambulance arrived, could not save his life. Even Meadowlands Hospital, with all its resources, could only sustain his life for thirteen days.

"I'm not saying anything bad about the Meadowlands Medical Center," Reilly said. "They did a fantastic job. But Joe's death and the vulnerability of our firefighters made me think about what we might be able to do to help protect our own people a little better, giving them something more to make sure they can be taken care of in an emergency."

Tagliani was not the first Secaucus firefighter to die in the line of duty. The names of the fire department's deceased veterans are engraved in stone in front of the town hall: John Keilp, March 12, 1930; George Bellis, March 15, 1935; William "Bo" Koenemund, September 2, 1985, and Tagliani, June 13, 1999.

Many of the elder members of the fire department remember the heroics of Koenemund, a man who, in the middle of the great Labor Day fire in Passaic, suffered a heart attack.

"It's a scary thing," Reilly says as he turns his car onto the first street ramp connecting Paterson Plank Road with Flanagan Way.

Reilly knows firsthand how risky a job firefighting is. In 1998, he had his own brush with death when he responded to a fire at Eighth Street and Centre

Avenue, only to find someone trapped inside the blaze. Reilly, a member of the department for twenty-five years, carried the eighty-one-year-old man to safety, fell, and collapsed when his oxygen pack expired while he was in the building.

"I got the idea that maybe the department needed [its own doctor] while I was visiting my doctor," Reilly says as he turns his car onto Flanagan Way, his radio rasping with the response of other fire vehicles, all of them converging on the corner of Hudson Avenue and Front Street. The voices of other firefighters already on the scene give the details: the fire started in the kitchen, apparently a result of unattended cooking. Reilly steps a little harder on the gas; the car moves a little more quickly toward the scene.

He talks as he steers the car, saying how he pondered the subject in front of his cardiologist, and the doctor volunteered.

"Dr. Rick Pumill is well known as a cardiologist," Reilly says. "He has offices in various parts of Hudson County and he has a good reputation. The fact that he wanted to do it delighted me."

Pumill, who will be sworn in next week as the police and fire doctor, will help make sure that an injured firefighter gets the proper care, guiding the man through the medical system. He will do this on a volunteer basis.

"He'll be on the scene or at the hospital whenever someone gets hurt," Reilly says. "He won't get paid unless the firefighter opts to use him as a primary physician. We just want him to make sure that all the proper medical steps are being taken for our firefighters, our police offices and the members of the Office of Emergency Management."

Reilly calls it an "extra level of protection," noting that police officers and firefighters already get physicals through the town's health care program.

"Yet, if someone has something they are worried about, they can come to Dr. Pumill for advice," Reilly says, steering the car finally to the scene of the fire, where four engines crisscross the streets and firefighters rush in and out of the house carrying fans and extinguishers. The blaze is out, but the smoke billows out the front door, carrying to the street the smell of burnt pancakes.

Unlike the blaze a week earlier a few doors down the street, no residents or firefighters are hurt, and no one has to withstand a wall of flames. Several firefighters, however, help calm a shaken woman who stands near the door.

"All fires are dangerous, even ones that seem as simple as this," Reilly says, returning to his car after a few minutes of talking with firefighters on the scene. He is in a hurry again, not to report to another fire but to make his way to the center of town before church lets out.

"I want to talk to this woman's daughter before one of the neighbors does," he says and swings the car around. "I don't want her to hear there's been a fire in her house where her mother is alone. I want to make sure she knows everything is all right and no one was hurt."

He says small details like these help make Secaucus the town it is, people caring for people, whether it means providing a doctor for firefighters or driving to church to help calm a worried daughter's nerves.

"This is what Secaucus is all about," he says.

From *The Secaucus Reporter*, Hudson Reporter Associates, 2000.

Saying Good-Bye

It was a gray day full of gray faces, the threat of rain hanging over the heads of police officers as they made their way out of the funeral parlor behind the casket. Storekeepers and customers under the shadow of the Parkway arches paused as the police lights flashed, car after car making the long way from Bloomfield Avenue to St. Thomas the Apostle Church just off East Passaic Avenue. Traffic halted just long enough to let the cars pass like a moment of silence that even the usual morning rush could not disturb.

Those observers who knew Detective Sergeant Thomas Bianco nodded gravely at the illuminated headlights and the long black car overflowing with flowers. It seemed like a small procession, with this small collection of cars holding a private pre-funeral ceremony, one that took Bianco on one last tour of duty, passing a portion of Watsessing Park, then onto Municipal Plaza where flags flew at half-mast for him. He had served as a police officer here for twenty-four years.

His route, however, did not take him past the schools in which he had played such an important role.

"We didn't just lose an outstanding police officer and detective," said Mayor James Norton said. "We lost a man who has had an important influence on the young people of this town."

Over the years, Bianco made frequent trips to the local schools to talk about his work.

"He did more than he had to do," Norton said. "He was a real humanitarian."

Any perception that this would be a small funeral ended when the procession reached the church where hundreds of police officers waited, their cars filling the wide side parking lot, cops from Glen Ridge and Belleville, Nutley and Newark, Clifton and East Orange, Wayne, Old Bridge, and others. Cops dressed in class-A uniforms, leather jackets for motorcycle work, crossing guards in their orange parkas, retired cops, nervous cops, some solemn and silent, some chatting quietly among themselves.

Bloomfield was well represented. Only those officers who had duty or were too ill had not come. Many of those who had been closest to Bianco went inside. Near the school, two girls stopped to look, as did one of the school workers, as police gathered on the steps, seagulls floating in the warm air between the steeples, the whisper of the Parkway traffic making its easy way through the leafless trees.

Anne Scherillo called Bianco "a good man," someone who had come to her aid about a year ago when she really needed help. And she had come to pay him tribute.

"It was a personal matter," she said. "I was really upset, and he knew what to say to calm me down."

Norton said Bianco handled himself well in a variety of situations.

"He was always fun to be with," Norton recalled. "On the outside, during a PBA function he was a real kibitzer."

But Bianco's mood always fit the situation. When he was doing police work, he was serious, Norton said. When Bianco was with his family, he was loving and caring. When Bianco was with "the boys," he was funny and companionable.

Officials and fellow workers will miss him. His wife, Cynthia, daughter, Valerie, mother, Sadie, and two brothers, Robert and Jerry, will miss him more.

Then, to the moody moan of the bagpipes, the casket emerged from the church, down through the lines of officers on the steps, sad-eyed, flushed officers with whom Bianco served, each raised their hands in tribute as along the street, the full regiment of other officers, stood at attention and saluted him, old and young, councilman and cop, mayor and civilian standing side by side as Bianco made his last exit, and, just for that instant, before the door closed on the hearse, one small ray of sunlight broke through the gray clouds casting soft golden light down on the heads of the mourners.

From *The Bloomfield Independent Press*, Worrall Community Newspapers, 1998.

Three Faces of a Cop

Terence McGrath chuckles when he sees early pictures of himself from when he first became a police officer on January 1, 1968. The young man who graduated from Bloomfield High School five years earlier still looked young, and eager, and—as he puts it—a little like Wally Cleaver from the television show *Leave It to Beaver*. It was an image that didn't fit well with the Flower Power hippie era.

McGrath seems to measure his thirty-year career with the Bloomfield Police Department by three different images of himself: that earlier innocent look, the in-between grungy look of his days working undercover on the narcotics squad, and the very eloquent man in blue, bearing two gold bars to signify his rank of captain.

Despite his distinguished career, McGrath didn't always know he wanted to be a cop. In fact, his first job after high school was in a slaughterhouse, where he worked himself out of the blood and guts and into the business office. He knew he wanted to do something with his life, he just hadn't made up his mind what. Then he got married and sought a job that he thought would provide him with a future.

"I took the test because I wanted something that was secure," he said, soon finding himself attending the Essex County Police Academy and then out on the street as a rookie cop. He remembers the lonely nights walking the center of Bloomfield by himself, walking past empty storefronts like a ghost.

Then, one night, as he passed behind some stores on Broad Street, he thought he heard something tapping, as if someone were chiseling at concrete. He called headquarters, and, as a result, began his long career with credit for breaking up a jewelry store burglary.

It was the beginning of a career worthy of a television police drama, with his name making headlines weekly for arrests that included gambling rings, murders, and drug and prostitution rings. He pursued rapists, busted people who tried to bribe him, and helped break up a plot by exiled Haitians who were attempting to overthrow the Haitian government.

In one week, McGrath broke a case of mailbox thefts, and while he was off duty, he nabbed a sex offender. In 1971, while he was on his way home from work, he busted suspects wanted in Glen Ridge. In 1978, he helped uncover critical evidence in a murder case in Glen Ridge. In 1974, he helped seize weapons from a man wanted for a Belleville bank robbery.

Over the years, McGrath has stood side by side with governors, mayors, and other dignitaries, yet was never too proud to do his share to help people in need. He was often involved in local charities.

As McGrath matured as a police officer, he saw the world change. His tours of duty revealed a rogue's gallery of people desperate for drugs. He knew them all, watched for them, waited for them to buy their next fix. He chased them from street corners, but seemed to understand that busting these people was only part of the cure. He went undercover, but even that wasn't enough. So later, when Joe Bogusz, then coordinator of health, safety, and physical fitness in the Bloomfield schools, asked for his help, McGrath agreed, and began to tour the schools in an effort to make kids aware of the evils of drugs. This was nearly a decade before DARE (Drug Abuse Resistance Education) became a national program.

In 1977, McGrath became a detective sergeant and began to realize that police work was changing around him, growing more intricate and more involved. Police officers needed to learn laws they had never needed to know before. That same year, he received his associate's degree in police science; three years later he received a bachelor's degree in criminal justice administration.

"I've always maintained the philosophy that my job is partly to help people get their lives back on track," he said.

McGrath believes he's helped many kids keep straight and sober, partly by pointing them in the right direction, partly by being a good example.

McGrath has achieved a lot in many years. His name has appeared again and again in newspaper headlines along with other legendary figures of the police department, people he has come to admire like Chief Jack McNiff or Captain Angelo Pizzino. He worked with the FBI, the DEA, the Essex County prosecutor and others, rising in rank from patrolman to captain.

When he was forty-three, he saw a light on in a house where he knew the family was on vacation. Even though he was off duty at the time, he went to investigate. While inside, he fell down a flight of stairs; his injuries—a broken jaw, a separated collarbone, and a fractured skull—put him in a coma. Thousands of people wished him well, and thousands of people sent Mass cards to Kessler Institute for Rehabilitation in East Orange, where he eventually wound up.

His recovery, some say, was nothing short of a miracle. He may even think so though he doesn't say much about it. Instead, he says he owes the place enough to volunteer his time, which is one of the things he intends to do now that he has retired.

"I'm going to do some teaching, too," he said, as a substitute teacher, giving even more back to a community to which he has already given thirty years as a police officer.

From *The Independent Press of Bloomfield,* Worrall Community Newspapers, 1998.

A Sense of Integrity

When Ron Cardone came back from a weekend at home to the Integrity House facility on the Meadowview Hospital Campus in Secaucus of which he is the director, he found that the crew assigned to clean up had painted all the stones gray—one of those small erroneous details that made him shake his head and wonder just what had gotten into the work crew, though for the most part, the residents at the long-term drug rehab facility had done a fine job.

"All the places where the curb should have been yellow were painted yellow," he said. "And the grounds looked clean. But the stones are supposed to be natural, so I sent them out to find new stones that looked natural."

A rule, after all, is a rule, and life at Integrity House is defined by rules, binding its members, a kind of military structure where chart boards, key hooks, and colored chips tell staff members where someone is supposed to be and what they are supposed to be doing. Work details roam the halls and the grounds and even wander out into town with the dedication of soldiers going to war.

Originally envisioned as a national model for drug rehabilitation, the "drug campus" at Integrity House may lose its federal funding. Under the current Congress, funding for both projects became part of block grants to the states, and Governor Christine Todd Whitman has not yet determined if the funding will continue.

"It's a shame," said a Hudson County spokesperson, who noted that Integrity House was one of the primary resources of treatment for county drug addicts. Almost all the current residents are from Hudson County, with a large percentage coming from Jersey City.

And there is a waiting list to get in. Cardone said the staff is selective about who comes into the program. According to founder David Kerr, the program receives about twenty-five requests a day from individuals in state prisons and county jails, as well as others looking for admission.

Everything at Integrity House is ritual and routine, from the pre-breakfast making of beds and cleaning of rooms to the evening lights out, from the eight A.M. meeting at which work details are assigned to the 8 P.M. ritual of evening games. For Cardone, his staff, and the residents, each day is a process of re-creating a new society, and each resident is an intrinsic part of that re-creation.

"Nothing is passive," said Cardone. "We insist these people develop social skills. We make them interact. We'll have someone stand up at our meetings and tell everybody about the weather or give us a summary of the news. Or we'll make them tell us a joke or sing a song for us."

Everyone, from Cardone to the newest admission to this long-term facility, learns how to work, from bending down to pick up stones to laying out projects for the basement print shop. People who lived on the outside as social outcasts with heroin and cocaine as their only companions, who fought with family and police, suddenly find themselves working side by side with others like themselves in an effort to find a place in society.

Everywhere along the walls of the facility messages of warning and encouragement can be found. "Don't break the structure." "Change your life." "Don't feed into negativity." "Think growth." "Hold your gut." "If you see something wrong, change it."

The halls buzz with nearly constant activity as work crews move through with specific projects, from polishing the floor to installing a computer, from painting a wall to cooking the daily meals. When a crew comes onto a floor, they shout out the fact in much the same way as trainee soldiers do at military boot camp. "Second floor, man on the floor."

This activity is a key part of therapeutic rehabilitation, a practice of long-term drug treatment that centers around the idea that people need to help themselves recover, to shape their own destiny, with staff members guiding them through the complicated process of learning the rules of civilized interaction. Here at the Hudson County branch of Integrity House, as in its sister facility in Newark, residents are expected to manage their own lives—once they learn the rules and regulations, giving back to the program, to each other, and to the larger outside society that has given each of them a second chance.

The concept for Integrity House came about in the mid-1960s when Dave Kerr, a Newark parole officer, sought to find a support system to help drug addicts ease back into society. When, after searching for three years, he found no such program existed, he decided to start his own, forming a kind of social club that met in garages and backyards until the group grew too large.

He then set up operations in a Belleville storefront. Eventually, the program moved to Newark, expanding to places like Berkeley Heights and, most recently, Secaucus.

Before becoming director of the Secaucus facility, Cardone spent seventeen years with the program, starting out in 1970 when he was admitted as a resident, a recovering heroin addict. After going through the initial program, he started working for the facility in 1971. It was his job to set up the facility in Secaucus after Hudson County offered space on the Meadowview Hospital campus. Cardone keeps framed photographs of what the place looked like when he first came, water-soaked walls, paint peeling from the ceiling, and mildew everywhere.

"And that was after we cleared the place out," he said, displaying the same stiff humor typical of drill sergeants and retired cops, though he actually served as neither. "The place was used for storage before we came, and it took a crew of ten three months to get it cleared."

Treatment at Integrity House consists of rehabilitation and education. The men and women here design many of their own social and work programs, get approval for them from the staff, then set out to make them work. It is an attempt to change the lives of these people from the ground up, teaching them how to make rules and keep to them, but, more importantly, how to live without drugs.

Every privilege here has to be earned. Residents must earn the right to send mail home, to get mail from home, or to go out on a weekend pass. Currently, the facility houses 144 residents in four sections, each section with lounge area, bedrooms, laundry room, and showers.

Indeed, the program itself is divided into four phases, though this has nothing to do with the size or shape of the facility. Residents start out with a thirty-day orientation period and work their way through the program to its reentry phase, learning about the program itself, the rules and routines, and then finally about themselves.

Their lives are recorded on data sheets, their complaints and concerns brought out in encounter groups. At each level, the balance between their personal needs and their responsibilities to other changes. They learn how to work together, then to think independently, slowly shifting from needing the program to making the program work for them. They talk to each other, help each other, and eventually begin teaching those who are just entering the program how to behave. They become part of the Integrity family.

"While we try to create a family atmosphere here, this is not something we want them to do for the rest of their lives," Cardone said. "The ultimate goal is to get the person to think clearly and make decent decisions. For many of these people, the only thing they thought about before coming here was how to get high. Many of them never learned how to choose. If they didn't feel like going to work, they didn't, and they rarely experienced anything without getting high."

But life here is not a constant grind, said Cardone, and the effort is to create good feelings that have nothing to do with drugs.

"Most of these people can't remember doing anything that isn't associated with drugs. If they went to the Shore, they went high," Cardone said. "We try to show how they can have a full life without drugs. You have to give people alternatives to drugs. You can't just take something away and not put something back in its place."

In fact, the staff members insist that residents here fill their days with drug-free distractions. They engage in sports of all kinds, and if they don't have a high school diploma, they must study for and get a GED. Among the numerous facilities the residents have built for themselves in the basement are a print shop, computer lab, and a classroom. The facility does print work for other programs on the Meadowview Hospital campus, and every resident attends class on a daily basis.

Randie O'Neil, the full-time teacher here, says she conducts classes on two levels: one level pushes to get residents their high school diplomas (one student may even enter a four-year college this year), and a second level helps improve their comprehension.

"Some people who come in here are functionally illiterate," she says. "We help them get some basic reading ability."

When residents finally reach the reentry phase, the program does not dump them out of the nest. They live here, look for work on the outside, seek and meet new friends, develop a network of activities, learn to budget money, set up a bank account, and then, eventually, move in with a roommate or a family member, or set up house on their own. Even then the program does not stop. It monitors the activities of its alumni, looks at their work habits, checks social habits, and takes routine urine analyses to see if the former residents stay clean.

These tests never end. The tests are taken frequently at first and gradually ease into longer intervals. Hundreds of graduates return to the facility whenever their names come up for a random test. Such monitoring continues indefinitely—for five, ten, fifteen, or even, as in Cardone's case, twenty-five years. In fact, Cardone's name came up this week and he had to submit to a urine test himself. After all, a rule is a rule.

From *The Secaucus Reporter,* Hudson Reporter Associates, 1996.

Facing the Outside

When Kimberly Maxwell stepped out of the Hudson County Correctional Facility in Kearny on October 5, a cold rain fell over the vast stretch of parking lot. The brick arch of the jail's front door protected her from the worst of the weather, although she was poorly dressed for autumn, wearing the same summer shorts and shirt she'd worn a year and a half earlier when she was brought here after violating probation. For a while, she stared out at the cold drizzle, asking several people for a ride back to Jersey City.

This was her second stretch at the correctional facility, a long, nearly unbearable eighteen months in which she said she nearly went stir crazy.

"The women only have one area; we don't get to walk around the way the men do," she said.

Maxwell is twenty-four years old. She has two children, a son, six, and a daughter, two. In that year and a half, she hadn't seen either one.

"I've talked to them on the telephone," she said. "But I didn't think it was right they should see me up here. I mean, my son is old enough for it to leave an impression."

Her first time at the facility, Maxwell served seventy-two days after being convicted of selling drugs. On the drive home, she stares out through the rain-peppered windshield and shakes her head at the familiar landmarks of her old neighborhood.

"It's scary seeing this place again," she said, her voice so weak you barely hear her. "Nothing's changed."

She's coming home to many of the same conditions she left when she went to jail, a modern kind of wasteland, where human potential is left in limbo.

"There are people with a lot of talent back in jail," she said as block after sad, dilapidated block passes, each street a marker signifying some important moment in her life, where she went to school, where she hung out as a kid, where she first met her dealer. She spent her whole life on these streets, growing up here, selling drugs here, eventually getting busted here.

The rain gives these streets an even bleaker appearance, painting them with a gray air of desolation, people scurrying to escape the wet look as if they are fleeing danger. Even the men who stand beneath store awnings stare out at nothing. They might be worried about getting work, or about getting a meal, or might be thinking about nothing at all. On the corner of her block, a billboard adver-

84

tises services at a local church: "Through Jesus Christ we shall overcome."

Maxwell rattles on about life in jail, and about the older women she'd met there, and how they scare her, too. She said she kept seeing the same people coming back, staying for thirty days this time, sixty days the next.

"Some women came in seven or eight times while I was there, women in their thirties, coming back again and again. I don't want to be like that," Maxwell said, staring out, her eyes a little sad. "I want to stay out this time."

Yet as appalled as Maxwell is about the recurrence, she's already started on the pattern, leaving the facility with only one large green trash bag full of private possessions, and no money for the cab fare home. She has no job. In fact, she has never had a conventional job. The only thing she knows about getting money is selling drugs, and she said that is something she wants to avoid. She said she wants to go back to school, take her GED, and get a vocation.

Ralph Green, warden of the Hudson County Correctional Facility, said many of the people leaving jail find themselves in the same condition as Maxwell. He calls it a "blindfold" release, in which no one asks where former prisoners will live or how they will support themselves, or even if they will have something to eat the night of their release from jail. Many of these people can't even go back to their families, since their families are disgusted with them for their earlier behavior.

"Often, they go back to the same people who got them in trouble," Green said. "They go back to the dealer and he gives them fifty bucks, saying: 'Go get yourself a meal and a place to stay, but remember who did this for you and what you have to do later.' That's the problem. They're right back where they started."

As depressing as that seems, Green said, the county jail doesn't have the resources many of these people need, and taking care of them after release must be the responsibility of the local communities, the towns and cities to which released time-servers return.

"These people need that aftercare," Green said. "All we can do here is help prepare them to get out."

Green said he has started developing programs to make sure people who leave the jail are better and perhaps more productive citizens than when they came in.

"But we can't do it all," he said. "The cities can't abandon these people. If there was better aftercare, many of these people would not come back, and instead of spending more and more money on jails, we could be spending money on schools."

The strategy for helping them begins with an effort to rebuild the family, enabling family members to trust these people again, rather than having ex-offenders fall back in with the criminal crowd. This is something jail officials try to do before releasing someone.

But many ex-offenders fear the straight world. In jail, they get a room, three meals a day, and medical care—things no one guarantees them outside.

"When they walk out of here, they get no support, many don't have a dollar in their pocket, they don't know where they're going to get their next meal," Green said. "But we can't solve every problem here. We put people in jail that we consider a threat to the community and society. That's where we draw the line. Our first priority it to protect the community."

Green started as warden of the Hudson County Correctional Facility in January 1993 after he had spent twenty-five years working his way up through the Washington, D.C., prison system.

Dressed in a black collarless shirt, he looks more like a tough priest than a prison official, down to the gold police shield that hangs from around his neck like a miraculous medal. He said he is a product of a progressive correctional system, a sharp contrast to the style of corrections in Hudson County before he came.

"I have a different philosophy when it comes to corrections," Green said. "Corrections is not just holding or warehousing prisoners. When someone comes in here, we have a responsibility to make sure that person [leaves] in better shape then when they came. Treatment and detention go hand in hand. We have to be more than a warehouse. The prison or jail must prepare the inmates for life on the outside."

While some people will continue to return to jail, Green wants to reduce that number. Through a variety of programs, he hopes to give people here an option, allowing them to see that there is more than one way to become important in and out of jail. In an interview done six years later, in September 2000, Green said that prisoners took on roles within a jail, building lives on jail jobs that did not prepare them for work on the outside. A prisoner working in the kitchen might barter food to other prisoners. A trustee might make money by selling cigarettes, candy, even drugs.

With fewer repeat offenders, the taxpayers save money, and former criminals become contributing members to the society. In this way, society gets a double benefit, no longer having to pay $35,000 a year to house, clothe, and feed these same prisoners, who are instead beginning to contribute to the tax base and uplift the communities in which they live.

"We still have a long way to go and a lot of people to convince . . . [including some of] the correctional officers themselves, who must now shift gears, learning this new approach," Green said.

Making these programs work depends upon finding out who can be trusted and who is too dangerous to trust. Some prisoners are a threat to society, a threat to other inmates, a threat to the guards, and a threat to themselves. But the numbers of these are remarkably small, accounting for about 150 out of a total jail population of 2,200, Green said.

"Those on the work program are screened very carefully, to make sure they pose no risk," Green said, noting that psychiatrist Dr. Oscar Sandoval works closely with him in making these determinations.

In the old Pavonia jail, prisoners used to vent their rage in numerous ways, Sandoval said. You could hear them at night, smashing their cots against the walls, or anything they could lift from the floor. They set fires. They rioted. They fought and killed each other. In the past, inmates had a difficult time getting to talk to people who could help them, such as the public defender. Frustration increased because they felt they were getting a raw deal or being mistreated by the system.

"We used to work with one psychiatrist and one social worker to classify and deal with prisoner problems," said Sandoval. "Now we have three social workers, and the prisoners are visited at least once a week."

These are regular meetings dedicated to dealing with problems they might have in their lives, like the death of a family member or a family member's losing a job. Sometimes they just need someone to talk to.

"This is a balanced approach and better than letting them burn mattresses the way they did in Pavonia," Sandoval said.

Serving as a support group for those who leave jail, a group of ex-offenders and this social support team attempt to let ex-offenders help each other work out the day-to-day problems that released prisoners will face out on the street and in their daily lives. Ex-inmates help each other to get and keep jobs, deal with the stresses that straight life presents, and cope when personal disasters strike.

"Some have already taken on jobs and become taxpayers," Green said.

Part of the solution to the problem of facing the outside world is to teach people good work habits while they are still incarcerated.

"Some people believe those incarcerated here don't want to work," Green said. "In truth, these prisoners are knocking down our doors to get jobs, and these jobs pay $1 a day."

But many of the prisoners don't know how to work. Many have never had a job, growing up in a culture where they don't even know what it means to get up in the morning to go to work. So any program designed to provide them with work also must teach new habits that center around reliability.

"Even if some of these people made $100 an hour at a legitimate job, they wouldn't know how to get up in the morning to get to it," Green said.

Once reliability and skills are learned and the prisoner is released, local communities must reach out and help provide the jobs. The jail itself has encouraged vendors it deals with to hire ex-offenders in order to set an example for others throughout the county. Mayor Bruce Walter in Union City has taken up the challenge, hiring ex-offenders there, and other mayors around the county, including Anthony Russo in Hoboken, have offered help.

"How can we expect other people to hire ex-offenders if we in the county won't?" Green asked.

From *The Secaucus Reporter*, Hudson Reporter Associates, 1995.

Down and Out in Hoboken

I never caught his name, if he ever gave me one. I was sitting in the emergency room at St. Mary's Hospital waiting for my mother, who had hurt her toe, when the man in the wheelchair started talking to me.

"All I really want to do is get back to the PATH station," he said. "I need to panhandle me some more money so I can get me some booze."

He claimed someone had mugged him there earlier and taken his money; he said his head hurt on that account, although I couldn't see anything seriously wrong with his head when he showed me his wound, a small red slash. It did not seem to cause him any pain.

"I had me enough to get drunk when they got me," he said, and gave me a wink. "People give me money to make me go away, all those people on the train platform shoving change at me so they don't have to look at me. Even after I was mugged and sagging there, they threw change at me, glancing back as if I was some kind of pervert.

"That's when the cop came along and tells me to move along, and I tell him I can't, cause I've been mugged. You could see he didn't believe me from the way he just stood there and sighed, and then starts talking into that two-way radio of his to call me an ambulance."

The man called over one of the passing male nurses. "Can you get some-one to get me another pair of pants," he said. "I messed myself in these and I really stink."

Then, the man looks at me again, winks, and says that for many street people coming to the hospital is like coming to a hotel.

"The bums fake getting hurt all the time so they can get a free ride here," he said. "It's free bed and board."

He pointed to several other men in the room he claimed to know from the PATH station and the McDonald's on Washington Street, where many of the street people hang out to keep warm, all of them looking nearly as down and out as this man did, though they stayed quiet when he couldn't.

"The bums think I'm crazy cause I don't like it here, or those ambulance dri-vers who tossed me around inside when they got me in, and tossed me out again when I got here, like I'm nothing better than a piece of baggage. Damn them."

He complained about being left in the emergency room to wait for some-one to see him.

"None of these people really believe me when I tell them I've been mugged. Who's going to mug a bum, eh?" he said with another wink. "But hell, even bums deserve better treatment than this, even if they're lying, waiting around, waiting for someone to come take care of them. It's enough to make you sick."

He said someone had cleaned up the blood from the cut on his head, some-thing they seemed to think he got by falling, though when he asked them how they thought he could fall out of a wheelchair and then climb back into it just in time for the cop to see him, they didn't have an answer.

"They say they can't treat me until my blood alcohol is down," the man said. "They've made me a prisoner here. I didn't want to come to this place, I didn't want to have to sit around here with mess in my pants."

Like many of the grim-faced men who occupy the streets of Hoboken, this man was a Vietnam veteran, though he didn't like to talk about it much, just cursing his luck at losing a leg overseas only to come home to find himself without a job or home or family.

"Bad enough I got to wheel myself around in his contraption," he said. "But doing it on the street?"

He squinted at me, as if studying the effect of his tale, then let out a long sigh.

"Look, I'm not going to hand you any crap. I've made up a thousand stories about what happened to me, all of them trying to sucker people into giving me one thing or another. I'm not proud. I don't care about anything much any more, except getting my booze."

He caught sight of a nun and called to her, using a voice so soft and ten-der and vulnerable I had to look twice to make sure it was the same man speaking. He tried to explain how he'd been mugged and how weak he was now and how he needed someone to roll him back up to the PATH station because his arms wouldn't last him half the trip.

"But what I really need is a pair of pants, sister," he said. "I been sitting in my own crap here for hours and it's beginning to bother me."

Like the nuns I knew in school, this nun had a look as if she had seen everything before, her steady eyes studying the ragged man in the wheelchair, yet not without sympathy.

"I'll get you some clean clothing," she promised, then marched off.

"She won't be back," he said. "I'll sit here in crap until the doctors take me and then they'll all look at me like it was my fault."

I didn't smell the crap, but I smelled the street on him, that same scent I had encountered when I rescued my uncle from his bout with homelessness in 1986, that smell of wandering and lack of washing. The man had the same gray flesh, typical of the street, from layers of dirt that had become immune to quick swishes of water and soap in the public toilets. His hair suffered most, slick with a greasy look that left stains around the inside brim of his baseball cap.

Like many of the street people, he seemed to have his own kind of logic. Most of the homeless people I had met over the years, especially when I was searching for my uncle years earlier, had a way of thinking that didn't quite match socially accepted reality. This man lied constantly to me, telling me things I knew not to be true, yet with such conviction, I had to think out the sequence of events in my head before I could sort out the distortions. He had told most of his lies so often that they had taken on the polished edge of well-rehearsed political speeches, with the pauses in all the proper places to allow listeners like me to react before he went on.

When I did not react the way he expected, with an offer to push him to the PATH station or give him money for a cab, he went on, seeming to invent new lies that I might believe, like how he had spent time in another hospital after the war, and how they hadn't just taken his legs, but his gallbladder by mistake, and how he was at that very moment suing the hospital for thirteen million dollars.

"They thought I was the guy in the bed next to mine," he said. "They came in one night, operated on me, and then when they brought me back realized their mistake. They had to come back for me later to take my legs off, too."

Eventually, when he realized I wasn't going to give him anything, he turned away, eyed the room, rolled his way over to someone who had just come in, and began to tell his whole tale all over again.

From *The Secaucus Reporter,* Hudson Reporter Associates, 1993.

Hero in the Emergency Room

I met Alan Spalding in St. Mary's Emergency Room early in January, just after a storm had dumped four inches of snow on Hoboken.

The Hoboken Volunteer Ambulance Corps had brought him in because the temperature was dropping and he didn't have any place to sleep.

"That's right, I'm homeless," he told me, when he noticed me looking at him across the room. He said this without shame or implied guilt, but as matter-of-factly as any newspaper reporter. "Me, Alan Spalding, Veteran of Vietnam, a man on the street."

Over the next hour of this talk, he told me he had served in Vietnam from 1965 to 1968, after being born and raised to an Irish family in Harlem.

"I grew up on 126th Street in Manhattan," he said. "I went to school in Manhattan, and when I graduated high school, I went to Fordham University until I went into the army in 1964."

He didn't say why he had joined. He didn't brag about how patriotic he was or how he might have thought the war was good and righteous, he just talked about joining, going overseas, and fighting "gooks."

"I killed a lot of gooks," he said, laughing, holding his T-shirt over his mouth as he laughed, as if he was hiding the laugh or the blush that resulted from it.

Now, thirty-one years after his discharge from the army, he looked less like a soldier than like one of the protesters who had stayed in college, but his long hair was white, as was his mustache. Wearing a new pair of sneakers and a Central New Jersey State Champion football jacket more suited for spring than winter, he was better dressed than most homeless men.

"I earned a Bronze Star and a Purple Heart in Vietnam," he said, talking about the wet, miserable conditions in which he had to fight, one of the unlucky men who was stationed in the rice paddies south of Saigon.

Over the years, I had talked to many homeless people, some of whom I once called friends, several right there in Hoboken who had lost their dogs to a Union City police captain who didn't think they deserved to have pets.

Spalding talked in the same rambling manner as most of those I knew, leaving it up to the listener to put the events in order, although he connected each disordered thought with "consequently" as if each came in some logical order no one else but he could understand.

"When I got back to the good of US of A, I tried to get back into Fordham," he said. "They asked me what my major was and I told them, 'Killing gooks.' They didn't like that one bit."

Over the next few years, he did well, although he wound up married to an alcoholic.

"I was an alcoholic, too, but I didn't know it then. But she and me got to drinking, and there ain't nothing worse than a woman who drinks. And she could drink. We spent a hell of a lot of money on booze. When I was in Vietnam, I never touched dope the way many of the other guys did. I didn't want to do that kind of stuff. But I drank. But when I was married, I drank a lot more. We'd go through as much as a hundred dollars each a day, and that was real money in those days."

During the 1970s, Spalding worked some very good jobs, mostly in bars, rising from bartending to managing a Wall Street club that was very popular during the 1970s.

"Sometime around that time, I decided to give the booze up," he said. "I'd come to realize what I was doing to myself. That's what busted up my marriage. I wanted to give it up, she wanted to keep drinking, so we went our separate ways. She's living in Florida somewhere. I don't know what she's doing. I haven't seen her since then."

To clean himself up, he went to AA at Trinity Church in Manhattan, where he met some of the people he'd been drinking with on the street.

"They all laughed when they saw me, and knew me by name. I asked. 'Do I know you people?' They said: 'Sure you do, we're the ones you've been drinking with all over Manhattan.' "

Spalding said he stayed straight for three and a half years, during which time he got an offer to tend bar in a mob-owned bar on Bloomfield Street in Hoboken.

"I didn't know the man was a mobster until I came over, but I didn't care. I made a lot of money there, and was really living it up."

Then, his brother died of cancer, and maybe his sister, too. Spalding was never too clear on this point, crying into his T-shirt as he mumbled incoherent details. But he was very clear about his best friend's dying, a man whom he had met during his return to drinking, someone to whom drink was an absolute poison.

"He was in the bed next to mine in the veterans hospital," Spalding said. "He couldn't take drink worth a damn. I mean, I can drink and drink. I got a resistance so high the doctors there couldn't figure out why I was still alive with how much I had in my blood. But this guy, he took one drink and he was in that hospital getting his blood changed."

Drink ruined Spalding, putting him out on the street, where he has lived for years, wandering here and there, mostly keeping warm in public places like St. Mary's Hospital Emergency Room, or the Hoboken train terminal.

"I'm not one of those shelter guys," he said. "People try to take me there from time to time, but I have to leave."

Spalding's left arm hangs in what is left of a sling, something he said he got during a previous emergency room visit. A few weeks earlier Spalding had undergone hip surgery at the veterans hospital; he said he hadn't quite recovered from it when he fell down a flight of stairs at the Staten Island Ferry Terminal in lower Manhattan.

"My hip just gave out," he said. "When I landed I heard it snap and I knew I'd broken my arm. It's just a chip, but it hurt, and I can't use the arm much."

In actuality, he seemed to use the arm most of the time, waving it around to make his point, the sling somewhat tangled in his armpit.

"The guys from the Hoboken Ambulance Squad brought me in," he said. "They all know me. They know I served in Vietnam. They know I'm not a mean drunk. So they take care of me when they can."

From *The Secaucus Reporter,* Hudson Reporter Associates, 1999.

Mistress of Modern Gothic

When National Book Award–winning author Joyce Carol Oates visited Maxwell's in Hoboken in July to give a reading, she visited a town she has only seen in the film *On the Waterfront,* a film she said had turned her on to film as art.

Strangely enough, the artistic image of Hoboken presented by that film no longer exists, and though Oates says she's heard good things about how Hoboken has been transformed over the years, the image versus the reality in Hoboken strangely echoes a theme that has been alive in her fiction for years.

Born in 1938, Oates was raised on a farm in an area of New York hit hard by the Great Depression. She showed an early interest in books, and when she was fourteen was given her first typewriter by her grandmother. Although she started her education in a one-room schoolhouse, she excelled in high school and won a scholarship to Syracuse University, from which she graduated as class valedictorian. She later earned her master's degree at the University of Wisconsin. She married and moved to Detroit in 1962.

"All over America a way of life is vanishing," Oates said. "Writers customarily memorialize the past, and I seem to be preserving the landscape of the twentieth century. Many of the people from the Depression era are dying off, taking with them the memory of what it was like during their time. Their experiences are very different from subsequent generations."

Oates's work, including her newest book, *Broke Heart Blues*, tends to bring back to life landscapes and characters from her days on the farm.

"I'm very interested in my parents and my grandparents, who were immigrants," Oates said. "The students I teach in Princeton today have no awareness or memory of World War II or the Depression."

Oates, who has been described as one of modern America's greatest writers, has covered other literary landscapes as well, making her mark in everything from modern Gothic and literature to poetry, plays, and nonfiction. She has published thirty-eight novels, twenty-four volumes of short stories, seven volumes of poetry, and four books of plays, as well several books of nonfiction.

While Henry David Thoreau's book *Walden* played an important role in her literary development, especially the simplify concept ("Our life is frittered away by detail. . . . Simplify, simplify," he wrote), which she claims she hasn't managed to live up to but still admires, Oates's time in Detroit transformed her writing. While teaching at the University of Detroit, she witnessed the riots of the mid-1960s, which she said shocked her.

"If I had not moved to Detroit, I might have been an entirely different writer," she said. "I would have likely written about rural subjects. But once I saw what was going on there, all the racial problems and how they exploded, my writing changed."

Oates said she suddenly became more concerned with the victims of economic deprivation and physical abuse, and through her modern Gothic novels she explores the nature of evil, which she described as a human tendency toward self-destruction.

"Civil unrest and discontentedness breeds it own destruction," she said. "Sometimes I think it is something in people's genes."

Oates has at times created characters dominated by their own drives; at other times, she has created characters who yield to circumstances; her tales show the process and pain of making uncomfortable compromises. Some critics have said Oates is most moving in her expression of empathy for America's lower classes. Yet she avoids being politically or socially revolutionary. She has been called the master of psychological drama, and she said these stories come out of the people and places she sees in her travels.

"Sometimes we meet another person and a mysterious connection forms between us," she said. "Somehow our lives are entwined, and I feel I owe that person something. I try to write out the mystery of that personality."

Oates said she's also been inspired by driving through towns and looking at the outside of buildings.

"Sometimes when I go through a small town something catches my eye, a store front or a small newspaper," Oates said. "I'll identify with the place. I'll ask who lives in that house or who planted that garden. Who works in that shoe store? I find that even in a small town where everything looks so peaceful there is something going on in people's lives."

Although she was raised on a farm, not all of Oates's works constitute a conflict between urban and rural.

"It varies from piece to piece," she said. "I'm fascinated with certain visual images."

In one short story, "Sky Blue Ball," for instance, she was struck by a place in New York that she used to pass on her way to her grandmother's. "I imagined a ball going over the wall," she said. "In the story, I have the girl throwing it over the wall, in a kind of dreamlike or supernatural setting, as if she is throwing the ball to herself."

Although drawn to William Faulkner and Ernest Hemingway, Oates has her own approach to heroism.

"It is based on individual behavior," Oates said. "In my new book, *Broke Heart Blues*, a young man sacrifices for his family to keep his family together, facing a family member's alcoholism. He is not a Christ figure, but he is being a savior. Part of his heroism is never explained."

Oates has used Christian imagery in her fiction and biblical infrastructures in the past, telling stories of redemption. In fact, critics claim she puts her characters through a kind of hell to bring them to that moment when their heroism can be tested.

In explaining her approach to family, she goes back to classical times.

"I do something similar to the ancient Greeks," she said. "People reveal qualities of their personality under stress."

This attitude is particularly evident in her nonfiction writing about boxing, and the lessons she derived from boxers she has interviewed.

"[Boxer] Floyd Patterson once said winning is easy, it's losing that takes courage," Oates said, noting she had gone to boxing matches as a little girl and even became friends with a middle-weight fighter.

"I was not thinking about it as a feminist, I was not judging it. I just saw it as revealing character. It must have had that meaning to me on a deeper level."

Over the years, interviewing numerous fighters, she began to see how losing often reveals an important part of a character, heroism in defeat.

"A fighter has to face his own character in losing," she said. "Muhammad Ali is great because he lost and then came back; Mike Tyson doesn't have that character. When he lost he gave up. That surprised me. I didn't expect him to give up the way he did."

She called it a kind of parable of life, the strength people bring to conflict.

Oates, critics have said, tends toward unhappy endings, a view she herself has helped foster by claiming in various past interviews that pieces with upbeat messages are better left for commercials. But not all her work has unhappy outcomes. She takes her work from the complexity of the world, its evil and its good.

"It depends upon the work," she said. "I have happy endings in a number of my novels. But my work tends to reflect life. Many are tragedies, [but] in some stories happy endings are possible."

From *The Hoboken Reporter*, Hudson Reporter Associates, 1999.

Images of Lisa

When Mark Twain moved into the Manhattan house at 14 West Tenth Street in 1902, his wife had just died, his daughter was suffering nervous stress, and his servants were stealing from him wholesale.

This may explain why one of America's best-known writers failed to notice the strange setting in which he lived. Nearly twenty years earlier, in the late 1880s, a husband had beaten his wife and children in this house, killing one of the children.

Even now, more than a hundred years after the event, the building has a morbid air, its huge shuttered windows staring down at the street around a

Diane Rolnick, whose images of horror made her a local legend during the mid-1990s, eventually moved west to New Mexico to paint scenes of desert life.

small, dented tin canopy that covers the front door. Walking along, people are drawn to it, frown over it, then hurry past it, as if knowing something dark had occurred there. Few of these people ever know the building's history, of the first child's death in the 1880s, of Mark Twain's misery here, or of the story of Lisa Steinberg who died here in 1987 as a result of being beaten by her father, Joel.

For an abstract painter named Diane Rolnick, it was not the house that created this eerie sensation, but the photograph of the strangely cheerful face of Lisa Steinberg on the front page of the November 8, 1987, issue of the *New York Post.*

So struck was she by the image that she tore off the page and immediately framed that face with another photograph, a blue-tinted storefront display of dolls for sale, a collage that seemed to sum up her own feelings toward Lisa at the time.

"Doll images are images of ourselves," Rolnick said. "I wanted to show Lisa frozen in time, a now-inanimate thing, no longer thinking, frozen the way the dolls were."

Although consumed by the image of Lisa's face, Rolnick was not yet able to transform her feelings into the images she wanted. She had been too long away from figurative painting. Although trained classically in some of the finest art schools on the East Coast, she had already committed herself to abstract art. The one or two experiments she did in figurative work during the late 1980s just did not work.

"I knew I wanted to do something with the collage," she said. "But I knew I wasn't ready at the time."

Whereas her abstract designs had slowly taken on more figurative features, semirealistic shapes beginning to fight their way out of the blocks of color, she knew she was not quite ready to take on the image of the face that had pressed into her mind from that photograph.

So the collage and the image sat for a few years, the pages of both the magazine and the new paper growing yellow and tattered yet emitting a strange radiance that Rolnick continued to detect.

"There was so much power in that expression, it sometimes reminded me of myself," she said.

While she says she was not abused as a child, she found herself isolated.

"People didn't know what to do with me," she said. "Somehow I connected with that expression. It has to do with being different as a child."

The expression reminded Rolnick of how she felt when she was very young and her aunt, a woman who had been as much a mother to her as her real mother, died. It also reminded Rolnick that even growing up in a middle-class environment, she had felt isolated, a dancer and artist whom people didn't understand. It was the mutual sense of isolation and the need to express it that made her follow the trial.

"It was a strange thing," she said. "All during this time I kept running into people who had something to do with the Steinbergs. I even ran into people who went out with Joel."

She read the articles and followed the television coverage, but it was the image of the face from that photograph that stayed with her, the image of a child who had been beaten to death at six years old, one smiling up to the camera. Then, finally, Rolnick could resist the image no longer, and she decided it was time to confront the eerie sensation that Lisa's face had caused in her.

But Lisa, Rolnick said, was only the impetus for something Rolnick herself had been contemplating for a long time, a jumping-off point into an artistic probing of the nightmare side of children's lives. For a long time, Rolnick had been looking for a way to deal artistically with the more personal side of her life and had been working out the details of such an investigation, when the image of Lisa came. In a way, the series of paintings she then began became a strange mixture of Lisa and herself, expressing through Lisa many of the fears she herself had felt over time.

In presenting Lisa's image on canvas, Rolnick said she sought to capture the vitality of the girl she saw in the photograph. In 1990, three years after Lisa's death, Rolnick began to paint.

At this point she sought out the photographer who had taken Lisa's picture at school two weeks before the girl's death. He had known nothing of the abuse she'd undergone at home. But like Rolnick, he was drawn to Lisa's face.

"All the other kids buried their heads in their arms when he came around," Rolnick said. "Only Lisa reacted well to the camera. That's the reason he took all those pictures of her."

The photographer did notice the black-and-blue marks on Lisa's arms and face, but he overexposed the film to bleach them out of the photographs. Rolnick went to meet with him a couple of years ago and traded some of her artwork for some of the photographs that had never been published, looking for more images of Lisa from which she could create.

"He spread the photographs out, I spread out my paintings, he let me take what I wanted, I let him take what he liked," she said.

Her first painting in the "Lisa series" largely imitates the collage she put together in 1987, combining the images of Lisa's face with the dolls, a three-by-four-foot work done in pastels. The second painting in the series moves away from the original image, using some of other photographs. This too, had been a more or less realistic depiction. Then, she began distorting the image, going inside to see how the child felt.

"I was looking for a specific effect, attempting to work out feelings figuratively, rather than abstractly," Rolnick said.

Although she started with Lisa, over time, she moved further from the original image. In three groups of artworks, Rolnick moved from a literal and exterior view of a child's pain to a three-dimensional expression of inner horror. In the first group, she used Lisa's face or variations of it, almost always adding animal figures around it. In the second series, she dropped Lisa's face, exclusively using the animal shapes to create the mood of a nightmare.

"Lisa led me to the feelings, and I reacted to her situation with abhorrence, from there I've moved on to do what I really wanted to do, to show how it feels to be a child growing up with terror," Rolnick said.

In describing this psychological state, she used images of animals and other shapes to reflect inner terror. Many of these paintings are huge, wall-size, with additional panels, an attempt to reflect the immensity of the psychological drama going on inside the child.

The third group has become strangely more literal, shifting from the image of dolls and stuffed animals to incorporating the dolls and stuffed animals themselves into the painting, a kind of three-dimensional mixed-media work, bringing nearly to life the twisting images Rolnick so far had confined to two-dimensional space.

"I'm trying to show how children have become throw-away objects in our society," she said.

Many of these dolls and stuffed animals Rolnick found discarded on the street. In one instance some had been thrown from the Palisades in Jersey City, where they sat for weeks and months. When she went down to recover them, a man actually stopped his car and asked her what she was doing.

"He asked me if I knew it was dangerous to be doing what I was doing," Rolnick said.

In all three groups of Lisa works, however, Rolnick said she is trying to make it clear that Lisa's death was not so singular a circumstance as people like to believe.

"Things like that happen to children all the time," Rolnick said. "And what I'm trying to show is that children are people, too, and as human beings we are destroying a valuable part of ourselves when we abuse children."

It's a feeling, she said, not a big crusade. She simply wants to point out the vulnerability, to make people aware of it.

"It's a power thing," she said. "I just want people to ask themselves how they can allow something like this to happen. I've seen it in Hoboken and all over the New York area, and we're losing something here. It's something I can get very upset about. By doing this, using these colors and these images, I'm trying to show people what it looks like from the child's side, and maybe then people will stop doing it."

She calls it a mirror of children's feelings and says that she is talking through Lisa.

"I don't want to be known as the Lisa Steinberg artist," Rolnick said. "This is just something I'm doing, part of what I do as an artist."

From *The Secaucus Reporter,* Hudson Reporter Associates, 1995.

The Seduction
of Howard Stern

For Rubberbaby, life as a member of the Howard Stern Chat Club on Prodigy has been a roller-coaster ride, so full of ups and downs, she still doesn't know where she is or where she's going, but when she made an appearance at the chat group's second live get-together in Secaucus last December, she was the star.

Rubberbaby doesn't look like a master of cybersex, a verbal vixen who has become one of the undisputed legends of the Internet with her on-line seduction of Howard Stern. Instead, she looks like a housewife and mother, which she is in the real world. Yet after two appearances on Stern's radio show, one appearance on his television show, and the reprint of her seduction scene in Howard Stern's 1996 book, she has rapidly become a celebrity in her own right, one of those virtual reality ironies she hasn't quite figured out.

"It's kind of strange," she says. "Sometimes I stand at a bus stop and realize that nobody there knows who I am. None of the other mothers waiting to send their kids off to school have a clue."

On Prodigy, Rubberbaby (who still refuses to divulge her real name, though many people now know it) withholds nothing; her on-line name allows her to play without the normal social repercussions. But with her appearances on TV, some of that is changing, and she worries about what this might mean in her daughter's life if news of it filters into school.

"People talk to people, you know, and we could have another "Harper Valley PTA" [referring to the song that was popular several decades ago] story here," she says. This sometimes makes her stop and think before she types her answers into the computer.

"I think some people expect me to be more mellow," she says. "But that's not me. I can't change now. Being careful about what I say is just not what I do, or what Rubberbaby would do, just doesn't work for me."

Rubberbaby signed onto Prodigy around 1989, just when the computer online service started marking its first real commercial push into the Internet. Although it has since been eclipsed by America Online, Prodigy was one of the first. People's ability to discuss sexual themes openly made it seem controversial at the time. "Back then you got the program when you bought a modem," she says. "Prodigy only had bulletin boards, a slow kind of chat where you had to wait for someone to type it in, send it, then you answered back later."

But even as early as that, people began hanging around on Prodigy, a new breed of cyber people who were emerging after the glory days of the computer hacker, people who grew more and more addicted to life on-line and spent as much time in front of a computer terminal as they spent doing anything else, like working or sleeping.

"My one brother was a complete computer geek," she says. "He was always telling me about the computer games he played."

When chat rooms emerged, Rubberbaby hung around one dedicated to her then-favorite writer, Stephen King. In fact, she was intimidated during her first trip into the Howard Stern chat room and thought at the time the people there were jerks.

"They were all talking nonsense," she says, "and I didn't want any part of it."

She claims part of the problem was her on-line name. She had selected something stupid, which made her vulnerable to every on-line jerk. When she reemerged as Rubberbaby, people gave her respect, though even then she still had a lesson or two to learn, and learned those lessons in one of the private chat rooms with four males.

"I didn't have a clue as to what was going on," she says. "But they taught me a lot about cybersex. It was blah-blah this and blah-blah that. You can fill in your own exclamation points and number signs. By the time I got out of that room I knew all I needed to know, and I knew that's where I wanted to be. 'This is it,' I said. I found a place where I belong and Prodigy gave me the platform for me to open my big mouth."

Of course, she's imagined herself as an actress from time to time. Who hasn't? And in an important way, Rubberbaby is a role she plays, someone other than herself. But the loud voice in the crowd has always been a part of who she really is, on the Net or in a room full of strangers.

"I'm the one you'll always hear over the din," she says with a laugh. "I even type louder than everybody else."

One day, a little over a year ago, Rubberbaby decided to hunt Stern down and seduce him on-line. Everyone knew Stern wandered around in his own chat room, taking on a different name every time in order to keep people from knowing he was there.

Fate seemed to lend her a hand when she broke her ankle on Memorial Day, giving her nothing better to do than sit in front of a computer.

"I thought, if he's not on now, he will be and I'll be there waiting," she says, though for months she ran into numerous imitators, fans and friends of Stern's who knew enough details about the man's life to put on a convincing front.

"Sometimes, you'd suspect you were talking to him, but you never knew for sure until he mentioned something the next day on his radio show."

Rubberbaby had long developed an on-line reputation for on-line cyber sex. People knew she was looking for Howard, too. And people kept trying to say they were Howard. Then she came into contact with someone she sensed was Howard Stern, and she decided to go all out, with an exchange of language so hot it is unprintable at a conventional press, though Howard Stern was so taken by the experience that he printed all of it in his book.

"People kept sending me messages saying it wasn't him," Rubberbaby says. "But I thought it was him and I was going in for the kill."

The following Monday, after a weekend of uncertainty, Rubberbaby called the radio station. Not only had she seduced Howard Stern, but he wanted her to come on his show and talk about it. She, still with a cast on her broken ankle, eventually agreed, only to find herself in a different kind of duel once she went on the air.

"He trashed me," she says. "But I held my own."

After Rubberbaby's appearance on the show, the people on Prodigy went wild. Rubberbaby became a star. She became the talk of chat line, sought out by its members. She grew in cyber stature when she appeared on Stern's TV show, but when her seduction scene was printed verbatim in Stern's new book, she became legend. At one of the book signings on Long Island, she nearly caused a riot, when Stern fans, waiting in the cold for hours, started calling out to her. Later, those people sought her autograph as well as Stern's. "It has all the feel of a fairy tale," Rubberbaby says.

This week the U.S. Supreme Court has agreed to look at a controversial provision of the new federal communications law that was passed by Congress in February. Under the Communication Decency Act, much of what currently goes on over computer communications lines would be curtailed. This has raised the ire of numerous free speech advocates, who are defending the right of people to speak freely over the Internet. President Bill Clinton and the U.S. Justice Department have agreed to withhold enforcement of the new restrictions until the high court rules.

The idea of censoring the Internet really riles Rubberbaby, especially talk about shielding kids from ongoing sexual conversations.

"That's all a lot of crap," she says. "People want things that have a sexual edge. I'm not a pervert or a deviant. Where are the kids' parents? Don't they watch what their children do? I have an eight-year-old daughter; I pay attention to her."

Rubberbaby says proponents of censorship are trying to sell the public on the idea that the net is like radio.

"But they are not the same thing," she says. "There is also a distinct line between being an adult and a kid. If adults want to talk about sex, they should have the right."

Penthouse and *Playboy* (which have their own on-line services) are on sale at most local magazine stores, she points out, and if kids are determined to get hold of such things, they can—especially if parents aren't there to watch out.

Rubberbaby says she monitors her eight-year-old daughter, making sure she doesn't sit in front of the TV watching cartoons all day. She makes sure her child doesn't use inappropriate language.

"She is not allowed to say 'stupid' or 'shut up,' " Rubberbaby says. "Those are our S-words."

For Rubberbaby, the whole cybersex issue is little more than play.

"That's the beauty of the whole thing. It's anonymous. It's all happening inside people's head. We can say whatever we like because none of it is real. There are no repercussions. No one is cheating on anybody. There is no emotional baggage to carry around."

But play or not, when it came time for Rubberbaby to meet many of the other members of the Howard Stern chat group, she had her doubts. The group held their first party last July in New York City.

"On the way there I wondered if I was crazy," Rubberbaby says. "Who are these lunatics and why am I going to meet them?"

But she found herself surprised. These people were exactly the same people with exactly the same personalities she'd come to like on-line, each bearing the same idiosyncrasies she'd come to expect.

"I knew what each person was going to say before they said it," Rubberbaby says.

The party was a huge success, with party pictures traveling along the Web from member to member. People on the chat lines could talk of little else for months. So they decided to hold the event again—in Secaucus, at a small bar called The Other Place in the center of town.

Rubberbaby says there is something special about the Stern fans on Prodigy, and over the years, people have come to her on-line just to talk.

"I've talked with everybody from thirteen to seventy," she says. "And from every walk of life. I don't have cybersex with everyone I meet. Most of the time, I just like bantering back and forth, a kind of mental fencing. But I always give people a reason to come back."

She says she likes to flirt, and that flirting is something harmless and fun.

"I'm no bimbo," she says. "And people understand that when they leave me. I enjoy talking about everything with everybody. I ask people what their favorite flavor is in ice cream, the last book they read, whether they like to swim in a river or an ocean. I have a list of questions, a kind of format, and I watch how people answer those questions, if they are funny or serious. It's the way people answer that gives me a feel for what they're like as people."

For her, cyberspace—or whatever you want to call it—is the perfect medium, stripping away the illusions that come with good looks or expensive clothing.

"You don't fool people as to who you really are. The truth about your character comes through. You're not judged by your weight or looks," she says.

And Rubberbaby says she seeks out people too shy to reveal themselves, trying to bring them out into the open and show them they are worth something.

"We talk heart to heart without physical barriers," she says. "Even if we don't go for a private chat, people seem to feel better after I've talked to them. I help anybody I can. I'm sort of on a mission to help people"—she says this with a deep and self-deprecating laugh—"just call me the Mother Teresa of cyberspace."

From *The Secaucus Reporter,* Hudson Reporter Associates, 1996.

A Summit of Hope

Just how long the idea for a summit was in Mayor Thomas Lincoln's head he cannot say. Perhaps it came about the way Superintendent of Schools Judy Conk said, during a conversation they had in September, or perhaps the idea had simmered in the back of his head for months and years, even as long ago as that fateful day nearly a decade ago, when Lincoln, then a councilman, heard the news about "The Rape." It was a time when Glen Ridge, a slightly upscale community focused on its kids, became a sideshow for national media, when groups from all over the country came here taking potshots at the way people lived, claiming the borough as a symbol of greed and privilege.

Some things are bigger than life. Names like Rodney King, Martin Luther King Jr., JFK, O. J. Simpson, Bobby Kennedy, Princess Diana, all resound with a vibration that reaches far beyond the act that made them famous.

Lincoln knows that when many people hear the name Glen Ridge, a mythological power begins to take hold of their imagination, and the gas lamp–lit streets and the beautiful buildings fade into a dull gray haze, and people envision a dark basement where several athletes huddled over a mentally retarded girl in 1989, raping her with a toy baseball bat.

This crime—as heinous as it was—has become a symbol so powerful in the minds of many people, and Glen Ridge has become so general a byword for reporting of related crimes around the nation, that the town and its goals, values, and accomplishments have become invisible.

Lincoln, of course, knows better, knows that Glen Ridge is made up of all kinds of people, some seeking to maintain property values, some seeking a good future for their kids, but few if an, ever condoning the kind of behavior that went on with those boys in 1989.

Perhaps through all the headlines, all the humiliation, one thought tumbled around in Lincoln's head, about the boys who have since been tried, convicted, and sentenced for their crime: "How could those boys think it was all right to do what they did? What made them think they had permission?"

It is a thought that has recurred to Lincoln several times since, when one kid after losing a baseball game in town said something racially outrageous, and then again—with the town under the microscope of the national media— several kids acted out a skit in school with heavy sexual overtones.

What made them think it was all right?

In some ways, the summit Lincoln has planned the end of January is taking on more than a community of eight thousand should, as if the sins committed by four boys in 1989 forced this community to tilt the windmills of a changing society to find truth. Glen Ridge, because it has been judged so harshly, can't just be satisfied with correcting the abhorrent behavior of some of its youth but must seek out the deeper reasons why its children think they have permission to act in the ways they do.

What makes a kid think he or she has permission to do wrong?

But the focus, Lincoln says, isn't on the kids at all.

Councilman David Kerr put it this way: "How surprised are parents when the three-year-old child they are raising blurts out an obscenity?

"It is a shock at first," Kerr says. "Where did that kid learn that? Most parents don't realize that they have little tape recorders growing up around them, taking down everything they say—not until it comes back at them."

Multiply that parent's shock by eight thousand and you begin to get an idea how Glen Ridge itself felt after "The Rape," and how Lincoln felt with each minor incident since.

What made those boys behave like that? What makes other children do the things they do or say what they say? Why don't those children understand they are doing something unacceptable?

In some ways, Lincoln's summit is an effort to begin something of monumental proportions, challenging the residents of Glen Ridge to look at themselves and honestly come up with answers that the world around Glen Ridge cannot. The mayor says he wants Glen Ridge to hold up a mirror to itself, to take one long and honest look at the kind of things it does and says to its kids, as parents, as a community—not so much the preaching, but the practice. What message are parents here sending to their kids by the way they act?

In sending invitations out to the forty or so community groups in town, from civic groups to churches, Lincoln hopes to find some answers. He knows that he and the town council can't dictate morality, but he thinks the borough needs to examine its own values, to determine if adults here are inadvertently sending the wrong messages to their kids.

Lincoln says he has pondered the question for a while, talking it over with others, trying to understand what makes kids do what they do. He knows that Glen Ridge parents wouldn't condone half of what goes on with kids, and yet the kids act as if they do. Why?

During a conversation with Conk in September, an idea emerged. What if Lincoln could get all of the leaders of the community together, to talk, to look at the town as a community, a mirror on itself?

"The concept was to focus on the adults," Lincoln says. "What does this community stand for? What are its values?"

Lincoln says some of his thoughts are simple ones, such as how to shape values so that kids don't get confused, how to make sure adults know the consequences of their own acts—on their kids.

"We have had incidents of anti-Semitism, sexual aggressiveness, and alcoholic problems," Lincoln says.

Glen Ridge, of course, isn't alone in any of these. America itself is suffering through a perceived loss of values, little old ladies running red lights as much as teenagers with hot rods. People everywhere seem to greet each other in traffic jams with obscene gestures. But Lincoln believes that Glen Ridge can face these issues as a community, its residents gathering to define its problems and possibly come up with solutions that will better handle situations such as the rape in the future.

"It seems we're beyond the point of holding open doors for each other," he says with a sad note in his voice, and yet when he speaks of the summit, a hopeful note joins this, as if he truly believes the borough can find an answer.

Part of what Lincoln, Kerr, Conk, and others hope to find is a consensus of opinion about what the community sees as its values. What will Glen Ridge tolerate? What do its residents see as wrong? By this, teachers, politicians, sports coaches, and other adults can learn to model their own behavior and perhaps shape the behavior of the kids.

Although the agenda has not yet been firmly set, Lincoln hopes that to have the groups bring up their concerns about the community's standards during the first night of the summit, coming to some consensus, then on the second night figure out what can be done to maintain those standards.

Oddly enough, no one spoke of the 1989 rape at the mayor's summit, even though talk went on for days.

"What we wanted to show ourselves is that we don't have to be the victim to negative incidents," Kerr said, looking back on the summit. "We do have the power to recognize things that happen in our community and do something about them. By meeting like this, we show people we have the guts to look in the mirror and do something collectively for ourselves."

People talked about what they thought was right in the borough and what they thought was wrong, and what they as a community might do about curing the wrongs.

"People seem to think that many of our standards didn't come from the community, but from television or radio or the world at large," Kerry said. "But what we discovered was that our standards came from a lot of places, from the police, parents, and institutions, and that many people didn't even know these standards existed."

From *The Glen Ridge Paper,* Worrall Community Newspapers, 1998.

Buzzing about Bees

When Bloomfield resident Joe Hansen ordered his first colony of honeybees from Sears, Roebuck thirty years ago, he didn't exactly know what he was doing. He had read about honeybees in a book, learned that they were the state's official insect, and decided he would like to raise them. He didn't know that in his lifetime the role of beekeeper would evolve into a vital role for agriculture—that three decades later whole crops would come to depend upon him and other beekeepers, amateur and professional. He simply liked honeybees.

But when those bees arrived, he didn't quite get a handle on the situation, and the colony died.

"I really made a mess of it," he said. "I just didn't know what I was doing."

Hansen, whose careers range from sailing on submarines in the navy to serving as vice president of a brokerage house, knew he needed information, and he found himself seeking out the Essex County Bee Society, where he found like-minded people who had a lot of experience. In 1982, Hansen became a Master Beekeeper, one of six or seven in the state and the only one in Essex County, certified at the University of West Virginia. This distinction, he said, required very specific knowledge about New Jersey's official insect, from gene studies to hands-on practical skills. In the years since his first experience with honeybees, Hansen has learned a lot, has met many important people, and in the process has won numerous awards.

"I've studied most of the time since I first started in the 1960s," Hansen said.

Ribbons hang from the wall of his den as proudly as the pictures of his sailing days with the navy.

"This is only a few of them," he said with a laugh, as if the ribbons were only a by-product of his real love, working with bees and extracting their honey.

This year, Hansen came away with about a half-dozen more ribbons from the 1998 New Jersey Honey Show. Over the years, his hives have produced many items including honey, mead, candles, even honey wine, and an unusual product that he sells locally to several supermarkets—creamed honey.

At the peak of his beekeeping activity in the late 1970s, Hansen had colonies all over the area, in Belleville, Bloomfield, Verona, and East Hanover; some of these were hired out to farmers who needed his bees to pollinate their crops. In New Jersey, honeybees accounted for the pollination of about $140 million per year in farm crops ranging from blueberries to pumpkins until 1995, when mites destroyed all of the wild honeybees and many of the managed bees. This major environmental disaster may have changed the landscape forever, since wild honeybees played a vital part in the pollination of numerous plants, and managed bees have helped pollinate acres of crops.

Since then, managed colonies like Hansen's have made a comeback, but it is a hard road for the managed honeybee, trying to make up for the work the wild honeybee did. Some believe it won't be possible. Some think the wild bee was never a predictable pollinator in the first place.

Hansen said his bees have made honey from many kinds of plants, from goldenrod to linden trees. Honeybees begin their season in April and continue until August or early September. Honeybee colonies generally survive through the winter, unlike the bumblebees'; they keep their hives warm by eating their own honey.

Hansen said while he couldn't attribute a personality to bees, some do get "grouchy" in rainy weather or when it grows cold. All bees seem to dislike the color brown.

"A beekeeper can wear white, red, and yellow, but never brown," Hanson said. "Perhaps it is because their predators are brown, such as bears."

For the most part, honeybees are reluctant to sting, except when their home is threatened.

While his bees generally recognize Hansen, beekeeping his hard work. Sometimes he has to lug around hives weighing as much as 150 pounds. This is too much work for a man who has retired already from his primary occupations, so at the age of seventy, he has begun to sell off some of his colonies.

"I'd like to see some younger people getting involved," he said.

From *The Independent Press of Bloomfield,* Worrall Community Newspapers, 1998.

In Search of Skunk

At first glance Al McClure seems to be a bit of a bloodhound, stalking through backyards, front yards, and the meadows of town with obvious urgency, a small wiry and energetic man always sniffing the air as if on the trail of some elusive scent.

Although his duties with the health department can vary, from pursuing wandering dogs to chasing down property-maintenance problems, autumn mornings it is usually the trail of skunk he follows. At 7:30 A.M. this Friday, however, the only smell in the air is one of rain, though for days people have been calling him with complaints about torn-up grass, the sounds of cats fighting and—ah, yes—the fine perfume of skunk wafting through their open windows just in time for supper.

As animal control officer in Secaucus, it is McClure's job to do something about the visitations of such nocturnal creatures as cats, skunks, raccoons, and dogs and if possible stop the conflicts and put a halt to the ruining of lawns by the skunks' hunting grubs.

Fifty years after winning a Bronze Star for duty in the South Pacific, McClure still dresses like a sailor, wearing his crisp blue animal control uniform as if expecting a military inspection. His hat is only slightly tilted to one

*Al McClure—pictured here in 1995—
continued to hunt skunks as the decade
turned, although his role expanded
to hunting mosquitoes as the threat
of West Nile virus descended upon the
Meadowlands area.*

side, giving him an official air even as he bends over a metal trap partially hidden by thick green hedges. His blunt work-hardened fingers feel carefully around the wire frame.

"Tripped," he says. "When it rains like this any small movement can set the thing off. If the skunk sniffs around or gets on top, the trap will trip."

Sometimes, the wrong kind of animal will walk into the trap. This morning, McClure found one of the neighbors' cats inside, a cat more curious than hungry since the bait McClure uses is peanut butter and chocolate chip cookies.

"Skunks love the cookies," McClure says with an infectious grin that makes him one of the best-liked men in town, "and the peanut butter keeps its smell for a long time."

The peanut butter is also sticky, which means the skunks can't grab it and run.

"They have to use both paws to pull at the cookie," McClure says, demonstrating how the plate beneath the bait moves when the weight is removed and the gates at either side of the oblong trap close down. This is what is called "a live" trap, one used to capture animals without hurting them.

Capturing any animal is a matter of patience and care. McClure says if he approaches a trap secretively and covers the trap before the creature can see him, the animal calms right down. He later releases it down in the meadows near the kennels, where there are no residential houses.

"We can't keep on destroying everything we see," he says. "These creatures were here before we were."

He gets called from time to time about stray dogs, former pets that people have discarded in malls and other places where McClure goes and fetches them.

"I've handled three or four wild dogs," he says, "but those I trap in a large cage, or if I corner them, I'll capture them with a retrieving pole, and when I get them to the kennel, I see if I can handle them. If I can, fine, but if they've been out in the wild for a long time, there's nothing you can do about them, and you have to put them to sleep," he says.

Sometimes, in really rough cases, he has to resort to the tranquilizer gun, which he keeps in a slot behind his head along the roof of the cab.

"It takes a few minutes for the animals to go out after I hit them with the dart. So I have to know what they're going to do before I shoot, I have to know that I can track them, and get back the darts I shot," he says.

McClure gets calls about cats, too, but there are no ordinances for managing cats—"free rangers," he calls them—and they survive on the abundant rodents in the area. Some residents feed the cats, leading to conflicts with neighbors who don't like the animals hanging around or screeching nightly.

Skunks, however, are a big problem in the North End. In other parts of town it may be raccoons or squirrels.

"But it's skunks, all skunks here, this time of year," McClure says, his salt-and-pepper hair hidden under his hat, as he checks the truck for his equipment, cages, birdfeed, traps, grabbing pole, gloves—and the tranquilizer gun.

This time of year, the skunks begin their ritual feed before the coming of winter.

"They don't exactly hibernate," McClure says. "They rest during the winter."

Skunks are the last really wild creatures in residential Secaucus. The raccoons, McClure says, have long been domesticated, feeding at houses where they know they can find food. Cat food is a popular treat for raccoons and skunks. They are attracted to the fish oils. But unlike most raccoons, a feeding skunk can get nasty.

"When you bother a skunk, he tells you," McClure says. "He does this with his front paws."

McClure begins a quick drumbeat on the steering wheel of his van with his hand heels. "You see that you know there's trouble."

The trouble with skunks became serious in the North End about two years ago when rabies warnings were issued. During the 1992 skunk season, Al McClure says, he must have caught as many as ninety skunks, many of them with rabies. This year he's captured five, none with rabies.

"They're a communal animal," he says. "If one gets rabies, the others are bound to."

Skunks don't usually bother people until fall, and then they come out looking for grubs, leaving tufts of grass torn up by the roots in the middle of people's lawns. McClure points to a wall at the end of the street where the base has been dug up.

"They'll find a tiny opening, open it up with their claws. They don't make their own nests, but they'll take over spaces like this," he says.

McClure, sixty-nine, grew up in Secaucus. He graduated from grammar school but quit high school in his senior year to work on a farm his father had bought in South Jersey. He worked there for ten years, and when the farm was sold, he worked for the Orange and Black bus line as a maintenance man and later a supervisor until the 1950s.

Since then, he's owned a diesel repair business in North Bergen, and retired from that to open a stationery store in New York City.

After his second retirement in the mid-1980s, McClure took a course in animal control given by the New Jersey Department of Health.

"Growing up in Secaucus when I did you learned to handle animals," McClure says in explaining how he could take on the job as animal control officer after such diverse employment history.

Over the years, McClure says he has avoided politics.

"As long as the politicals leave me alone in my job, I'm fine. I do what people ask me to do, and if their ideas don't work, then we try something else," he says. "If people want to attack me, I walk away, I don't say anything that I'll be sorry for later."

As a property maintenance officer, however, he's rubbed a few residents the wrong way. People don't particularly like this part of McClure's job. But the law's the law, he says, and if something's in the maintenance code, he has to enforce it. On his way through his rounds, he points to the places he's helped clean up.

"People have to get used to the idea of doing things legal," he says, noting that he's had to warn a few of his own relatives.

From *The Secaucus Reporter,* Hudson Reporter Associates, 1994.

A Little Tender, Loving Care

As often as not, visitors to the Secaucus Animal Hospital are greeted by a one-eyed, tiger-striped cat named Rocky. Sometimes he patrols the waiting area, a dignified official of the hospital staff who has taken upon himself the duty of checking out each and every visitor.

The kittens awaiting adoption in the cage do not bother him. The dogs of various shapes and sizes that come and go do not bother him. He knows them all. Sometimes, Rocky sits in one of the letter trays and yawns with uninterest, a supervisor of medical proceedings who has utter confidence in his staff.

As well he should, for according to Dr. Richard Brady, who took over as owner and chief veterinarian of the hospital earlier this year, this staff is one of the best, dealing with most of the routine pet problems with professionalism and kindness.

Brady himself has become one of the most revered pet people in town, second only, perhaps, to Animal Control Officer Al McClure.

Whether it is informing an owner about a pet's terminal illness or of a more hopeful prognosis, Brady carries on with the same calm, caring manner that has won him high praise from his patients and their owners.

A large man with a broad face and huge hands, Brady seems perpetually conscious that he is dealing with people as well as with pets, and he often recommends options for treating the most pressing problems.

"I know that people skills are as important as my 'pet side' manner," Brady says. "When dealing with a sick pet, people can be very emotional, and you have to understand that."

As he moves from treatment room to treatment room, he knows each pet and its owner. He is a soft-spoken man who often lingers longer with each pet owner than he should, trying to make sure owners understand their pets' problems and options for treatment.

But it is the challenge of dealing with animals that inspires Brady more than other types of medicine he has dealt with. "Pets aren't like people, they can't tell you what is wrong," he says. "You have to figure out how they feel."

In an era of high-tech veterinary care, with machines as sophisticated as

Dr. Richard Brady continues to leave his mark on the local community, becoming the person to whom most of the locals turn when their pets are in pain.

those used in human medicine, the real solutions are still contained in the skill of the doctor. While he can use an assortment of treatments, Brady often recommends a slow approach, even for something as debilitating as cancer.

"I could recommend chemo or radiation," Brady tells one concerned pet owner. "But why put the pet through all that pain and you through all that expense? Let's just see if this works first, then we can discuss something else."

Brady, forty-seven, came to Secaucus from Texas four years ago with the idea of taking over the Secaucus Animal Hospital. Although he had practiced as a veterinarian in Houston before his arrival, Brady had done significant medical research and instruction at Texas A&M University, in a much more human-oriented medicine.

Although he had always worked toward the goal of becoming a veterinarian, Brady found himself involved deeply in biochemistry and molecular biology while at college, an involvement that continued through studies for his master's and doctorate. He earned his Ph.D. in 1980, then embarked on six years of research.

But he grew weary of a pursuit in which he hardly ever saw the practical results of his work.

"I felt out of touch," he says.

While he could have just as easily become a doctor, Brady was attracted to treatment of animals. Something about their inability to communicate their ailments drew him to them. Like many kids, he had had his share of hamsters, fish, and other pets. When he visited his grandparents' home in Oklahoma, he became acquainted with their horse.

He says treating animals gives him a satisfaction he's not sure he would get from treating people. Their helplessness makes his efforts seem more significant.

Brady treats the usual assortment of pets—rabbits, cats, dogs, hamsters. Despite his exceptional training in biochemical research, he has been confronted with a few pets he could not handle—like the hedgehog someone brought to him when he was still in Texas.

"I didn't know which end was which," he says with a laugh. "I had to send it somewhere else."

He did once treat an ostrich that was being raised on a ranch near him.

When he first came to Secaucus, he says he was under significant pressure. The well-informed and well-trained staff, however, smoothed the transition of ownership. Including a bookkeeper, receptionists, and technicians, fifteen people work at the hospital.

Since he became a vet, Brady says, the profession has become much more sophisticated. A hospital like his, which provides general pet care, now offers ultrasound, surgery, radiology, EKGs, and other medical devices and procedures not thought necessary only a decade ago. The hospital is also open seven days a week, something very unusual in the past, and he has increased the size of his staff to include two other veterinarians, Kimberlee M. Young and Michael B. Goldmann.

"My goal here is to provide a high-quality medical diagnosis and medical care in the most congenial manner possible," Brady says. "I want to eventually have the hospital open twenty-four hours a day, providing care any time of day or night."

From *The Secaucus Reporter,* Hudson Reporter Associates, 1997.

See Ya Later, Alligator

Secaucus had some remarkable visitors last week as the firemen's end-of-summer carnival rolled into town, full of its usual display of games of chance, wild rides, and small sideshows.

At the east end of Buchmuller Park residents were greeted by a huge red-sided trailer straight out of Big Top movies of the past, with the painted jaws of an alligator gaping to reveal razor-sharp teeth. Inside, past the ticket vendor and the drooping curtain, guests were greeted not by Crocodile Dundee, but by Alligator Bill—Bill Knox, that is—and four black-backed alligators named Alli, Ruby, Eli, and Little Buck.

Ruby and Eli are each about four years old, three-and-a-half-foot-long alligators staring out from glass enclosures that resemble fish tanks. Their eyes are open, but they look rather sleepy, the glass of their tanks steamed a little from the system of warm air and moisture that mimics their native environment of Florida. Farther in, two side-by-side picture windows look in on a sixteen-foot-long swimming pool–like tank. Alli, a great deal older and four times larger, stirs in the water, a huge black-backed creature with one eye frosted over with what looks like cataracts, though the other clear reptilian eye is hardly endearing. The giant lizard stares out at spectators as if they are chunks of meat.

Bill, who rushed in with his rapid verbal presentation, is taller than the character from film *Crocodile Dundee*, but he has all the other mannerisms, as well as the same thin and muscular shape and sun-browned face. An ex-military man, ranch hand, and all-around outdoor type, Bill says he looked for something that would keep his interest. Raised on an Idaho cattle ranch and holder of a degree from Boise University, Bill has been everything from a cowboy to a deputy sheriff.

"After twenty years in the army, you know I'm not going to be happy flipping hamburgers at Hardee's restaurant," he says.

Curious spectators crowd around the picture windows staring in through the glass as Bill pokes at the thirteen-foot Alli with the tip of a broom. The spectators ask the usual questions. How was he caught, where was he caught, does Bill actually go into the tank with Alli?

"Of course, I go into the cage," Bill says gruffly. "Who do you think washes the windows?"

*Although Bill Knox risked losing a finger
by sticking it into the open jaws of this baby
alligator, he continued to travel around the
country over the last decade, introducing
the public to alligators of all shapes and sizes.*

"Doesn't he bite?" one spectator asks, while another asks if Bill plays with the creature.

"Yes, Alli bites, and no, I don't play with him," Bill says. "Alli is a wild animal and always will be. You play with him and things can get terminal quick."

Alli, who weighs 850 pounds, is about sixty years old and was captured by Bill and several other men in Florida in 1990. Alligators have been recorded up to nineteen feet, though size is shrinking as the larger beasts are killed off. The normal life span runs upward from eighty, though this has been cut in half by the encroachment of humans into their natural habitat and the spread of pollution.

"Alli should live a full life with the controlled environment he's in," Bill tells the spectators, the younger of whom ooh and aah at the large beast's movements inside the tank.

"What does he eat?" one kid asks.

"Raw meat, about twenty-five pounds a week," Bill says. "If you look in the water you'll see a rack of ribs."

(Among the laziest animals on the planet, alligators don't need much food, despite their size.)

The kids look; the raw meat moves along the bottom as the alligator shifts.

Bill says Alli was scheduled to be killed because he had grown too large for the area he was in. The Florida Game and Fresh Water Fish Commission gave Bill and his two companions a week to flush him out of the swamps. No drugs were used in capturing Alli. The three men kept at the animal until he was exhausted, then brought him in.

Bill draws Lucy out of the smaller container, pets her neck, whispers calming words then carries her outside where more spectators gather, twenty or thirty faces exclaiming over the display of teeth, though Lucy is as calm as a kitten compared with the more cantankerous Alli. Alli's teeth are three times the size of a German shepherd's. Ruby's—with two years to go until she is full-grown—are more the size of a full-grown dog's.

Then, with a surprise that delights most of the kids, a small reptilian head pops out of Bill's shirt like a flashback to the movie *Aliens*. It looks around, twisting its neck to see the crowd. It is the size of a large lizard, though it still looks like an alligator.

"This is Little Buck," Bill says.

"Where did you get it?" one very curious kid says, reaching out to pet the small head. "Crossing a road?"

"I got them all in Florida," Bill says, letting Little Buck crawl up his shoulder. "These critters are very intelligent. They respond to verbal commands. They like affection. Tender loving care is the key to handling these critters."

At Bill's home base in South Georgia, all four alligators wander around the backyard.

"Only when we're on the road are they in a cage," Bill says, noting that this has as much to do with their need for warmth as it does for safety. Since he has taken the show on the road, he has gone deeply into the North.

"It gets cold up here," Bill says. "These critters are used to warmth."

Bill worked with experts to design the tanks, which he says keep the alligators comfortable and healthy. Environmentalists actually bent over backward to help him, he says, encouraged by his positive approach to alligators.

"They liked the fact that I'm giving people an education wherever I go," Bill says.

But as much as he talks about environment and the creatures' health, Bill is a carnival man, and this is a sideshow—managing through care and attention to his animals to transcend many of the negative connotations people associate with that kind of life. He started thinking about this as a business during the late 1980s, and calls it "a roll of the dice."

"I had a couple of friends in the carnival business," he says. "We talked over the idea. We thought about bear, buffalo, or elk, but decided those animals were too dangerous."

Bill says he likes New Jersey and the response he's gotten here, and would like to book more shows. He came to Secaucus from the month-long Meadowlands Fair, and has hooked up with a local contractor, Cook's Entertainment, which books the acts for most of the area fairs. Bill brings his act north in late April and stays until it gets cold.

"I'm an entrepreneur," he says. "I like the business, but it's in a struggle mode right now. But I think it'll get going good soon as word gets around."

Bill sells jewelry on the side, made from alligator scales Alli has shed, and he displays his wares—earrings and such—with something of a shy grin, like a man selling candy at a dentist's convention.

Bill says he wants to go home someday.

"I was born and raised near a ghost town in Idaho," he says. "There's a hot springs sixty miles away. I'd like to buy a house there and settle down. But I don't have the money right now."

So until he does, he says he'll keep the show on the road.

From *The Secaucus Reporter*, Hudson Reporter Associates, 1994.

Beeping

The peeping and rumble begin at 7 A.M. as the trucks start up, metal strikes stones, and backhoes dig holes just yards from the side of Bernard Antonovich's home.

The workers are digging up tons of contaminated soil from Carteret Park. The constant beeping, banging, and bumping of metal goes on until nearly 6 P.M., and Antonovich's house shakes most of that time.

"If it's not a dump truck banging, then it's something else backing up going beep, beep, beep," Antonovich said, standing outside his house, two yards from the fence that hides the digging. He said his windows rattle and his drinking glasses shake, and the floors of his home hum with the movement of the trucks up and down the street.

The U.S. Environmental Protection Agency (EPA) has been cleaning up the ninety-acre, radium-contaminated site in Glen Ridge since early 1989, although officials discovered the problem in 1983 when tests showed high levels of radon gas and radon decay products, as well as excessive levels of indoor and outdoor gamma radiation.

Antonovich bought his house in 1982, a year before the nightmare began.

While the EPA installed temporary radon ventilation systems and gamma radiation shields in thirty-eight homes in the area, it wasn't until 1989 that it began the systematic removal of soil from homes, selecting the most contaminated properties first. In these cases, the homeowners were relocated while the cleanup moved ahead.

Unfortunately for Antonovich, the EPA found a home for him and his family in West Orange, which made it difficult for him to transport his children to school. So he went looking for a house on his own in a nearby neighborhood, then waited out the five long months until his own property was declared safe.

On April 15, Antonovich stood at the edge of his driveway in anticipation of Congressman Bill Pascrell, who came to look over the site and possibly nudge the EPA into hurrying up the cleanup of the park and surrounding streets, the last large pieces of real estate in need of soil removal.

Up and down Carteret Street, a small yellow street sweeper swished, moistening the ground over which the trucks rumbled—part of the cleanup's dust suppression efforts.

Antonovich said the vigilance is a recent effort, noting less energetic attempts in the past. For him, the cleanup has been plagued with problems. Once he came out to find his driveway gone, lost as the soil beneath eroded under the digging claws in the park next door. Another time—after the EPA had cleared the contamination from his land—a dump truck fell over into his yard, spilling tons of contaminated soil onto an area where his children play. Now they do not play in the yard while the work is going on.

In fact, almost every time Antonovich steps outside, he expects to find some new disaster waiting, such as the open sewer line he found when EPA contractors tore up the street, a line no one believed he saw until he practically pushed officials' noses into it, he said. Another time, work uncovered a gas line in front of his house, twisting it a little. Had the pipe been metal instead of plastic, he said, the area might have seen a significantly greater problem.

Antonovich keeps a collection of photographs in his car as visual documentation of each incident. But in all this, he knows he is not nearly as badly off as some of the residents along Lorrain Street, where the backs of garages threaten to fall away under the constant erosion of soil.

The worst part for the whole neighborhood, however, isn't these incidents, he said, but the wait. Although neighbors here have met monthly with EPA representatives, no one told the residents that the project would take a year longer than originally projected. Then, when the EPA proposed another year's extension, many residents like Antonovich felt betrayed. This was more than having contractors hook up his sewer to a dead line, it meant another year of listening to the constant beeping, and living with the fear that another dump truck might roll over into his yard.

Antonovich has no complaints with local officials; he said Councilmen Steve Plate and Carl Bergmanson have pressed the contractors to hurry while at the same time keeping residents informed. But the cleanup has left life in a constant uproar. For Antonovich, even pulling his car out of his driveway is a chore as cars from other neighborhoods zip both ways along Carteret Street.

While dealing with the EPA has improved greatly since John Frisco came on as deputy director of the project, Antonovich says residents are hoping Pascrell can do what local officials could not—make the nightmare end.

From *The Glen Ridge Paper,* Worrall Community Newspapers, 1998.

One for the Record Books

A funny thing happened to Richard Koeppen while fishing in the Duck Pond in Secaucus: he found himself in the roughest freshwater-fish fight he'd ever had, the result of which put him squarely in two national record books.

Normally, Koeppen comes to the pond to relax before work. He brings his coffee and throws a line in to see what he can catch. In the past, he's caught carp and catfish, and thrown them back. Then, one day, his line went crazy.

"I heard the fish grinding on the hook," Koeppen said, noting that it took his float down like a bullet. He didn't know what it was, but he had to scramble up from his seat on the bench and pass his fishing pole around two trees in order not to lose it. Even then, the fish dragged the line out for about thirty yards, trying to tangle it in the reeds.

"He knew the shore," Koeppen said. "He shot straight through two rocks as if he'd been through this before."

When Koeppen finally got the fish to shore, all he saw were teeth: two sets of what could have been human teeth and they were sharp.

"They could have cut through my line easily," he said. But the hook had snared the fish through the lip and the six-pound test line managed to avoid getting cut.

Seeing the teeth, Koeppen began to suspect the truth and grabbed up the fish by the forked tail. The eyes bothered him.

"Its eyes bulged out on the sides," he said. "They looked human and they looked right at me."

Koeppen, who fishes at the pond almost every day before going to work, never saw anything like it. Neither did his workmates at the Upper Hackensack Bridge, where he works as a lift operator for New Jersey Transit. He didn't throw back this fish, he said. He knew he had something important here. It was. It made the record books as the second largest red-bellied piranha caught in the United States.

"It's unbelievable," he said. "I've been fishing since I was seven years old and I'm fifty-one now. Of all the places I've fished, and I got into the record with a fish from a pond."

A friend at work volunteered to put the still-twisting fish into a live-catch

Since setting a national freshwater record in 1993 for catching a red-bellied piranha in a local pond, Richard Koeppen has continued to fish there at lunchtime, though he hasn't caught anything nearly so interesting since.

tank in the trunk of his car, but Koeppen refused, throwing it into the freezer where he knew it would be safe.

"I've never had that kind of fight from a freshwater fish," he said. "It's a very odd fish to catch."

How the fish got into the pond is a mystery, though Lou Fallivene, owner of Maplewood shop where Koeppen had the fish weighed, said it was likely dropped into the pond by an aquarium owner when it grew too large for the tank. He believed it was probably put into the water during the spring or summer when temperatures were high enough to support a tropical fish native to places nearer the Equator like Brazil. But the seventeen-inch-long fish weighed in at four and three-quarters pounds, large even for red-bellied piranhas, which generally grow to about a foot. Koeppen and some town officials say the fish had to have been in the pond a while to know the bottom.

It isn't the first piranha caught in the Duck Pond either. A few months ago, a smaller fish was caught, then thrown back. No one believed at the time that it was a piranha. The state department of fish and game said this type of piranha does not pose a danger to residents or children. The red-bellied piranha mostly eats other fish, though it is wise to be careful when handling them. Koeppen said other fish he had caught had cut marks on their sides which he believes now came as a result of the piranhas. Both Koeppen and Mayor Anthony Just wonder if the fish is responsible for several missing baby ducks.

From *The Secaucus Reporter,* Hudson Reporter Associates, 1993.

A Natural Haven in the Heart of Bloomfield

Lois Ross watches seven eggs hatch into frogs, tiny green creatures huddled together on the bottom of a clear tray, their dark eyes seeming to reflect the world around them, trees and houses along the northeastern edge of Bloomfield.

Sometimes she lets them out, giving them space on the lawn of her back-yard, easing them toward the moment when she will set them free, giving them a taste of nature rare near the speeding cars of Watchung Avenue and the Garden State Parkway. They are in many ways seven small miracles, yet part of the daily life for people like Ross who live on or near the banks of Clark's Pond.

Almost every evening, Ross and others can count on a parade of creatures through their yards—muskrats, geese, opossums, rabbits, chipmunks, turtles, snakes, even bullfrogs showing up to prove nature isn't dead even this close to civilization.

Unless you know to look for it, Clark's Pond, a space bordered by houses and trees on three sides and the fields surrounding the middle school on the fourth, is invisible to the general public. It is one of those remarkable spaces modern environmentalists have come to call "urban wilderness" and one of the focuses of the state's preservation efforts, a rich snapshot of what life was like in Bloomfield when the Native Americans wandered here, before the Dutch and English came to build around it.

Ross grew up nearby and remembers Clark's Pond as a vital part of her childhood social life, providing opportunities for ice skating, fishing, and other activities. When she returned to Bloomfield five years ago, she was thrilled to find the pond still thriving, a hidden natural treasure that once more has become part of her life.

Clark's Pond rests at the bottom of a slope leading down from her backyard, and she makes the trek down to its shore at least once a day, ducking under low branches, to the water's edge where fallen trees and thick clumps of bushes make up the habitat for numerous species: bullfrogs and salamanders and turtles. She has managed to glimpse many of the more elusive secrets of this place simply by learning to be quiet.

Through the leaves, you can see the water, and the mud and trees that make up the island at the north end of the pond. A few kids have managed to get to it from time to time, young Tom Sawyers and Huck Finns who often leave a trail of bottles and other junk in their wake. Ross has not been to the island, but some of the other members of the Friends of Clark's Pond have during the cleanups that have removed tons of junk, including everything from old tires to rusted bicycles.

Clark's Pond is part of the Third River, which runs south from Garret Mountain in West Paterson in a long zigzag route. The pond—as it is now seen—was the result of an earth-and-concrete dam from what local residents in the 1850s called the "last natural bird sanctuary." Bloomfield had other such sanctuaries, such as Oakes Pond and Davey's Pond, both of which have vanished beneath the insistent blade of the bulldozer and development pressures.

History suggests that a more naturally formed pond existed here for many years before that, a product of beavers when the Yanticaw tribe of the Lenape Indians used these grounds to hunt and feed as well as to store their canoes.

Although the pond itself is only three acres in area—a long, narrow body of water about one-third of a mile long and one-sixteenth of a mile wide—the total track of land around it makes up eleven acres. The Sigler family owned it during the Revolutionary War. When the Morris family took over, they put a gristmill at its end. Over the years, the name of the pond changed with each new owner. It has been called Upper Morris Pond, Mesler's Pond, Riker's Pond, Kierstead's Pond, Van Winkle Pond, Brownie Pond, even Poor Hour Pond. Lumber from near this site was used in building ships. George Washington's troops may have even soaked their feet in its waters in their famous retreat across the state. Its current name came when the Clark Thread Company purchased the property in 1922 because of its pure water. After World War II, the site was purchased by the San Giacome Paper Company, and later by Scientific Glass. Bloomfield purchased the site in the 1950s, and under the guidance of then Mayor John Dinder and Councilman Gary Davis, the town sought to preserve the wooded area and pond, constructing a recreation area at the south end, dredging the sediment to control the mosquito population. Plans included the construction of an environmental education center at the middle school to study the pond, complete with a weather station, nature trail, and outdoor museum, with tent platforms, water life studies, and tree identification programs. Only a portion of these ideas ever came to fruition, although the middle school and its current principal have been very active in studying the nature around the pond, according to Ross.

As a biomedical engineer, Ross has had some experience in using technology and hopes to use computer programs to establish an inventory of wildlife around the pond. The goal, she says, is eventually to get the pond listed for preservation. She and the other Friends of Clark's Pond would like to see a nature trail built along the pond and they have been talking to members of the local board of education with that in mind.

While as many as seventy to one hundred people—from middle school students to students from a local school of Chinese culture—have shown up to help clean the pond twice a year, the Friends of Clark's Pond has a core of about eight people struggling to maintain the natural feel of the place. In the past, Ross says, people have used the pond as a dump, something she noticed when she first moved back, and vowed to stop.

"We actually started by cleaning up our own backyards and realized that we couldn't do it all ourselves," Ross says. "So we asked our neighbors to help, and then we distributed leaflets."

The group is now planning a fall cleanup, just to keep the place in shape, and Ross talks about possibly getting the pond dredged again since it has been rapidly filling up with silt. As she talks, several great egrets strike dinosaur-like into the muck, so white that their shapes stand out sharply against the backdrop of brown and green. Nearby, about forty Canada geese have taken up residence, although these are only a small part of the total number that stop here during migration two or three times a year. Sometimes hundreds blanket the site, leaving breathless any observer who watches their takeoff. School officials find the geese an annoyance and have struggled to find ways to keep the birds off the sports fields at the nearby middle school.

Ross says she would like to take a canoe trip north to follow the Third River to its roots, just to get a complete picture of the cycle of nature to which the pond belongs. "This is an amazing place," she says, kneeling down near the water's edge, the wind blowing a loose strand of hair across her face. "We would like to make sure people in the future will still be able to enjoy it."

From *The Independent Press of Bloomfield,* Worrall Community Newspapers, 1998.

The Hackensack Gets a Keeper

Captain Bill Sheehan is a white-haired man with a baseball-style hat and a moustache straight out of Mark Twain's autobiography. He rides the Hackensack River as if he owns it.

"Own it?" he has said more than once while sailing his boat through the intricate waterways of the Hackensack Estuary. "Sure I do. Everybody does."

This sense of public possession of the nation's waterways has made him dedicate a good portion of his time to protecting the river, watching out for the encroachment of trash, manufacturing, or human waste, and—more importantly lately—the threat of development.

Monitoring the Hackensack River is no part-time job, something else he has repeatedly said over his thirty years of wandering this river, first as fisherman, then as river tender, and now as one of only nineteen River Keepers across the United States.

"The ecological importance of the Hackensack River estuary has long been recognized by local, state, regional, and national organizations and agencies," Sheehan says. Yet, he notes, the river has been targeted for development since Colonial times, when the Dutch first settled here and began to build dikes. Only about one-third of the original wetlands here still remain.

After years of doing volunteer work for the Bay Keepers, an environmental activist group under the auspices of the American Littoral Society, Sheehan set up the Hackensack Estuary and River Tenders Corporation (HEART Corp.), a nonprofit environmental watchdog group determined to keep an eye out for the ecological interests of the Hackensack River.

*Since first taking on the task of
protecting the Hackensack River,
Captain Bill Sheehan has set up offices
at Fairleigh Dickinson University.*

Sheehan says he was inspired by an environmental conference he attended where he had met people from all over the country, many of whom were defending the environmental integrity of streams and rivers imperiled by development and pollution in much the same way as the Hackensack River. When he and a North Bergen friend started HEART Corp, they wanted to preserve the river's history as well as its ecology, making the public aware of its ecologically significant areas. At the time, Sheehan says, the organization was founded on the premise that the Hackensack River and its estuary are in the public trust, and that current governmental organizations are not honoring that trust.

Sheehan, a one-time rock-and-roll drummer, has worked as a dispatcher for a North Hudson cab company for years to support his home and family in Secaucus. When he is not working, he is sailing the river, attending meetings of groups with river-related interests, or reading up on the latest proposal from the Hackensack Meadowlands Development Commission (HMDC).

Since declaring himself the Hackensack River tender in 1995, Sheehan has worn numerous other hats, including director of the Hudson River Fisherman's Division of Environmental Affairs and chairman of the Secaucus

Environmental Advisory Committee. He has been a volunteer member of the Bay Keepers for years, monitoring the river changes as well as local publications.

But the role of watchdog has taken more and more time, shifting from a part-time volunteer effort to something requiring his full attention. While he has been lucky over the last two years, getting grants to cover some of the costs, time has always been a factor.

"Watching the river is a full-time job," he said. "And now, as the River Keeper of the Hackensack, that's what I can do."

While warnings about the plight of American rivers go back as far as 1870, when a naturalist named Veplanck Covlin warned against land clearance in the upper Hudson, more modern focus on the river is credited to the 1962 publication of Rachel Carson's *Silent Spring* and Robert Boyle's 1969 book *The Hudson River: A Natural and Unnatural History*. Groups such as the Scenic Hudson, the Hudson River Fisherman's Association, and the Hudson River Sloop *Clearwater* came to the understanding that the Hudson (and later other rivers) needed someone in particular to watch over it.

In Britain, River Keepers have traditionally protected fish and habitat, but the concept was something new to America, where the rivers served as a means of discharging waste. Thus in 1973, environmental groups hired Tom Whyatta as America's first River Keeper. The move failed partly because of finances. Then, in 1983, the Hudson River Fisherman's Association hired John Cronin, providing him with a boat with which to patrol the river. Since then, other River Keeper programs have been established across the country, and the name was trademarked against unscrupulous people who might use it in an illegitimate way.

"Until I was named River Keeper of the Hackensack, there were eighteen other programs across the country," Sheehan said. "Mine is the nineteenth, and I'm flabbergasted that they would allow me into that select company."

Sheehan said the influence of Boyle's book has been felt through all nineteen programs.

"In his book on the Hudson River, Boyle said every river in America should have a Keeper," Sheehan said. "Where fish are biting, it is up to the River Keeper to protect the interest of the natural resource from people who do them harm."

The Hackensack River program is an outgrowth of the one established by Cronin in the Hudson, as is the Bay Keeper program, which has been active throughout the Newark Bay complex.

The Hackensack River is part of the Newark Bay complex, and the Hackensack Meadowlands are well known throughout the region for their vast wetlands and diverse wildlife—more than two hundred species of resident and migratory birds live here for all or part of the year. For a large part of the twentieth century, the river and the meadows were used as an open sewer; the practice ended with the passage of the Clean Water Act in 1972.

The river recovered remarkably well. Tests show a steady increase in the amount of dissolved oxygen in the water, and this has attracted more fish species and other wildlife to the estuary. In fact, the National Marine Fisheries Service has declared the Hackensack an Aquatic Resource of National Importance, and the U.S. Fish and Wildlife Service has called it an important stopover for migrating waterfowl, shorebirds, and raptors. The Environmental Protection Agency also considers it a "key priority habitat range."

"For the past couple of years I've been doing volunteer work on the Hackensack River through HEART Corp. That was basically serving an apprenticeship," Sheehan says. "Last January I was invited to a meeting of all the River Keepers. . . . I talked to John Cronin who told Andy [Wilner, the Bay Keeper] to set up a River Keeper program on the Hackensack."

Sheehan, after he filed paperwork to have his program incorporated as a formal nonprofit entity, received the distinction in June.

"What a keeper does is the same as what I was doing as a volunteer, only on a full-time basis," he says.

His mission is partly to watch what happens on the Hackensack, but more importantly to make sure the residents, municipalities, and others know what is going on.

"I'm the voice of the Hackensack River," Sheehan says, claiming that once the program is fully established he will be able to work full time on river-related issues. "This means dedicating myself to the river, attending all public meeting, hearings, committees in order to bring the message of the river. People will know that somebody will be on the job, a full-time paid advocate. It is like a dream come true. I'll be giving up everything but work for the river."

As River Keeper, Sheehan will monitor the entire river from its most southerly point at Paulus Hook in Jersey City to its northernmost extreme in Rockland County, New York, where two streams combine. Sheehan says he has already contacted conservation groups upstream, but early on, he says, he will concentrate in the Meadowlands area, because he fears that is the area most in danger.

He believes the estuary here is threatened by massive development disguised under the "Special Area Management Plan," a twenty-year projection by the Hackensack Meadowlands Development Commission that calls for more office buildings and factories in the Hudson County portion. This amount of development, he says, would certainly require the filling of wetlands.

Sheehan says he will continue to set up workshops for organizations along the water in both Hudson and Bergen Counties, seeking venues where he can continue to call attention to the potential and existing threats to the health of the river.

From *The Secaucus Reporter,* Hudson Reporter Associates, 1997.

An Organized Man

It's not popular to talk about former Mayor Paul Amico in Town Hall these days, at least not approvingly. A pall hangs over the building and its employees as if they were mourning the end of an age. Longtime employees who served under Amico are hesitant to put their names in print for fear of what the new administration will say. But even so, they speak in awe of the man who sometimes treated them as a father would.

"Organization" is one key word they use in describing what made Amico successful.

"He was the most organized man I ever met," one town employee said. "Nothing in his office was out of place."

But this went beyond mere paperwork. Amico seemed to struggle to keep himself in order; his office walls were filled with mottos on how to improve himself and the town. "Try harder," said one, though according to those who worked for him, he seemed to have a motto for every occasion. He even carried index cards in his pockets for things he needed to remember. One card said, "Praise, do not criticize." A soft-spoken man, Amico even had a sign to remind him to speak up into the telephone.

People who didn't work with him or those who were outside his political sphere sometimes believed him cold and unfeeling, especially compared to the more gregarious Mayor Anthony Just who is his successor. While Just bears an almost folksy air when he greets constituents and emphasizes parks and how Secaucus used to look, Amico seems more aloof, a dignified statesman whose vision seems dedicated to larger issues like the changing nature of Secaucus over the years. But many employees say Amico had his personal side. Many came to him with both town and personal problems.

Since his retirement in 1990, former Secaucus mayor Paul Amico continued to play the role of advisor, giving young people the benefit of his political experience.

"Amico never made promises. He didn't build up false hopes," one employee said. "If he delivered, that was great, but if not you weren't disappointed."

Amico came to Secaucus in 1919 at the age of six. His parents had moved out of Little Italy in New York City seeking elbowroom. His father worked for a railroad company based in New York. At thirteen, Amico started to work for Marra's Drug Store behind the counter. A year later, he was working full time. Although he didn't finish school, Amico soon graduated to his own business, and it is this to which he credits his organizing skills. In a small diner, the only way to make money is to create volume. He built the counters so that he and his workers could provide quick, efficient service.

Providing service became one of the chief motivations for him over his twenty-eight-year mayoral career. It was in seeking increased services that Amico transformed the town from a backwater world of pig farms and trash deposits to one of the most successful business communities in the state.

The initial spark toward politics did not come from a vision for the future, but from genuine anger at the way things were done. Returning from the Army after World War II, Amico found things about local government he detested. Local politicians seemed to treat people with contempt. While he didn't run for office until the 1950s, he watched and learned, and then organized a personal political machine capable of beating politicians at their own game.

The remnants of this machine remain like a White House war room in the basement of his house, an elongated room with tiled floors and typing work stations. The ghosts of old campaigns linger in the dustless air as if waiting for a chance to rise again.

Old-time campaigners call the place "the bunker," and it has become a symbol of Amico's organizing skills. Desks and cabinets glow under florescent lights. A four-desk configuration was the heart of the operation. Amico still uses one desk to type out press releases from time to time. Behind him, forming a U, are three other glass-topped desks with sheets listing the town's registered voters. Card files above each desk list every house in town, who lives there, their political status, and other vital information that was revolutionary in the pre-computer campaigning of the 1950s. Even unregistered voters were part of Amico's informational base.

"When we sent out campaign literature, we sent it to everybody, even people who weren't registered," Amico said. "Those people might not vote, but they talk to those who do."

Information, then and later, became a fundamental tool, and one central criticism he has for the current administration is that it makes decisions without getting the facts. Accurate information was pivotal in Amico's first election victory, when the margin was only four votes. Before a recount, his opposition claimed Amico had lost by a single vote. Out came Amico's accounting of absentee ballots. So impressed were the officials that they searched long and hard and eventually found out Amico was right.

For Amico information equals credibility, and credibility was the biggest part of shaping the future of Secaucus.

"Paul Amico was always sensitive to the quality and diversity that this town provides," said one town official who had worked closely with the mayor over the last twenty years. "He has always been conscious of what the town looked like before he took over and what it looked like later."

Even before he was elected mayor in 1963, Amico had set goals for himself in terms of improving the school system, providing kids with recreation, and expanding municipal services to the town. He wanted to attract development that would employ people and create a tax base with which to pay for improvements to the town.

"I wanted to create an atmosphere in which developers would feel comfortable investing in Secaucus," Amico said. Hudson County had a bad reputation.

"My goals were not to have the biggest police force or the best schools or the best streets," Amico said. "But to have all of them at a high level of quality. It's like being dressed up. You don't want the best tie or shirt or suit, but you want to have everything you need to look good."

Over his career, Amico replaced the grammar schools, built a high school, expanded sewage treatment, and provided one of the highest levels of services in the county to Secaucus residents. He saw the lack of these things as limiting the ability of the town to grow.

Development, Amico believed, was a necessary evil that allowed the town to give the residents a better way of life. The more industry that came into town, the more services the town could provide. He compared it to a family trying to send its kids to college.

"How do you get money? The father gets a raise. The mother takes a job. Unless the town gets ratables, there's no fresh money, and paying for services would have to come from the people living in the town," he said "Or you can resort to what Reagan-Bush did by sweeping the problem under the rug and not facing up to it. A family might take out a second and third mortgage and have things look all right for a time."

While many opponents criticize Amico for overdeveloping Secaucus, loyal supporters say it isn't totally the former mayor's fault. In 1969, Secaucus lost control of its own destiny when the state formed the Hackensack Meadowlands Development Commission.

"Amico went to court early," one town employee said. "But he couldn't stop it. Then, seeing that development was coming in whether he wanted it or not, he said why not make the best of it."

But many townspeople, even those who respect Amico, criticize him for his pro–Allied Junction stand. Some who have been his staunch supporters in the past have backed away from him on this issue, saying he might be right in the long run, but he seems out of touch with the wishes of the population. Allied Junction, a four-million-square-foot commercial enterprise, has been proposed to be built on top of New Jersey Transit's Secaucus Transfer station. Amico said he treated Allied Junction the way he did all incoming development.

"I took more time on Allied because it was more complex," he said. He gathered the facts. "Then, when it was time to decide, it was easy."

He discounts many of the arguments made against Allied, saying they are emotionally charged, but not based in fact, especially those regarding the volume of traffic the project would bring through Secaucus. He accuses his opponents of seeking short-term solutions to problems facing Secaucus.

As an example, he noted how Town Hall had passed over an opportunity to buy property in the Plaza, which could have been used for parking.

"They said by letting someone else buy the property it would mean more ratables," Amico said. "That's short-term thinking."

The former mayor said if the town had built parking, other businesses might have opened in the center of town, rather than going to other communities where there is ample parking.

"It's Amico's basic philosophy," a town employee said. "In the long run, the best thing he can do for himself politically is to do the best thing for Secaucus. He's always taking the long view on things."

Amico's career can be divided into two epochs. In the first fourteen years, he was in total control, wielding a majority on the council that allowed him to decide Secaucus's fate. Current and past opponents accuse him of being too close to the county, something he denies.

"I was on good terms with them, but I kept my distance," Amico said. "You can't be antagonistic. You have to be careful and very selective, considering the long- and short-term interest of the town before you get involved to any extent."

But he had no qualms about admitting he liked the early years, when he could operate more freely, better.

"If you're not strong, you can't lead," he said. "If you can't get momentum, you can't be effective. If a good person is a strong politician, he can move a program."

In 1977, however, the Democratic Party made inroads into the council, taking the majority vote away from him.

"While the Democrats were not in harmony with each other, they voted together, and in that position, I couldn't be awfully effective," Amico said.

In truth, the nature of his position changed. Some believe he was more effective during the second half of his career when he built coalitions rather than pushing his agenda. There were betrayals. People he'd helped turned on him and worked for the opposition, yet somehow he overcame them all, even when he was accused of hiring supporters for key jobs. Some believe there was no real opposition to him at all. Even when the Republicans rose from the dead in 1982, forcing him to unite with the Democrats, many Republicans voted for him.

"The man was practical," one employee said in explaining some of Amico's ability to work with people. "If you went to meet with him and ranted and raved about a problem, he would sit and listen, then he would turn around and say: 'Now we know what the problem is, what's the solution?' He expected people to come him with some sort of answer in mind."

From *The Secaucus Reporter,* Hudson Reporter Associates, 1993.

From Out of Obscurity

With Fran Holland, her face says it all, bearing an expression of subtle pride. She is a success story in the legal profession, rising from the obscurity of being a part-time student at Jersey City State College to being a one-woman performer in the state's highest court. In less than a decade, Holland was a college student, Secaucus town attorney, and then special attorney for Secaucus and North Bergen appearing before the New Jersey Supreme Court. But it was no easy ride. Her climb up the legal ladder was accompanied by doubt and personal pain, and though she is now doing well, she says, there were times when the pain nearly overwhelmed her.

In an interview held at the offices of Rosenblum & Rosenblum in Secaucus, Holland sits stiffly, as if not quite comfortable with her success. In many ways, she seems a bundle of contradictions. Her clothing is fashionable, but not in the outlandish designer styles that many prosperous people wear to broadcast their achievements. Although thin, she says she loves to eat, listen to country music, and has from time to time toyed with the idea of learning to line dance. She expresses fascination with simple things, yet also expresses a distinctly urban touch, saying she'd like to attend classes at the New School in Manhattan if she can ever find the time. While claiming to like Conrad, Yeats, Burns, and medieval Italian poets, she says she now prefers to read nonfiction.

"I like real life and things that have happened to people," she says. "I like to look at life and see how it can be expanded in different ways."

She sees herself as being very human; a sensitive individual who had at one point in her life lacked the calloused edge to deal with the public.

"Not that I'll ever be callous," she says. "I'm just learning to balance out my life, taking things more objectively than personally. Some things are painful. My husband was extraordinarily good, a prince who kept me somewhat cloistered. Now I'm out in the world on my own, and finally coming of age as a person and a professional and I feel more real because of it."

For Holland, the legal profession is fascinating, something she got a taste for as a little girl.

"In fact," she said with a wholesome laugh, "my life seems to be a history of Hudson County."

She boasts of being a lawyer groupie, hanging out with the big boys of the Hudson County legal profession before she even left high school. Yet long

Although suffering ill health over the last few years, Fran Holland continued her legal career.

before high school she was the little girl selling Girl Scout cookies to the men in gray suits.

"I used to sit and listen to all the lawyers shoot the breeze," she says.

It must have been something in her blood, she says, noting that she grew up in the Granville section of Jersey City, where lawyers and politicians visited with the frequency of family.

"I learned from them," she said. "Even at the time I realized it was an unusual experience for any kid growing up."

Her parents were involved deeply in the roots of protest in the county, and she laughingly says they were a big part of the anti-Hague movement. Her mother was a founding member of the Living Theater, a world-famous theatrical troupe specializing in street protest performance. The troupe began these activities in the late 1950s in reaction to anticommunist hearings in Washington, D.C., and ongoing development of nuclear weapons. Both her mother and her father were part of the now-legendary late 1940s sit-in when parents struggled to establish a PTA in Jersey City schools.

"Mayor Kenny wouldn't permit the formation of a PTA," Holland says. "He wouldn't permit teachers to be part of any organization. The people met in my living room."

Road construction protests, liberty park protests, and many others, Holland was there, a Hudson County red diaper baby, learning what law means from the ground up.

Her father was an anti-Hague man who was as involved as his wife with the local political scene. Through him Holland met many of the top names in Hudson County legal profession, and still has strong ties with some of them.

She recalls her father's struggles with Hague goons as he mounted political opposition, challenging votes in election fraud cases against the legendary Hague corruption. Each legal battle eventually led her father to victory in the courts and a bigger moral victory that later won even Hague's begrudging respect.

"Hague told someone that my dad was the one person he'd ever met that he had complete and utter respect for," Holland said. "He said my dad was not afraid to speak the truth and move forward regardless of the consequences. He won on strength of character."

Holland says her parents became two strong role models in her life.

Another hero of hers is former Secaucus mayor Paul Amico, who she said was a particularly strong influence on her.

"He played a special role in my life by putting faith in me," she says. "He and the governing body gave me a chance to show what I was made of and what I could do. They allowed me to expand, show my ingenuity and effort. I tried to rise up and meet their expectations."

But she said with Amico it was never an obligation. She learned to put loyalty to the town first when her husband, Louis Holland, was town attorney.

"Lou never used his position to forward an economic agenda or personal power," she says. "He was tremendously loyal and he imbued me with the same sense of responsibility. Even when things aren't expected of you, you have to think of the best interest of the town."

She says it was this aspect that Amico seemed to admire in her when, after her husband died, she took over as acting town attorney.

"Mayor Amico never demanded anything from me, or expected me to rule in favor of any policy," she says. "My duty was to find legal decisions that would benefit the town, and while I was there, I did my utmost to uphold that standard."

Holland married very young, and had two kids by the time she was twenty. While balancing the chores of motherhood with working, she struggled to study law. Over the years she worked as an English teacher and as a legal aide for the Constitutional Law Clinic at Rutgers. Eventually she received a law degree from Seton Hall. "It took me a long time to finish," she says. "I kept getting sidetracked by advocate work with my husband."

She and her husband lived and breathed legal matters. She discussed tactics with him, worked on his briefs, often sat in on the legal discussions between various attorneys.

"It was a very good tactical education," she says.

Amico brought her husband, Louis Holland, on as town attorney shortly after taking office early in the 1960s. Many of the cases Holland has taken to the state Supreme Court were ideas she and her husband had worked out in those early years. In the mid-1980s, however, her husband got hurt in an auto accident. After eight months in the hospital, he died. Holland was named acting town attorney in August 1987 and remained in that capacity until July 1988, when she was named town attorney.

For Holland, that whole period of time was a trial. One of her children—though cured later—was believed for a year to be terminally ill. Then came her husband's accident, and four weeks after her husband's death, her father suffered a heart attack and died.

Through it all, she says, she focused on being responsible to the town, her clients, her husband, and her children.

"Somehow I had the strength to do what needed to be done, and each thing I did gave me strength to do the next thing. It's through hard times that you learn what you're made of," she says, though admits she wouldn't want to repeat the experience regardless of how strong it made her.

Apparently, Holland did not inherit any of her parents' political feistiness. She says neither she nor her husband ever took a political position in town.

"I'm not political to this day," she says, though she dodged the question of whether she thought of serving as Secaucus mayor. "I'm a good consensus builder, which I believe is sorely needed in this town and I hope that after things get settled in town hall, I can be of some assistance in building a consensus here."

She says Secaucus needs someone without political affiliation to help it get the business done and run the government in a sensible manner.

Since she passed her bar exam in 1983, Holland has handled a continual stream of cases. She describes her practice, which covers commercial, municipal, real estate, zoning, land use, tax appeal, general practice, and appellate cases, as "pretty intense." She currently sits on the Community Advisory Board of the United Jersey Bank, as well as serving as special counsel for various cases in Secaucus and North Bergen—a position she had held since stepping down as town attorney in February 1991.

One of the most significant victories of her career came on February 22, 1994, when the New Jersey Supreme Court struck down county tax exception to Bayonne, forcing it to pay its full share of taxes toward the upkeep of the Hudson County vocation school. She currently has another case pending against the Hackensack Meadowlands Development Commission.

"It's not common for an attorney with a solo practice to be heard at such a level," she says. "While things are a bit freer in New Jersey than in other states, it's usually the larger firms with five or six lawyers that get involved with the state supreme court."

Holland now has six of her cases recorded in the state law books—another rare accomplishment.

Last December, Holland got a message from Mother Nature to slow down. While the heart attack wasn't as severe as it could have been, it told her she isn't made of steel.

"I can't keep trying to push things too far," she says,

To relax, she intends to travel. She says she wants to kick around and explore the New Jersey Shore, visit museums, and see her kids. She has been jogging, walking, using the rowing machine, even taking tennis lessons.

"I feel good," she says. "I'm working on becoming more balanced and trying to keep myself from getting emotionally cut off from the world. But I'm an energetic person and I'm used to going full tilt."

She's not going to let the heart attack stop her. She likes the public sector and says she believes she has a talent for this kind of work. She says she's never made an issue of being a woman attorney, yet notes the significant strides women have made in New Jersey politics and in its legal community.

"I've never let people's perceptions of my being a woman interfere with what I needed to do," she says. "I have something to contribute, if not in one way, then in another. I want to leave my mark on the world, but in keeping with my own personal style."

From *The Secaucus Reporter,* Hudson Reporter Associates, 1994.

A Matter Bigger
Than Books

On any given day, the Secaucus Public Library is a hive of activity, a hustle and bustle of daily routine that includes everyone from pre-kindergarten kids to seniors. The copy machine whirs, computer keys click, people whisper into telephones answering inquiries.

"This man wants to know about certificates of occupancy," said one worker, excitedly thumbing through a thick volume of state statutes. "I can't seem to find anything here to help him."

"Tell him to call Town Hall," another worker said. "The building inspector can help."

As the town information center, the library refers questions that can't be answered from information in its books, computers or tapes to others in the town, county, or state who can provide suitable data. Yet over the years, the library has been more than questions and answers, offering residents everything from art shows to musical performances, or a place for people with mutual interests to gather.

From the sidewalk, the red brick building looks as though it comes straight out of a 1950s civics text, fitting that era's image of public buildings, with pitched roof and arched doors. Inside, its narrow aisles weave through an assortment of features the building was never intended to house, with computers to one side and whole shelves dedicated to videotapes. Downstairs, the basement serves as meeting room, children's library, and classroom for pre-kindergarten children.

For many residents, the library is more essential to their lives than even Town Hall. For morning commuters passing through the town on the New Jersey Transit 190 bus, the library is the face of Secaucus, its brick visage surrounded by the green lawn of Buchmuller Park. Now nearly forty years old, the library marks the town's transition from pig farms and trash dumps to one of the most successful business communities in the state. Through that transition, little has changed in the building's outward appearance, although inside it has shifted with the changing times, adapting to the community's needs. Much of this is credited to Margaret Grazioli, who celebrated her thirty-second year as director last month.

Despite her deep desire to see her library expanded, Margaret Grazioli died in early 1998. A new library was planned to start construction in fall 2000. The library trustees said they intended to name the children's wing after Grazioli.

While there are daily, weekly, even monthly rhythms to the library—books in and out, kids coming for morning and afternoon sessions of story hour, group meetings, and other events—the one most lasting influence on library life has been Grazioli. Although thirty years from now people might not remember her, Grazioli's impact on the library will still be felt.

"She continues to bring us into the twentieth century with technical advancements, literary programs, deaf awareness programs, and cultural events, while she still maintains a home town atmosphere," said Kathy Steffens, who has worked with Grazioli at the library for over ten years. "It amazes us that she finds space to do all these things."

Grazioli is not a local phenomenon. She has been involved with programs throughout the county and state. She has twice been the *Jersey Journal* Woman of Achievement and has served as vice-president to the Secaucus Board of Education and president of the Hudson County Library Association, Secaucus Woman's Club, and Weehawken Garden Club, as well as in a variety of other posts in both Secaucus and Weehawken. She is listed in *Who's Who among American Women* and has received awards from the Girl Scouts, Boy Scouts, Secaucus Jaycees, the Red Cross, and the town of Secaucus. She has chaired scholarship funds, presided over PTAs, received awards as an outstanding citizen. She is treasurer of the Essex-Hudson Regional Library Cooperative and a trustee at the Weehawken Library; she has taught religion, been active in many charitable organizations, and yet has remained above the fray of local politics.

"I've been privileged to travel with Margaret to meetings throughout the state," Steffens said. "They respect her knowledge and her years of experience. She is considered a valuable resource throughout the state."

Grazioli's face tells the story of her life as director, with lines set in a perpetual hopeful smile. But she sits now with less comfort than she might have in the past, hands pressing into the arms of her chair, as if assuring herself of its stability.

"I'm not in pain," she said. "It's just hard to see sometimes. I've had the lights changed here [in her office] and that helps."

While she walks less surely than she might have in the past, her slow gait suggests great dignity, each careful step following a well-worn path through the narrow library aisles. Her office has the same sense of dignity, though with a mid-1960s sense of elegance with cushioned chairs and patterned wallpaper, suggesting a sense of time suspended.

Court administrator and Secaucus history buff Dennis Pope said Grazioli is a well-respected figure in town.

"She always put the library first," he said, noting that when politics began to dominate the school board, she left, refusing to let any of it interfere with her more primary concern, the library.

"While there was talk about her running for town council, she never did," Pope said. "She would have made an excellent council person. She's very classy and very, very dedicated."

Thirty-two years ago, however, Grazioli declined initial offers to become director. Although at the time she had worked for five years as the children's librarian in Weehawken, she originally went to school to teach. Then, when asked to fill in as a librarian, she found she loved the profession, going back to school to get certified. Then, out of the blue, the superintendent of Weehawken schools called.

"He said the Secaucus library needed a director," Grazioli said. "I wasn't really interested."

Weehawken and Secaucus have had a close relationship for years, so when Secaucus needed a library director, Weehawken's director was glad to help find someone to fill the post.

Fate seemed determined to take her, and a few days later the superintendent of Secaucus schools called and asked her to come down for an interview, and though still not enthusiastic, she agreed to come to town and talk about it. The library had been up and running for two or three years already.

"They had trouble keeping a director for some reason. Library directors were scarce and moved around a lot," she said. "Once I saw the building, I changed my mind. It struck me as so beautiful. I told them I wouldn't mind doing it for a while. But I had to talk with the board of trustees at the Weehawken library.'"

She did stay awhile. She stayed thirty-two years. Weehawken, however, understood just how valuable Grazioli was. While they couldn't keep her on as an employee of the library, they could make her a trustee in Weehawken, which they did.

"They just wanted to keep me on in some capacity," she said.

Secaucus was a challenge.

"When I first got here there was a big empty area and very few books," Grazioli said. "I saw it as a challenge and began to build it up myself."

She said she learned a lot as she went along, but was innovative from the start. In 1967 she started Story Hour for young kids. Like its name, it originally lasted one hour a day, but got so popular that parents asked her to increase it.

"Their children used to cry when they had to go home," Grazioli said.

This was the first of its kind in the state and became the pilot for programs in many other libraries.

"People came here to see how we operated," Grazioli said. "Some of the children who came to Story Hour then have their children in here now."

Physical changes occurred within the library over the years.

"When I first came, the whole top floor was the library with the children's room in back," she said. "As we went on, we moved the children's room downstairs because so many children came. The back of the library became the reference area."

In the early years, the library had to struggle along. There was never a lot of money.

"Since there was no [state funding] formula then, we were low on the totem pole when it came to funding," she said.

Then, in the early 1980s, state law required libraries to be funded according to the ratables in town. Since the town's ratables had skyrocketed since 1969, the library funding rose at a fantastic rate.

"We saved money," she said. "We were always very conservative in our spending."

In the early 1970s, however, Grazioli began to see the strain. While the rest of the town changed, the library did not. Harmon Cove came, as did other condo developments. The daytime population of the town increased, and so did library use. The library needed to expand.

"Nobody wanted to spend the money. It wasn't until ADA [Americans with Disability Act] came that anyone paid attention," she said. There was some discussion about moving the library, but the trustees hired a consultant and came up with a surprising result: the library was already in the best location.

In December 1992, the trustees reviewed plans that would have the library expand outward. With ramps and other features, it would then meet ADA requirements and also provide additional space.

Mayor Anthony Just, however, did not agree with the plan, questioning the cost of an outward expansion, offering preliminary sketches that would create another floor and leave the attached firehouse undisturbed.

Former Mayor Paul Amico had proposed moving the fire department out entirely and giving the whole building to the library, a plan that would have met the needs of the library, reducing the costs of expansion without increasing the building size or reducing the land area. But that plan was never implemented and might have gathered more support if Amico had introduced it while he was still mayor. A proposal suggested by Third Ward Councilman Sal Manente would relocate the library to a new facility on Route 153. But as of today, no plan has been approved, and if the library trustees don't act now, there might not be time to avoid federally imposed fines.

Grazioli pointed out that many events begun in the library had moved out for lack of room. Art shows formerly displayed here are now given yearly in the halls of Panasonic headquarters on the other side of town. Many of the current town senior programs began under Grazioli's care.

"I start a lot of things, and then they move on to someplace else," she said. "But it doesn't feel right, even if we're sponsoring the effect. It's not the same as holding it in the building."

Even with many programs exported, space pressure mounts. More and more kids are attending the library programs as the town's younger population increases. Housing planned by Hartz Mountain Industries would bring two thousand more families to town. Already the library serves a wide variety of people, from professors to schoolchildren, providing a host of new features. Videos have become the hottest item, with a heavy demand for space.

"People use the library who live here and work here, companies have taken out cards for their employees," Grazioli said, noting many ideas that have been put off until expansion is finished, like a music room where people can listen to CDs, and more computers for patrons' use.

"People don't understand just how important the library is, how we serve people from birth until death," Grazioli said. "This is the cultural center of the town."

After twenty years of hoping and planning, the expansion has become Grazioli's biggest dream. But it is one she may not get to see. A few years ago, Grazioli discovered she had glaucoma. One day she saw flashes across one eye. A medical examination discovered significant damage. Now, after numerous laser operations, she cannot see out of her left eye and lives with the constant fear that the blindness will spread to her other eye.

"I hope that before I retire I can see the library expansion done," she said. "Now I don't know. We started the thing, but it's not moving ahead. I really want to be able to see the expansion while I still can. I'm very afraid I won't be able to."

From *The Secaucus Reporter*, Hudson Reporter Associates, 1994.

Not a Taxing Job

Nothing about Jim Terhune fits the stereotypical model of a tax assessor: the suit and tie man carrying calculators, seemingly more interested in numbers than people.

In fact, a glance at him in passing would define him as anything from a truck driver to that kindly uncle who brings cake and cookies every holiday. Standing behind the counter of the tax assessor's office in Secaucus Town Hall, Terhune looks out of place. Even in his suit and tie, the jacket of which remains on the back of his office chair, he seems ill at ease within four walls.

He is a broad-shouldered man, and as he leans over the counter, his large hands spreading out building plans, more the image of a field supervisor to some massive construction project, one gets the impression he is about to roll up his sleeves to mix concrete and place bricks rather than calculate assessments. Yet he handles himself with an unusual grace, part of the ballet of property and values to which people are understandably sensitive. He says there's no secret to his skillful handling of people.

"It's a matter of making people realize that we're trying to be fair," he says.

Jim Terhune continued his tax assessments as land values increased in the late 1990s, witnessing one of the greatest economic booms of the century.

"Everyone assumes they are paying more taxes than anyone else, and no one likes to pay taxes."

In most cases, Terhune has an amiable approach to people, dealing with citizen or professional in the same straightforward manner. All seem to feel Terhune has done his best to help them. "Helpful," is a word the Hackensack Meadowlands Development Commission people use. "Down to earth," is a phrase one local real estate broker used in describing Terhune. The worst criticism people seem to have is Terhune's brutal honesty when it comes to facts and figures.

"The man just won't fib for you," says one of the well-known political pundit. "If Jim believes a property is worth X, that's what he tells you. You might not like it—especially in these times when we're scrambling to bring ratables up—but if he believes he's right, he sticks to that number no matter what."

Terhune grins at the lack of significant criticism.

"I like to hear that," he says. "Nobody likes to make enemies. Do I make mistakes? Sure. That's why pencils have erasers. But I'm as quick as anyone to correct my errors."

Part of his ability to function as tax assessor, Terhune says, comes from his having an open mind, as well as an aversion to politics.

Like other offices in Town Hall, the tax assessor's office is a series of cubicles that divide one office into many small compartments. The door from the hall opens onto a small counter behind which Terhune secretary works. The main computer is to one side of this space; Terhune's office is a twist and turn around a barrier into still more secluded space with windows that overlook Paterson Plank Road.

Messages and letters are taped to the wall above his computer. He has pictures of his kids on the wall; a picture on his desk includes his wife. His paperweight is a crystal with two pennies sealed inside. Everything is orderly and in place, with only the day's work on his desk.

"You have to like dealing with people," he says, in one of his startling shifts between humor and philosophy. "You have to like people and like finding out the unknown."

He claims each assessment is like a puzzle.

"You have to come up with a value," he says. "Some people can look at a property and tell you what it's worth. But proving it is another thing. I can look at it, tell you what it's worth. But better yet, I can prove it. You develop an instinct over time, and learn how to look at things and translate them into value."

He says the computer upgrade done about a year ago has changed the way he does his job, and he fiddles with the computer, calling up files to show the new system. In "the good old days," the tax assessor went out into the field, took measurements, did calculations, and then came back to the office and filed it on a newspaper page–sized card.

What he has called up on the computer screen looks much like the card, even down to the sketches, which advanced technology has allowed his office to add to each new file.

In the old days, there was much more room for error. The assessor had to calculate all the room sizes, and other details about the house, property, or commercial building. Now he puts in the figures and lets the computer figure out the details.

"It does away with a lot of the human error," Terhune said. "But it gives us a lot more than that."

Information is compiled not just into that single file but also into a large database from which the assessor can determine market trends on houses, condos, or corporate properties. With a push of a few buttons, valuable statistics roll up onto the screen in ways that would have taken months or longer to compile without the computer.

"You can classify a house in a neighborhood, adjust and fine-tune all your calculations within seconds," he says.

It was by computer that the town did its last assessment, he says.

When he talks about computers, Terhune's face takes on the expression of a teacher trying to simplify a difficult concept.

"It's not that computers save us a lot of time in day-to-day operations," he says. "We still have to spend time putting the information in. But it's when we need to calculate things, when we need the results of something, that's when the computer is impressive. We can compare 5,000 entries in a matter of minutes when in the past we couldn't do that at all. We can compare data on the whole town just by pushing a button."

Holding up a tape cassette slightly smaller than a VCR tape, Terhune says it contains all the appraisals, records, and tax information for the entire town.

Like many businesses, the tax assessor's office does work in season: added assessments in October, information on the budget in January, and preparing tax books in March. Yet investigating appeals, watching over improvements of property, and keeping track of sales keep him busy all year long.

"Every time a property is sold and a deed recorded, we have to keep track of it," he says. "It's important for tax collection that we keep our books up to date."

In preparing the budget, the mayor and council rely heavily upon information from the tax assessor's office.

"You have to know what they have before the mayor and council can work out what they can afford to spend," he says.

As remarkably closely as his office works with other departments in Town Hall, Terhune says he really not responsible to the mayor and council.

"The town gives us space here. It provides clerical help and pays the salaries, but who we are answerable to are the Hudson County Board of Taxation and the Division of Taxation of the State of New Jersey. They're the ones who look at our work schedule and how it is done."

Terhune is the most senior town official after Town Administrator Phil Kieffer and Town Clerk Claire Grecco. He came into the tax assessor's office under then Mayor Paul Amico in 1975.

"Secaucus has changed a lot in that time," he says. "It's bigger in some ways than it was in 1975 when I came back into town, and it will keep on changing, but I don't think it will ever lose that small-town feel."

Now fifty-four years old, Terhune grew up in Union City, went to Union Hill High School, and studied for two years at Rutgers, where he majored in real estate. Then he took the state exam to become an assessor. He began working as an appraiser in 1961, and a decade later started at the part-time assessor for Guttenberg—a position he still holds.

He moved to Secaucus in 1965 and moved out three years later, only to move back again in 1975. He lived in Fairview for a while, owned a home in Weehawken, then began to look for a house in Secaucus.

"I found out by accident that the town was looking for a full-time tax assessor," he says.

Behind the mask of tax assessor is a much different Jim Terhune, who says his private life is not quite as active as he would want. He likes films and draws upon famous film characters for comparisons. He also likes to build models of airplanes and trains. His father was a brakeman on the New York Central Railroad, and Terhune recalls going with his father to the big city.

"He knew how to get around New York City underground through all those passages. You remember that Superman movie with those underground tracks? That's what it's like down there."

His father, who died in 1977, was born and raised in Kearny, and Terhune is constantly accosted with questions about his relation to other Terhunes throughout Bergen County, particularly the Bergen County sheriff. The questions come often enough for him to look into the history of his name, tracing it back to the original Dutch settlers.

"The name Terhune is Dutch," he says. "Ter means 'from.' Hune is a town in Holland."

A few years ago, Albert Terhune, a writer, wrote a book tracking the name in American history. Terhunes were deeply involved in the American Revolution. One was an aide to General George Washington.

"But some of them were Tories, too," Terhune says with a booming laugh. "Not all the Terhunes were patriots."

From *The Secaucus Reporter*, Hudson Reporter Associates, 1994.

The Human Side of Legislation

They stop him on the street asking, "Hey, Tony, how are you doing? How's the family?"

Old women with gray hair and stories about vacation trips, young girls driving their parents' car, mothers driving through town with infants in the back seat, waving, beeping, reaching out to shake his hand.

*Year by year, Anthony Impreveduto
continued to make his hometown proud,
becoming one of the most senior Democratic
members of the state assembly.*

"Hey, Tony, how are you? Good to see you," they say.

Everybody here seems to know Anthony Impreveduto by sight. He's one of the town's success stories, the son of a son of an Italian immigrant, who can brag that he has stood with and shook the hand of governors and presidents.

"Hey, Tony, how are you? How's the family?"

Before being elected to the state assembly in 1987, Impreveduto was criticized—perhaps unfairly—for not being accessible. People called him, his critics claim, and he'd be too busy to get back. Any accessibility problem, however, ended the day he opened his assembly office on Old Route 3. Almost from the minute he walked through the door, the phone rang, and it hasn't stopped since.

"The first call we got was someone on the line for information about an IUD," Mary Waller, Impreveduto's legislative aide, said. "After that, we knew we would be in for the ride of our lives."

And what a ride it has been.

People have continued to call about everything, seeking housing, seeking jobs, seeking help to solve a problem with sales from highway discount stores.

"People come to us when they can't find anybody else to help them,"

Impreveduto said, sitting in his office on Plaza Drive, kind of nostalgic about the years that have led up to this election.

Although he served with distinction as a Second Ward councilman, Impreveduto came into his own when elected to the assembly in 1987, finding himself above the petty mudslinging so typical of local elections. And although he is one of the leading legislators in proposing and passing bills into law, it is the everyday activity of dealing with people that has surprised him. He has found himself more deeply immersed in people's lives as an assemblyman than he ever imagined as a council member, almost as if people expected someone on a state level to have all the answers.

People like the family whose husband and wife both found themselves out of work as a result of a corporate downsizing have called, saying that they are using up their savings in order to make ends meet, and now, with a three-year-old child, find themselves being evicted. Or the older man whose wife has been suffering from a debilitating mental disorder, and he, ten years older than she, doesn't know how she will survive when he dies. Or even the local family whose income doesn't quite manage to pay the bills and who find themselves with phone service cancelled.

"One woman who called was dying of cancer and couldn't afford chemotherapy," Impreveduto said. "What do you say to people like that? How can you tell them you won't help? Sometimes I don't know how to help, but I try. I make some calls. I find people who can help. But it's not always easy."

And there are the letters. The mail comes in with bags full of requests. Some seem like small matters compared to the huge decisions made on the floor of the state assembly in Trenton; some of the letters even raise questions of significant social importance, yet Impreveduto has come to understand that the author of each letter has turned to his office for help.

"It's not me; it's the office," he said. "Most legislators are faced with these same requests."

Many of the letters come from people with older family members seeking to find some way to take care of them. Many more people write seeking jobs, asking Impreveduto where they can go and who they can talk to. In most cases, he can deal with a letter by making a phone call or two. His years in office have allowed him to develop a network of contacts, public agencies, business leaders, and others he can utilize in solving problems.

"That's where the theory of term limits falls down," Impreveduto said. "When you're in office year after year, you meet people, you learn about their services, and you can call on them when one of your constituents needs help."

Not all letters and phone calls come from constituents. Although the Thirty-second District includes parts of Jersey City, North Bergen, Secaucus,

Harrison, Kearny, East Newark, Fairview, and Edgewater, Impreveduto has received calls from other areas.

Sometimes he is outraged by what he hears or reads, as he was when he received a letter from a state prisoner in a Secaucus detention center who claimed raw sewage was running beneath his living quarters. Some letters even inspire legislation, such as the letter from the Hoboken attorney whose client has spent eleven years in jail for a crime he didn't commit, was proven innocent, but couldn't sue the state for loss of income or the family time he had lost.

"He could sue the state if he had been wrongfully convicted," Impreveduto said. "But he was mistakenly convicted and there is a difference." This was a legal distinction. Apparently, a person could sue previously only if he could prove someone had lied or fabricated evidence.

Still, this year is different. This year Impreveduto is running on his own, running for office in a kind of vacuum after the death of his father, Rocco Impreveduto in 1996. Rocco started Anthony in his political career when he urged him to run for town council in 1978, and since then, Rocco had been the solid force behind him, helping him to keep moving.

"It feels strange not having him around," Impreveduto admitted, also noting the loss of another good and supportive friend, Daniel Flanagan, who died in a fire last August.

The loss of his father and friend seems to have cut him off from an important part of his life, his family history, a history that included his grandfather who saved enough money for a first-class steamship fare for his family to come to America after World War I. His family has always been his strongest support system, people who loved him and believed in him and helped him move ahead, coming with him when he arrived in Secaucus at age ten in 1957 after living in a three-story walk-up in Union City.

This was farm country then, and he didn't know anything about farms. The kids here were different; they didn't play box ball the way kids did on Union City streets. They hunted muskrat in the Meadows. It was cultural shock watching kids carry their morning kill up the street, watching them slip into a friend's garage to skin them. Then, when he got his own junior hunting license, he found himself truly immersed in Secaucus culture, a culture that has evolved over time, a culture that has faded slightly, leaving him more than a little nostalgic.

From *The Secaucus Reporter,* Hudson Reporter Associates, 1997.

PART THREE

The Arts and Sciences

Blast from the Past

When Robert Lynch opened the March 12 edition of the *Independent Press,* he found himself fact to face with the past, with an image he remembered vividly from when he coached the Demarest boys' basketball team in 1963.

He couldn't recall all the names to match all the faces, but he knew all the faces by heart. They were part of one of the best years of his life.

Even though Lynch moved out of Bloomfield to take a job in Old Tappan in 1965, he kept in touch with the town and its sports teams, checking in on them from time to time to see how the schools and people were doing. He even knew one or two of the people on the current Bloomfield Board of Education.

Lynch was born and raised in the Watsessing section of Bloomfield and lived on East Passaic Avenue until he married in 1965. He began teaching in Demarest in 1959 after graduating from Seton Hall.

Those years were magical, he said, and thinking back to those times still brings a smile to his face.

"Those were perfect classes," Lynch said. "They were bright, eager kids and I was young and enthusiastic. I used to see pictures of people from the past and think about how people would remember when. Now I'm the remember-when."

In seeing the team photo from 1963, memories came flooding back to Lynch, bringing such a deluge of nostalgia that he had to visit the *Independent Press* to contribute some of the names of the players in the photo. He joined many other readers in providing names after the paper asked "Do you remember when?" in the March 12 edition.

Though so many years later the faces are more familiar to Lynch than the names, he remembers that the sports programs in the 1960s were strong, and he said he was glad to have played a part in them.

Over the years, he kept many reminders of those times—the sixth-grade yearbooks and even some of the grade books he used. Some of the lesson plans he used in Bloomfield he brought with him to Old Tappan when he was hired there.

"I got a lot from those kids," Lynch said. "My five years here were some of the best—a great staff, a great principal, and a great group of kids. They really set a mood."

Leaving Bloomfield was hard, but it was also a wise career move. Lynch eventually raised eight children and went on to become the principal of Old Tappan's middle school and, for a time, acting superintendent. Yet looking back, Lynch said it was those first five years of teaching that set him in the right direction.

In 1996, Lynch retired after thirty-seven years in education, though he now works with retirement funds for schools, helping to provide teachers and educators with tax shelter plans.

He is fiercely loyal to Bloomfield's sport teams even though he lives in Ridgewood now, and he cheers on Bloomfield teams whenever he gets a chance—with one glaring exception.

During the championship football game for the 1995–96 season, his son was quarterback for the Ridgewood High School football team. He scored the tying touchdown that sent the game into over time, and then later, the winning touchdown in overtime.

Lynch says he'll never forget his years in Bloomfield as a teacher and coach.

"Those are rich memories," he said. "If any of the guys and gals from that era are still around, they should get in touch with me."

From *The Independent Press of Bloomfield*, Worrall Community Newspapers, 1998.

Stretching Out the Walls of Education

People who have come to know William Koenig over time call him "Columbo" because he isn't what he seems at first meeting. While "mild-mannered" doesn't quite capture the image of the man the way it does Clark Kent, there is a sense of a quiet around him that is deceptive.

As acting principal of Secaucus High School, he seems a quiet volcano to many students and teachers, an efficient man who patrols the hallways and classrooms with a pocket notebook, noting the details of the day, things that need improvement, ideas that come to mind during routine procedures.

Although William Koenig retired as high school principal in 1997, he continued to lend his expertise to local school officials. He also continued to fly his airplane.

Dressed in a suit, tie, and vest, he is the classic picture of what a principal should look like, though his gaze is never fixed; he studies details of things even when he is seated at his desk, as if seeking some solution to a puzzle whirling around in his head. Students say he is a stern taskmaster, yet he also has a sharp sense of humor that isn't afraid to target himself.

Conversing with him is often a study of human nature Lenny Bruce–style, each joke tinged with a slice of truth. But when it comes to education and his plans for the future, Koenig is all business, his expression and gaze fixed upon some vision that he is formulating in the air before you, less trick or puzzle than a master construction.

In the secretary's area outside Koenig's office, a small sign stands among the calendars, school notices, and yellow marks of old Scotch tape: "Education is not a spectator sport." Even the room has a feel of a hands-on approach to education, the small office space lacking every bit of luxury that other schools afford their principals, speaking of constant activity, of people coming and going, of letters and memos being typed, of issues being argued and proposed. In the midst of all this, Koenig ponders the future, just now outlining long-laid plans that will change the course of how students are educated in Secaucus High School.

After thirty-three years in education, Koenig is hardly a newcomer, yet he says he feels that there are things he can learn from talking to students and the community.

"I can't take credit for [my] ideas," he says. "The school improvement committee has been talking about them over the last year."

But now he is reaching beyond the teachers and faculty for ideas that might be waiting outside the walls of school, and with his own background in media, he see the direction as a positive one.

Koenig has been in the Secaucus school system his entire teaching career, starting as a part-time teacher/part-time librarian at the old Lincoln School. When the high school was built, he went on to it.

He was born in Hoboken and went through the Hoboken school system, then to Jersey City State College, Rutgers University, William Paterson College, and Montclair State, his degrees covering everything from administration to media, though media is his specialty. For a time he taught at Jersey City State, William Paterson, and Montclair, but the workload became too much.

There is no mystery about his wanting to teach. He decided on that career path when he was still a senior in high school. He said he saw things that could be done in education and weren't.

"We're talking the 1950s," he said.

Even as far back as that, he believed it was necessary to provide more opportunities for kids to get directly involved with their own education.

As acting principal of Clarendon School twice, Koenig got early experience that helped him when he came to Secaucus High School, teaching him how to analyze the school system and propose improvements.

Others in the school system seem him as a strict disciplinarian, something he does not disagree with.

"I set a standard of behavior and shift some of the responsibilities of the school onto the student," he said. "I set up simple rules, explain the rules to the students, and then consistently enforce those rules."

He believes other people see him as strict, but fair and consistent as well.

"I think students know what to expect from me," he says. "I'm willing to grant almost any privilege they ask for as long as they accept responsibility for it."

As an example, he notes a problem that occurred in the student lounge last year. There are rules in the lounge against eating and drinking. The rule was broken, and the seniors came to Koenig and asked that the lounge be closed for a week.

"In this case I believe they handled their responsibility quite well," Koenig said, noting that he has worked with the student government in the past, giving and receiving suggestions as part of improving the quality of education. "Students have to be responsible for their own education and play a major part in it."

Yet in spite of his love for education and his ideas for improving students' ability to learn, Koenig does not take his work home with him. While, oddly enough, he teachers outside school in his spare time, he doesn't teach the stuff found on the bookshelves in his high school office. His second life begins the moment he leaves school, and school is forgotten for a few hours.

"That's my other life," he said. "I don't worry about what happens during the day. I know I'm going to start over tomorrow."

Part of the reason for his nickname, Columbo, is the apparently drastic change in lifestyle. Instead of finding him in a classroom after house, you might find him sailing high in the clouds above the Hudson River, at the controls of a small four-passenger airplane. While he doesn't have the time to teach students to fly from scratch, he does give instruction to help polish their skills and qualify them for upgraded licenses.

Flying and skiing were two things Koenig put off for years, saying that he would get to them later in life. Then, about ten years ago, two of his close friends died, and something clicked inside him. He decided to stop putting off things he wanted and needed to do.

Flying is a hobby that he gets paid to do, and he has visions of doing work for the Federal Aviation Administration someday, when he finally does decide to retire from his more conventional life as principal and teacher.

He said he loves to take people flying.

"I like to see their faces the first time they go up," he said, though he notes that people are awed by the sights only after they've calmed down.

Flying for his own pleasure, Koenig has traveled up and down the East Coast from Canada to Miami.

"It's more fun when you have a place to go than [when you are] circling around in the air," he said.

When he is not flying or skiing, Koenig reads. Novels are a staple of his literary diet. But so are books about flying. He said he gets caught up in authors and might read consecutively everything written by a single author. Currently, he reads detective novels, which is only fitting, since to many people in and out of the school system, Koenig is a bit of a mystery.

From *The Secaucus Reporter,* Hudson Reporter Associates, 1993.

Rocket Man

"Is everybody clear?" John O'Hara shouts, glancing around at the boys in the field; some are watching the launch pad, others the sky for signs of planes. "Are we ready to launch?"

When each waves or yells "all clear," O'Hara leans over an electronic control panel he designed and built thirty years ago, a four-switch apparatus from which wires lead to a metal platform about ten yards away.

"We're launching from number one," he announces, then slowly counts down from ten before he flips the switch sending an electronic signal to the first of four foot-high rockets on the launch pad. For a moment, there is only the sound of hissing, then a pop as the first of the rockets soars skyward in what is deemed a successful launch; high up in the sky, its parachute suddenly opens, letting the craft sail slowly back to earth.

The students waiting to test their rocketing skills come from high schools in West New York, North Bergen, Secaucus, and Kearny, and gather as part of a field trip arranged to bring them together a few times a year.

O'Hara, who is a physics and math teacher at Kearny High School, developed the program in Kearny in 1970. In 1996, the number of students grew as Hudson County introduced its interactive television broadcasts.

Six kids from Secaucus as well as similar numbers in the other schools get to school every day for the 7:30 A.M. transmission, so they can explore various aspects of flight, from the physics of flight itself to the psychology behind the design of an instrument panel. Students explore flight, aircraft and navigation instrumentation, the science of rocketry, the physics of satellites and orbital payloads, astronomy, meteorology, aircraft and spacecraft physiology, and living in space for extended periods.

O'Hara usually starts each year with the history of flight, going from the Wright brothers to the present.

"We even cover health issues, like vertigo and how to keep people alive in space," he said. "What would be the impact on someone going to Mars."

O'Hara calls the program a "paradigm of imagination and creativity," in which the traditional model nineteenth-century classroom is converted into something more contemporary through collaboration and interaction.

"The classroom will be run like a business, modeled after successful corporations like NASA, Lockheed, and Rockwell Corporations," he told the class in his outline at the beginning of the year. "The focus is on teamwork, building interactive skills, and on learning, not teaching—and on sharing information through technology, in particular through ITV."

In this project, the traditional classroom has been re-engineered. The monotonous rows of desks are replaced by high-tech telecommunication equipment, fiber optics, real-time video and voice communication, fax machines, modems, computers, video cameras, control panels, and large screen monitors.

"The 'I lecture you listen' approach to teaching is replaced by definite, well-defined goals," O'Hara said. "Students are continually aware of the goals and their progress toward achieving them."

Students don't do all of their studying or communicating in the classroom; they share projects with kids from the other schools via telephone.

The classes are divided into teams, with students possibly participating in a variety of roles depending upon the project. Teams hook up to complete one project, then move on to others, or do other projects at the same time. At any given point, a student might be a physical scientist, life scientist, social scientist, mathematician, engineer, technician, engineering designer, or technical communicator.

O'Hara got into teaching about aerospace by accident. A few kids approached him while he was student teaching at St. Aloysius School in Jersey City in 1968 and asked if they could build a model of the Apollo spacecraft.

"That was before we had landed on the moon," he said. "I thought they wanted to build a small model, so I told them to go ahead. Then they started dragging in sheets of plyboard, and they planned to land it in Roosevelt Stadium."

The experience remained in the back of his mind until 1970, when he secured his first teaching position at Kearny, where he convinced the administration that students would enjoy this kind of experience. Over the years, he has gathered information from numerous sources, ranging from books and magazines to NASA workshops

While some of his students have gone on to careers in the aerospace industry, most simply go along and enjoy the experience.

"Their motivations differ; some are interested in aerospace, some just come because they hear about the class from others," he said.

The group meets several times a year for field trips, some like this one to Secaucus where they launch rockets they have built, sometimes to other schools to build wind tunnels where they test wing designs. They also take field strips to various public facilities where they might see planes and rockets.

Joe Serrano, a student from West New York, built his own launch system, as well as rockets, shooting off from an alternative launch pad.

"We're using a solid fuel," he said, noting that it him took a day to build the pad and rockets. "I'm thinking about becoming a commercial pilot and wanted to learn everything I could about air planes."

Dewey Whitley, of Kearny, said he built two rockets, one from a kit, one from parts he had collected. He wants to be a mechanical engineer in aerospace, with rocket design as one of his ultimate goals.

"I heard about the course from others, and I knew I would be studying the material in college and thought I should take it."

Frank Tollack, of Kearny, has been accepted to Stanford, although he is uncertain whether he will seek out aerospace as a career.

Tollack's rocket, however, was larger than most, carrying a raw egg he hoped would survive the launch. The rocket veered off course and crashed in the nearby ball field, where it was recovered; the egg—thanks to packing material—remained undamaged.

"I'll try it again later," he promised, heading off to refuel his rocket.

From *The Secaucus Reporter,* Hudson Reporter Associates, 1999.

More Than Numbers

For students like Ali Kalu, one of the many sixth-graders who took the special class earlier this year, accounting is a lot of work, yet something he never realized gave so much to the public.

"It seemed confusing to me at first," said sixth-grader Chasun Lee. "But when it was over it was a lot less confusing."

Both Kalu and Chasun and others said they never realized that accounting involved so much or that accountants had to work as hard as they did.

When accountant Felix Addeo first started in 1995 to teach kids what it means to be a certified public accountant, he brought them to his office on Paterson Plank Road. It was just a handful full of kids then, and he walked them through the operations, showing them everything an accountant did.

Before becoming a CPA, Addeo was actually a teacher, who taught in Manchester for three years, after which he said he sort of "fell into the accounting profession." In Secaucus, he served as the board of health's accountant for nine years.

"I've always had a good rapport with kids, not only as a teacher, but as a coach and parents," Addeo said, noting that he was a basketball coach for three years.

His lessons on accounting became an immediate hit, so much so that kids started asking to come to his office. Then, one year, more than forty-five kids called, and he decided maybe it would be easier if he took his show on the road and brought the class to the school instead.

Principal Pat Coccuci jumped at the chance. He said he'd been trying to get people from various professions to come in and talk with the kids.

"I believe kids look up to coaches and parents as role models," said principal Pat Coccuci. "By [our] bringing people like Mr. Addeo in, the kids learn about more role models and what people are doing in their community."

As part of the school-to-careers effort, Addeo came in to teach these sixth-graders again earlier this year. As president of the Hudson County chapter of the New Jersey Society of Certified Public Accountants, Addeo looked at his own business operations to show students how accounting works. Over the last two or three years, the program has evolved into a curiously entertaining lesson.

Addeo begins his lesson, not with mathematics but grammar.

"I break down what a certified public accountant is," he said, "splitting the words up to show that it is a accountant who is certified by the state, and that he or she works for the general public rather than a private company."

While CPAs are most often associated with taxes, they are often much more, learning about the professions they help.

"So we learn a lot about law when we deal with attorneys, and a lot about what engineers do when we deal with them," Addeo said. "People sometimes say that if you're good in math, then you should become a CPA. But numbers are only part of it. CPAs can be investment advisors, tax advisors, and other things, and often have to learn new things all the time, through journals, weekly tax alerts, and other means."

This means accountants have to read a lot to keep up with the most current information about their profession, but it does not mean that a student can slack off in math or science.

"I bring a computer and show them the insides," he said. "We talk about the hardware and the software and how each works. I even take apart an external disk to show what that is like. It piques their curiosity."

As part of a lesson plan he tries to make sense of what are to many people, two of the great mysteries of modern society: taxes and deductions.

With laser pointer and an overhead projector, he goes through each level of the tax table, forms, and gets them a refund.

"It's all hands-on," he said.

While taxes are an important part of an accountant's services, so is helping someone set up a business. For kids at school, Addeo picks a kind of business many of them might like to run: an ice cream store. He goes through the details of what it takes to open a business, run it, and in the end make it succeed.

"For instance, I ask them would they want to open a ice cream store next to an existing ice cream store," he said. "They tell me no, of course not."

Where do they get the money to open their business? If they borrow it, then they have to pay it back—with interest. And this along with rent, supplies, and other operating expenses has to come out of the gross receipts, or money taken in with sales before the owner can show a profit.

"I show them the scheduling for how to pay it back, the interest costs, and budgeting," Addeo said. "I know it is a lot to digest, but it is surprising how much the kids can grasp when you put it in terms of ice cream."

He even delves into such things as the effect of raising the price of the product. Will it chase away business or increase profit, and can a business owner make more money by lowering the actual price or by making the product more attractive by adding more ice cream to the cone in the hope customers will purchase more.

If that wasn't enough, Addeo also gives these kids a lesson in the stock market, handing out five hundred dollars in Monopoly money so they can learn what it means to invest.

"They can buy stock or not buy stock," he said. "One student decided he was going to keep the money. Another one sold his stock for one thousand dollars after it paid him dividends. These kids had all heard of the stock market and knew a lot more than they are usually given credit for."

This year, Addeo's class included his own son in his class, who seemed to get a better appreciation for what his father does.

"It's a lot of hard work," he said, and like many of the kids in the class seemed impressed by the presentation, especially the talk about the computers.

From *The Secaucus Reporter,* Hudson Reporter Associates, 1999.

A Twist of Fate

From the moment you meet Michael Gehm you sense how special he is. This has nothing to do with his growing up in the South or the fact he teaches civics in Secaucus Middle School. It doesn't even have anything to do with the wheelchair with which he propels himself around the halls of the school.

He is known to pop wheelies with it from time to time. He is also known for his stories about roadkill and for lecturing drivers who park illegally in handicapped zones. But these things can't explain the sense of faith he seems to carry around as conveniently as a pocketwatch, pulling it out from time to time to show people just how marvelous a place the world is. He doesn't mind talking to people about himself during what other people might have thought the worst time of his life.

Teachers who work with him know how special he is—especially the teachers he has helped over the fear-of-technology hump. He says he takes it slow with them. He says teachers unfamiliar with the gizmos fear they might blow up the computer lab if they push the wrong button or do something else wrong. He says it is a matter of overcoming their fear.

And that is something he knows as much about as he knows about computers. He says he's living proof of how a person can overcome fear.

In 1990, when he was hanging fifty-five feet above the steel deck of the USS *Normandy,* Gehm's safety harness snapped, and, as he fell, he saw not his life passing before his eyes but the end of his naval career as a fire control technician.

Even though he knew every circuit and every system that made up the missile radar system, he could not continue to do his job with a broken back, nor could the navy afford to keep him. They had spent too much money training him to have him work at a lesser job.

"I had a critical rating," he says, seated in one of the Secaucus Middle School work areas, giving the kind of shrug that says he didn't think it so important now, but seven years ago, when he found himself in the hospital without the use of his legs, he was bitter. "They couldn't transfer me. I wasn't trained for any lesser job."

He had counted on the navy to provide him with a lifelong career. Like most kids growing up in small farm towns like Bennettsville, South Carolina, he had plotted to escape what he thought of then as limited opportunities.

Michael Gehm has become one of the most popular teachers in Secaucus High School, involving himself in nearly every aspect of the educational process despite his handicap.

And in the navy, he had found himself in a brand-new ship traveling to brand-new places, able to count on something so he could begin a family of his own.

But his fall ended all that, and he wasn't in a mood to talk to anyone, even the navy chaplain who made daily visits to his bed. He spent a year staring at the walls.

"During that first year, I was ready to give up," he says. "I was a real tyrant."

But his pregnant wife was a saint. She didn't give up on him, even though he kept mumbling things about how they'd married for better or worse, and how she'd ended up with the worst.

"There's nothing tougher than a navy wife," he says, giving that infectious southern grin that has won the hearts of his students and fellow teachers. "She had faith in me even when I didn't."

The navy chaplain had a different kind of faith and a different approach to breaking Gehm's spell of self-pity.

"He told me I had done this long enough," Gehm says. "He told me he was sick and tired of my feeling sorry for myself. 'You have a wife and baby now,' he told me. 'It's time to get your act together.' "

Deep down, Gehm knew the chaplain was right. His parents and grandparents had taught him better, raising him with the kind of pride that didn't fit in with self-pity.

Yet even though he'd made up his mind to do something with his life, Gehm didn't know what he wanted to do.

Since the navy had trained him in computers, he presumed he should follow that up. He tried, enrolling in Stevens Institute of Technology in Hoboken, where he ran into a history teacher who intrigued him. So did the subject matter: the American Civil War. Only when Gehm read the text, he discovered the book had it all wrong from the way he'd been taught. The professor said: "Fine. You teach the class the way you see it."

Gehm did, and discovered he loved teaching.

In retrospect, Gehm realizes that teaching came naturally to him. While he was in the navy, he worked with people on various programs.

"I always enjoyed helping new recruits, teaching them different parts of the department," he says. "I loved that part as much as I did trouble-shooting."

The history professor encouraged Gehm to take up teaching, and Gehm enrolled at St. Peter's College in Jersey City. The choice seemed right. He felt good. And he didn't just get through college; he stormed through with a 4.0 average, graduating in 1996 as the class salutatorian.

"I shocked myself," he says. "Here I was a country boy from a hick town and the first one in my family to even go to college, and I was making a speech."

Some of his family came North, though his eighty-year-old grandmother couldn't make the trip. His success was their success. His family, particularly his grandfather, had always raised him with the belief that if he did something, he should do it right.

"With status comes responsibility, my grandfather told me, and if you did something, you had to do it 110 percent," Gehm says.

Gehm is not an easy teacher. Even he'll admit that much. He says he challenges everyone, making them stretch their abilities. But he also says this raises his students' level of enthusiasm, letting them learn in new ways. This is the way he learned, pushing himself, making himself grow.

"You can't say I can't do something," he says. "I go out and do it."

Gehm doesn't like limiting any aspect of his life. When he's not teaching, you might find him playing basketball, or down at the gym doing his daily forty to fifty laps in the swimming pool. Although he currently lives in Jersey City, he will soon be bringing his wife and two daughters to Secaucus. He loves this town, which he says has the texture of the town where he grew up.

"You're not going to find many men like Michael Gehm," says Middle School principal Pat Impreveduto. "He is an inspiration, someone who has won the respect of the kids and the faulty. And he has an incredible energy. He is constantly thinking up new things. His civics class developed their own constitution. He's taken his students to Ellis Island. He's planning a trip to Philadelphia to reinforce what they've learned in class. He is quite a teacher."

The oddest thing about it all is how Gehm now feels about his accident. Looking back, he says his fall may have actually served a good purpose.

"If it wasn't for that accident, I wouldn't be here right now," he says. "And I love what I'm doing now."

From *The Secaucus Reporter,* Hudson Reporter Associates, 1997.

Moving On

Anthony D'Elia, principal of Clarendon School, had a few pleasant little surprises in store for him the week before he retired. Students from pre-kindergarten to sixth grade began to flood his offices with messages.

"You're a nice man and you care," read a typical message, bringing a slightly startled but obviously pleased expression to the face of the man who had served as principal since 1987.

"You can't ask for much more than that," D'Elia said, looking over the latest handful to get dumped on his desk. Over the last seven years, he has become a very philosophical man, setting goals for himself and his school with the hopes that with hard work and intelligence he can achieve them.

This week, however, he was struck in a way he did not at all expect, an emotional outpouring from students, teachers and parents that was not in the goals he set for himself when he first became principal here.

"The response has been so great that I almost wish I wasn't going," he said, with a look in his eye that says he means it.

Since 1987, when the school board named him principal, he's spent a lot of time with the kids, looking in on classrooms, sampling their lessons like a good cook sampling dishes being prepared under his charge, stopping at the art or history, math or English classes just to see how the kids are getting on.

*Anthony D'Elia,
although suffering
through a serious illness
after retiring, bounced
back, still jogging a
significant distance
each day.*

"I must walk about five miles a day," he said. "I'm hardly ever in my office."

The Clarendon School PTA acknowledged this when they put on a "This Is Your Life" program as a tribute to a man who gave them more input into the education of their children than ever before. They said D'Elia had three things all good principals should have: "Love of children, vision, and respect for teaching."

For D'Elia, who will leave at the end of this school year, Clarendon School will travel with him.

"There must be a million small incidents I'll remember about this place," he said, noting that he had come in that morning to find over a hundred kindergarten students putting on a mini-series about a day in his life. "My wife helped by giving them information."

The performance was more than liberally spiced with humor in its attempt to capture D'Elia's typical day. Science class, as they depicted it, included a rendition of the 1960s rock-and-roll comedy classic "The Monster Mash."

"What made it most wonderful is that I hadn't expected any of it," D'Elia said.

In many ways, D'Elia has fulfilled the classic American dream, going from playing football in the street in Jersey City to being principal of a Secaucus grammar school. Along the way, he served as president of his Dickinson High School graduating class, captain of the football team, and even married a cheerleader—one he claims he nearly didn't date because of his shyness. From high school, he went to Seton Hall University, where he eventually got his degree and later his master's in education.

Many people, however, will remember D'Elia as a man who loved to sing. His cousins recall him singing "Prisoner of Love" to them when they were young. Others say he would sing at the drop of a hat, from the chorus in grammar school to the coffee room in high school. One Christmas he even sang on the radio. Nor did he lose the urge to sing when he came to Clarendon School, where he has been known to break out in song at the slightest provocation. Once he walked into a reading class and started to sing the song the kids were reading. In April of this year, he started to recite a poem for Arbor Day and ended by singing it. Over the years, he has been an active member of the local theater group, CAST, taking part in many of their musicals.

Had he ever had dreams of making music a career?

"No," he said. He was always too practical for that, choosing education over other fields. "I liked to work with kids and that was the big key, I wanted to do something with kids."

D'Elia started teaching in 1957 as a permanent substitute for Public School 37 in Jersey City, and he called it "a real experience." In 1959, he became a sixth-grade teacher in Roselle Park, then moved in 1965 to the Teaneck school system, which was then on the cutting edge of education; there he taught science, saying he wanted to try something new.

"I remember going up to observe some of the team-teaching programs they had there," said Secaucus Superintendent of Schools Gus Scerbo. "The principal at the school directed us to Mr. D'Elia's class. He told us we would get to see a master teacher at work."

D'Elia's arrival in Teaneck coincided with the district's period of racial integration, and D'Elia recalled the experience as "teaching science in a fishbowl" with so many people and friends coming to watch him teach.

In 1968, D'Elia came to Secaucus as a science and physical education instructor. He said the district's new science program attracted him. He taught in Huber Street School for two years until Clarendon School was built in 1970.

"Clarendon School had just opened, and it still lacked a few things," he said. "Like hoops for the basketball courts. We had to use trashcans. We put trashcans on the tables and let the kids shoot balls into them."

Then, in 1978, D'Elia had to make a hard choice. Superintendent of Schools Arthur Couch asked him to run the Secaucus Recreation Department football program and the adult school. The move, while a challenge, meant giving up teaching—something he loved.

Yet he loved football in a different way. Football had helped shape him as a boy in Jersey City, where he played it in the street as well as at the high school. He knew how well sports could help shape young lives in conjunction with education. Nor had he been idle. Years before taking on the role as recreation coach, he, Couch, and Ed Rittberg had struggled to make the Secaucus Recreation football team into a competitive force in the Meadowlands.

"When we first started, Secaucus was the joke of the league," he said. "We got beat regularly by towns which had bigger boys."

Not so coincidentally, just about the time D'Elia took over recreation, the team began to peak, securing the Meadowlands District Championship for two consecutive years, and remaining in the running for years afterward.

"Football is the love of my life," D'Elia said. "I'm very proud of what we did here."

In 1987, D'Elia was named principal of Clarendon School, a position he had wanted for a long time, a new challenge after teaching and football. Yet coming back into the school system was culture shock. He had been away from the classroom setting for nearly a decade.

"In those ten to twelve years, the whole society changed," he said. "Here I was in a school that now had to deal with a new divorce pattern and one-parent families, as well as many social problems."

He said coming back provided him with a real education on how much school systems needed to change to meet the growing need.

"People are asking more from the school system than they did years ago," he said. "Parents have abdicated much of their responsibility, and the school system has taken it on."

D'Elia said it took him a few years to adjust. The first thing he did, however, was to set goals for himself, goals designed to improve morale and create pride in the school system. He also wanted to strengthen the basic elements of education, emphasizing reading, writing, and math.

"I used to tell the kids, we may not be the best yet, but we're going to be, and then later, I would tell them we almost made it," D'Elia said. "Then finally, I told them we were the best, and I believe that."

Under his administration the PTA got much more involved. He wanted and needed input from the parents and needed them to understand how the system of education worked. He said he has incredible respect for mothers, who, he believes, play the most important role in a child's life.

"I really sincerely feel that the mother is the most important part of every family when it comes to raising kids," he said. "I'm not saying the men aren't important. In our own way we are, but I still think that if the mother has the goals and the standards and the rules and the regulations and the guts to raise the children properly, those kids are going to grow up great. If you read some of the biographies of some great men, lots of times you'll see great mothers behind them."

Yet in the 1990s, economic considerations have pushed the mother out of the house and into the workplace, D'Elia said. Now both parents have to take an interest in the child's education, and there's an active interchange between parents and the school.

"This has to be parents and teachers working together," D'Elia says. "That's something I've tried to stress during my time here. Children are wonderful little things, but they're very shrewd little things, also, and they can sense when there is some kind of division. They can sense when a parent is saying one thing and a teacher is saying another, and if they can squeeze in through the middle, they will. It is important for teachers and parents to talk to each other and understand we are working together for our children. They have to put aside petty little differences, like who has what schedule."

D'Elia attributed much of his success as a principal to the great staff of teachers, and said that his biggest job was providing motivation. In leaving this year, he said the school staff is in great shape.

"Some of these teachers are as good as I've ever seen," he said.

D'Elia will be sixty-two this month and has opted for an early retirement package. He has a theory that people should change their situation every seven to ten years.

"After three years, you get proficient in whatever you're doing," he said, "After seven you need to look for new challenges."

D'Elia, who was once called "Touchdown Tony," loves sports, and also loves to read—something he has had little time for over the last few years. In retirement, he has mapped out a reading program for himself, books he's always meant to get to over the years. His favorite author is Rudyard Kipling, a writer whose early Asian work had a romantic edge tempered with realism and emotional impact, often celebrating modern society with such poems as those on automobiles. In many ways, this dual image of romanticism and practicality seems to fit D'Elia as well. He loves history and reads a lot about the American Revolution and World War I, two periods of time he believes the general public has neglected. He is intrigued by the fact that soldiers in World War I wrote poetry in the trenches.

D'Elia also loves education, and over the years as studied his own profession, mapping out its patterns and its limitations.

"Every era is critical for education," he said. "People are never happy with the educational system of their time. They're always saying it's not like it was ten or fifteen years ago. But twenty-five years ago, the Russians put up a satellite and people screamed that the schools weren't up to date. We're always under the spotlight, but in many ways, the schools today are better than ever."

Quoting from a book called *The Troubled Crusade* by Diane Ravitch, D'Elia said the schools have changed to meet current social needs.

"We've constantly had to keep improving, to bring things up to date. Change takes a long time, but the changes in the school system have been tremendous," he said. "With each decade, there are new problems for the schools to face. Before World War II, immigration was a problem, with the associated language and health issues. Now, we're in a financial crisis. Budget cuts have a serious effect on the schools today."

He said technology is an important part of today's education process, noting that computers and calculators are now becoming as valuable tools to learning as the pencil and the slide rule were in the past. But even things as apparently simple as the telephone have changed the shape of modern education.

"We don't rely on sending notes home from school any more. People don't read them," he said. "We always have to follow them up with a telephone call."

He said that after teaching in five school systems, he has come to realize that Secaucus offers as much to its students as anyplace else, despite the fact that other school systems may send more of their children to fancier schools, like Princeton or Harvard. This, he says, has more to do with family background and financial status than with the local educational system.

"Secaucus is Hoboken West," he said. "People here have middle-class values and middle-class expectations, and the school system gives its kids what they need to survive."

Over the years, D'Elia has taught many students. Some of their children now attend his school; others he meets in various places.

"That's part of what makes this so rewarding," he said. "When you run into former students and they remember when you taught them years before."

From *The Secaucus Reporter,* Hudson Reporter Associates, 1995.

A Global Perspective

Some people in the American education system frown a little when confronted by seventeen-year-old Nathan Van Kouwenhoven. In a society where kids make the obligatory trip to a classroom from age five, educators react with some alarm when confronted with self-taught people.

"They just don't fit into the predetermined boxes the education system has built for students," said William Paterson College professor Jim Hauser, who claimed such people always drive him nuts. "You can't predict what will come out of them the way you can with other students."

This "what do we do with him" question plagued the admission office of Hudson County Community College (HCCC) when the young Hoboken resident came to sign up for some classes. They looked at Nathan, asked for his social security number, then balked when he said he didn't have one. All he had was a passport that said he was born in Canada, the son of American citizens.

"They just didn't get it," said Nathan's father, Jon Van Kouwenhoven, who was a little upset by his son's first confrontation with standard bureaucracy. "We told them he was an American citizen, but they still asked for his green card, and finally decided to charge him the price they'd charge for legal immigrants."

While admissions officer Diane Thompson from HCCC, when contacted for comment, said this was an unfortunate mix-up that she had already straightened out, Nathan must have seemed as alien as a Martian. Here was a boy who had not learned the art of filling out forms or waiting on line, or enduring the routine hassles of bureaucratic red tape.

Nathan has studied almost entirely outside the traditional classroom, and had only fifty hours' contact with local school systems while earning his General Equivalency Degree. How could Thompson or any of her aides, used to more traditional students, understand that this boy of sixteen had finished in the top 3 percent in the nation on his GED without the benefit of a teacher or schoolbook?

Out of a possible grade of 300 on the GED test, Nathan got 294, in a state where the GED testing process tends to be more rigorous than most. Although he had to go through the fifty hours of prep time at Hoboken High School, Nathan spent only one year in a classroom and that was in Vienna. Yet regardless of the reaction of the educational bureaucracy—or perhaps in spite of it—Nathan is part of a national movement to take kids out of the classroom.

"Home schooling is growing rapidly in the United States, with thousands of children now being taught by their parents at home instead of public or private schools," said Karl Bunday, a national advocate of home schooling. "The decentralized nature of home schools makes accurate estimates of the numbers of home schoolers difficult; moreover, some persons estimating the numbers purposely err on the low side."

The most current estimates show about 1.2 million American kids study in their homes. Some parents have opted for this because they fear the reported violence of urban public schools and can't afford private schools. Others teach their children because they disagree with the curriculum. Nathan's parents largely sought to create a friendly atmosphere for their child. Nathan's father is a violinmaker, and his mother, Deborah, is a writer. Both have traveled extensively around the world, and the home schooling was as much a necessity in some respects as it was a choice, since by teaching Nathan themselves, they could take him wherever they went.

"We were a little worried about the test," Van Kouwenhoven said. "But we have to thank the people at Hoboken High who helped him get ready for it."

They shouldn't have worried. Nathan's reading of technical books honed his ability to comprehend, making him a perfect candidate for the GED, which is centered around reading. In fact, in each stage of testing, he said he finished first.

In some ways, this family helped pioneer the home school movement. Even the most optimistic count by supporters of home schooling shows fewer than 300,000 students being taught at home in the United States before 1986, a number critics claim was exaggerated even then.

"It wasn't as trendy when we started as it is now," Van Kouwenhoven said. "Years ago, we felt in the minority."

Maybe they were a little scared, too, taking on the enormous responsibility that is normally consigned to schools. They wondered if Nathan would miss something important by not spending his time in a classroom like other kids his age. Yet now Van Kouwenhoven believes that not only did Nathan not miss anything, he may, in fact, have come away with something many other students lack.

"This allowed us to keep in touch with our son, watch him as he learned," Van Kouwenhoven said. "And it really enhanced the unity of our family. The whole idea of quality time with kids seemed wrong to me. Fathers would spend fifteen minutes a day with their child and think they were doing something good. I didn't feel that way. We've managed a kind of bonding. We've spent an absurd number of hours together."

In fact, for a long time, they hardly separated.

Of course, one of the primary criticisms of home schooling is the lack of socialization that comes from daily interaction with other children. But supporters of home schooling have disputed this argument, saying that children actually find more socialization within the family structure, grow closer to family members, rather than face possible humiliation and alienation in a traditional classroom. A good home school program allows children to learn in a supportive atmosphere.

Nathan says he has no trouble interacting with kids, even though he had little contact with them when he was younger. He spent most of his early years in the company of adults, especially when traveling abroad. His father calls Nathan "miraculously social" and says he in no way fits the stereotypical image of the "protected child."

"He has street smarts," Van Kouwenhoven said. "When he goes out onto the street in Jersey City, he can handle himself."

Nathan says he hangs out with kids and doesn't feel isolated because he didn't go to a traditional school. In fact, he finds the other kids are fascinated by him.

"They are always very interested in where I've been and what I do," he said, "asking me about what I did in this place or that."

Because the elder Van Kouwenhoven is a violinmaker, he felt he could handle the responsibility since he would be home all the time. The family lived in Jersey City and Weehawken before settling back in Hoboken two years ago. Van Kouwenhoven wanted his son to learn in a low-pressure situation and wanted to dedicate a lot of time to him, and his occupation helped.

"While I was building violins, he sat at my side and made airplanes out of the scraps," he said. "I felt I was in on the process."

Van Kouwenhoven didn't limit the subjects. Anything Nathan wanted to study was fine. He could feel his son's hunger for knowledge and he fed that hunger as much as possible. When Nathan became interested in something, building a model or a guitar, he read everything he could about the subject, from aerodynamics to the working of sound. Van Kouwenhoven did not set up a formalized study ritual the way some parents do. Many of the programs available on the World Wide Web function largely in the same manner as traditional classrooms, setting specific hours and studying particular subjects during the day. For the most part, Van Kouwenhoven let his son's interests dictate the lesson plan, imposing no set structure on the boy's approach to learning.

"He is an incredible reader," Van Kouwenhoven said, "especially when it comes to technical reading."

Everything that interested Nathan involved the same basic subjects he would be required to learn in a traditional classroom. To build something required math and reading, and he would study every aspect of the material.

As for guidance, father and mother covered the full spectrum of subjects. Father taught Nathan the vocational aspects of education, mother, as a creative writer, taught him the humanities.

"He knows a lot more about the environment than most people, and he knows about electronics from the fundamentals up," Van Kouwenhoven said.

Early on, the family didn't push reading, but let Nathan explore phonetic sounds at his own pace.

"It took him a little longer to learn how to read that way," Van Kouwenhoven said. "But once he started, he never stopped."

Van Kouwenhoven, in fact, made wooden puzzles, which allowed Nathan to shift the letters together and practice the sounds. Nathan's mother taught him history, but in a way that most kids would envy. Nathan didn't just read about events, he saw where they happened, learning about the history of Europe, for instance, as the family traveled through.

"When we went to England, I didn't really want to go over to Ireland, but I was glad I went," said Nathan, remembering the rough ferry ride and the amazing green when he arrived. "And I learned about the history of that place."

He learned about Austrian history in Austria, Italian history in Italy, Belgian history in Belgium, working his way through Europe country by country.

"It gave him a global perception," Van Kouwenhoven said.

While very technical-minded, Nathan has not been deprived of the arts. He admires Jackson Pollock and Picasso, has examined their works, read books about them, and even painted his own pictures. Although he spent a lot of time in Europe and learned a lot from his father and mother about classical music, Nathan loves Jimi Hendrix. But he didn't just learn to play guitar—he built his own, learning everything about the instrument from the wood up.

"He has a great talent for adapting," said Van Kouwenhoven "But isn't that what intelligence is?"

While Nathan was a little turned off by his first encounter with bureaucracy, he says he still intends to seek out college, something technical in nature, something electronic maybe, but definitely something with a creative twist. He and his family see him as artist and technician, someone who encompasses the whole spectrum of knowledge. Most recently, he discovered the automobile, and purchased a 1951 Chevy from the owner of a shoe store in Hoboken. As with everything he has ever done, Nathan is throwing himself into the project, reading everything he can about how cars work, before he breaks out the tools and begins to dig in, taking it apart piece by piece—then, putting it back together again.

Has he ever not been able to get things back in working order?

"Sure, I've screwed things up," he said. "But that only means I need to learn more."

Yet in many ways, Nathan is no different from most teenagers. When asked what he wants to do with his life, he shrugs and says, "I have no idea."

From *The Hoboken Reporter,* Hudson Reporter Associates, 1996.

The End of a Double Life

For the last twenty-three years Dennis Pope, former municipal court administrator, has lived a double life. Not only has he worked as everything from swimming pool director to assistant town administrator before finding himself in court in 1991, but Pope, who has a Ph.D., has also taught law in college.

A mild-mannered man, Pope exudes professionalism. He credits this not to his formal schooling but to an education of a different kind. "I learned lessons of life from [former] Mayor [Paul] Amico," Pope said. "He was a unique individual to work for and if there was one ultimate experience, it was my working with him." Pope announced his retirement in June to dedicate more time to his teaching.

When Pope first started working for the town full time, Gerald Ford was serving his last year as president and Paul Amico was halfway through his eighth term as mayor.

"I actually started a few months before July 1976, but I was just finishing graduate school and I was looking around for a job," Pope said. "Mayor Amico has asked me a couple of times if I was interested in working for him. But I wanted to finish my dissertation first. Then, when I was done, I went and talked with the mayor. He said I would have to wait two weeks until he found me a desk."

Pope was twenty-eight years old at the time and had already been teaching college for three years while pursuing his doctorate.

*Dennis Pope, seen here fishing at the
local pond, teaches at several colleges and
universities, thus fulfilling a lifelong dream.*

His first assignment involved the proposed swim center for the north
end of town. He was supposed to test the sentiments of the community. But
Pope's work often involved jobs that no one else wanted or could do. He was
often the person the mayor sent to talk with other local municipal govern-
ments. Later—because of his experience with the swim center—Pope inher-
ited the ice skating rink, where he served as recreation facility director for
six years.

"I feel very lucky that I had such a varied career in municipal government,"
Pope said. "I never burned out in a job, and I learned a lot about everything."

In 1985, Pope became the assistant town administrator and took on even
more responsibility, such as coordinating activities between the town and the
Hackensack Meadowlands Development Commission, working on the municipal budget, and shaping the town's recycling program. In 1991, when the
court administrator was indicted, Pope took his place and helped the court
to catch up with ninety thousand unpaid tickets and other legal notices.

Getting into court fused the two aspects of his life: his love of local government and law. Over the years, Pope has taught everything from basic American government to his more specialized fields of constitutional law, judicial
process, and public administration.

With his appointment to the court, he moved from the theoretical to the practical and began to bring to his students specific examples of how law worked on an everyday basis.

"Nothing gets the concept across better than a good example," he said. "It brings a degree of credibility to the lesson as students know that this came from real life, not out of a book."

Although he was contemplating retiring this year anyway, Pope's career at the court came to an abrupt halt in 1998, when changes in state law and local politics sent him into a bureaucratic tailspin. Pope, who had been instrumental in cleaning up the court, was faced with new regulations that required the understaffed court to keep two sets of records, one for the state and one for the town. His requests for additional help went unheeded, and a brief investigation by the town and county resulted in a confused report that initially claimed money was missing. Months after Pope took a leave of absence from the court the truth came out: there was no money missing nor evidence of any other wrongdoing.

By then, however, Pope had made up his mind to retire, taking his accumulated sick time before announcing his intentions.

"It has always been my ultimate goal to dedicate my full efforts to lecturing and research on the university level. Pursuing that is my reason for retiring," he said.

Pope said teaching at a college level allowed him to work out hunches and theories, giving him a kind of laboratory where he can toss out ideas and get responses from the students. He expects to continue teaching at Kean University in Union, and will likely teach classes at Bergen Community College and William Paterson University.

Pope said he will not be fading from all civic activity and will look into changing the charter that established the town's current form of government; he noted that the staggered two-year terms now have half the town government up for yearly reelection.

Municipal government had always held some interest for Pope. His uncle, Herman Pope, served on the council for ten years, from the mid-1950s to the mid-1960s.

As a young boy Pope got to watch a new generation of politicians emerging, with the rise of his uncle, Paul Amico, and Howie Elwell.

"Many of these were veterans who had come home, made new lives for themselves, and in their thirties and forties decided they would run for office," Pope said. "While Mayor [Anthony] Just bemoans Secaucus's lost generation, I was part of that generation—the last generation who learned to swim in the Hackensack River or camped out in Schmidt's Woods. We grew up as the town grew."

His first experience in politics came when he was ten years old, when he stood on a street corner handing out flyers for Howie Elwell, Jimmy Moore, and his uncle. In 1960, when he was eleven years old, his uncle gave him a huge poster urging voters to elect John F. Kennedy president. "My mother was a registered Republican," Pope said. "She made me keep it in the garage."

Although he loved politics he ran for office only once, vying for one of three seats with nine other candidates in 1972. "I came in fifth," he said. "I beat out Tom Troyer by two votes, and over the years we've ribbed each other about it."

While he found politics exciting, he preferred working behind the scenes, doing political writing and advertisements. One thing he finds unfortunate today is the lack of grass-roots organizing; he claims elections are now run by public relations professionals.

"I enjoyed old group meetings at which people sit down and talk about what to do the following week, how to react to a situation," he said, noting that his political activities ended when he was appointed to the court.

"Politics are a remarkably fluid system, with fluxes, shifting in alliances— something similar to professional wrestling," Pope said. "One day people might oppose each other, the next day they're on the same team."

From *The Secaucus Reporter,* Hudson Reporter Associates, 1999.

Metaphors of Life

My grandfather, who was a boatbuilder for thirty years, had a unique metaphor for life: "You set sail, you sail around, and then you sink."

Metaphor is how humanity understands the greater questions of life, those that science and mathematics struggle to define, and metaphors for life and reality are the heart of Doug Depice's teaching in a unique new class at Secaucus High School.

In trying to explain what he does, Depice sometimes talks so fast that your mind reels listening to him. It's as if he has so much to say that he's afraid he'll forget it all if he doesn't get it out quickly. But when he teaches, he moves through his lessons like a magician pulling rabbits out of his hat, talking about

Doug Depice has made significant strides in the 1990s, teaching art in the Secaucus school system as well as opening his own school in Hoboken. In 1998, he received a fellowship from the Geraldine Dodge Foundation.

cosmic issues the way mathematicians might a number sequence or an English teacher the construction of a sentence. And even when the room grows warm with the smell of books and paper, students stare at him, caught up in his spell. These are honor students from English, biology, physics, and social studies, each catching something from his remarkable sleight-of-hand, as he takes them through the complicated maze that makes up infinity, unity, and the random creative urges of chaos.

"Give a man a hammer and use the world as a nail," Depice says with a glint of a sideshow artist in his eyes. "But give that same hammer to a child and it becomes a hundred different things, and that's what I'm teaching here."

Indeed, when Depice makes his routine visits to the variety of honors classes around the high school, he drags behind him a cartload of props, objects he has discovered have multiple meanings to him and can help him convey his complicated ideas. For one lesson, Depice might draw out of this bag of tricks a huge plaster model of a human ear, something that may or may not be an ear. It all depends on who is looking and what that person is looking for. On another occasion, he might drag out a saxophone still in its case and ask his students what it is they see. The ones who are used to nothing but facts and figures may tell him they see nothing but a saxophone in its case, while others, much more adventurous, might say it is a baby in its womb or a golden snake half curled in the curve of a rotting forest log; for a student more metaphysical in nature, the saxophone might be beauty hidden inside something that appears ugly on the surface.

Then, to emphasize his point, he draws out a fist-sized ball made up of hundreds of rubber bands, asking them what this thing means to them. Students, now a little more accustomed to Depice, will raise their hands. One might say it is a collection of orbiting planets around a star. Another might say it is the workings of a complicated atom with electrons racing around a proton-heavy nucleus. A third, more socially oriented student may say it is a complex human situation from which you can peel away each rubber band and never come to its core.

"I'm not teaching these kids the ABCs," Depice says. "I'm teaching them that life is not sequential, but a cluster of feelings and images, desires and wills, everything happening at one time. You can look at the rubber-band ball as a metaphor for that. Life is connected. Everything is united. Each rubber band might be a strand of something working in unity to make up a human life."

Depice's vision of a whole universe didn't begin with this class, though he says he's discovered a lot about connections since he started. For years he has pondered the way kids get taught and has struggled to find a new, more comprehensive way to make them understand that life is not divided into subjects, and that English doesn't end where mathematics starts or science stop when the bell rings for history.

Over the years, the education establishment has fostered a kind of linear thought, Depice says, one that says things go from Point A to Point B without alternatives, like driving Route 80 from New York City to San Francisco without understanding the concept of television, telephone, satellite links, airplane travel, train travel, or even space travel as alternatives, or sailing around South America to get there, and Depice says half his bag of tricks is an effort to show students how they can see the universe in a drop of water, and how their lives fit into bigger, more fascinating patterns.

Indeed, Depice says he's still finding these things out for himself. Like the time he was photographing a spider web in his back yard and noticed that for some reason it reminded him of something else. Later, when he was putting together slides for his class, he projected the slide of the spider web and one of the solar system and noticed they fit exactly. As did a cross-section of a tree

185

trunk showing the rings of the tree, and another showing the pattern of magnetic fields. That's the kind of discoveries he's trying to teach kids to look for, not just in art class, which until this year he routinely taught in Secaucus, but in every class and every subject, since he believes all subjects are connected by the same invisible strands as the images of the web and the solar system.

Even before he won a grant from the Geraldine R. Dodge Foundation last summer as a working artist and teacher, Depice contemplated a means for teaching students a more holistic approach to knowledge. For more than twenty years, Depice has been concerned with the change kids go through as they grow up, and how they lose the artistic vision of youth.

"I believe all kids are artists and all people are special kinds of artist," Depice says. "When you're young center of the world and every expression is important to the people around you. But along the way, we start teaching kids to categorize, and kids find they are no longer the center of things."

In a society with these overtones, kids begin to lose their ideas as well as the creative way they look at things, Depice said. As they grow up, they begin to look for firm answers to everything, and instead of gauging an experience from what they see and hear, they start applying logic or formulas to experience.

"There are things larger than logic, like life and feeling," he said. "But people, especially adults, are not comfortable with non-logical things. Kids, seeing how uncomfortable adults are, try to conform."

An educational system that emphasizes survival over vision, Depice says, creates a kind of split personality, in which art is seen as inferior.

"This is a kind of educational toxicity," he says "Where children learn to become divorced from themselves, putting their experiences and their feelings into horrible categories in which those things are considered either not important or something for which they should be ashamed."

Creative experience deals with things that are not quantitative, he said.

"It's very difficult to grade experience. With math or science it is very easy to see whether a formula is correct or incorrect. Yet when it comes to the intangible it is difficult to make those kinds of judgment," he noted, calling this sensual experience the "Poetics of space."

"In the past most education has been linear. Students might be taught how Monet painted during a particular time period, while Romantic poets were writing these poems, and Mozart was creating that piece of music," he said, calling this a piecemeal approach to education rather than showing how all these things work in conjunction.

"Where is the emotional part of math, that part of the student when he or she discovers the key to a mathematical problem, or can sense what is the right process?" he asks. "What happens when a botany teacher tells his class that they are going to study plants from da Vinci's *Annunciation*. In it he or she can show them the plant life behind the Angel Gabriel and how it is different from the plant life behind Mary. Since Leonardo painted nothing without researching everything first, everything within the frame of the picture is relevant."

Depice is particularly enthralled with da Vinci, the Renaissance artist who exemplified this teacher's ideas of united knowledge, showing metaphors for the human spine as the mast and workings of a sailing ship, thus showing in a single image how each serves the same purpose and uses the same pattern.

"When da Vinci drew an ear or hand, he was using other things like mathematics, science, structure," Depice says. "He learned everything he could about what he drew before he drew it, seeking to get more into the work than just an image, seeking the soul of a subject. His studio was a place of discovery, a science lab, he sees poetry as analytical. Da Vinci searched for parallels in all the forms of life he saw. And it is that kind of vision I'm trying to teach, trying to open windows of creativity, by letting students see objects used in a different way."

Depice says he's trying to teach students a way of seeing.

"I'm asking students to take a leap into the apparently illogical," Depice says, "To admire the beauty they find in books like *Alice in Wonderland* or *Gulliver's Travels*. I'm trying to teach a kind of imaginative seeing, something comes out of people's dreams. Einstein had a dream. He saw the universe on a beam of light, and then thought up multiple dimensions no one else could see. You can see the universe in the movement of water, if you know how to look."

From *The Secaucus Reporter*, Hudson Reporter Associates, 1996.

Building Community

Luthier Jon Van Kouwenhoven's talk on the violin-making process at the Hoboken Barnes and Noble covered more than just the making of a musical instrument. After years of quietly contemplating his craft, working in relative silence and obscurity, Van Kouwenhoven has finally decided it is time for people like himself to speak up about art, life, and the increasingly disposable society in which we live.

Luthier Jon Van Kouwenhoven's instruments have become desired by musicians around the world over the last few years, although he has involved himself in numerous other socially beneficial projects as well.

Standing in his Hoboken workshop, Van Kouwenhoven looks the model of a European craftsman, and seeing him without a violin, one would easily guess he worked with his hands. Part of this comes from the sense of seriousness chiseled into his face, and the thoughtful way he has of looking into the distance as if searching for his words in the air around him.

He and his family have just come back from two years in Europe, where, he said, they spent their time viewing America from the outside. But this was only one step in a quest for a place in which to put down roots. Recently, he and his family spent another year traveling the roads of the Continental United States, from the Deep South to the Northwest, only to wind up back in Hoboken.

"We put thirty thousand miles on an old Volvo, taking a tour of cities to get a close-up look," he said. "When we got back we wondered what we were doing here again."

Part of the attraction here are the roots laid down by his ancestors, who came from Holland in 1628. Now, after seeing other parts of the country and the world, he has settled in Hoboken, where he works and lives and hopes he can begin the long, slow process of building a modern-day community here, one with the same sense of purpose his forebears must have had when colonizing this area.

Van Kouwenhoven has been making violins, violas, and cellos since the mid-1970s, but he started out as a sculptor and a violinist. He studied music in Denver under Le Yeignst, a world-renowned instructor and performer.

Interest in making violins came to him when he was on tour in Canada with a string quartet. Although he'd been involved with music all his life, it wasn't until he met Otto Erdesz that it occurred to him to build violins.

"I was performing with the National Ballet Company and was looking for a viola," he said. "I wasn't happy with the one I had. So I went to Otto, who was an instrument maker in Toronto."

Erdesz, he said, was a real character, one whose energy and work left a strong impression on Van Kouwenhoven, enough to inspire him to consider learning the other man's craft. He watched Otto as he worked. It wasn't formal instruction. Neither man spoke much, yet Van Kouwenhoven got a chance to watch through the whole process and learn.

This was a rare treat. Instrument makers are incredibly secretive about their methods, where they get their wood, and the kind of varnish they use, and for one to show another his or her art is a matter of great trust and friendship.

Then, Van Kouwenhoven went away and came back with a violin of his own, finished and—surprisingly—quite well done. Although Erdesz was amazed, Van Kouwenhoven was not. He was already a sculptor. He knew how to shape things with his hands. Watching carefully, he was able to take away from his sessions with Erdesz knowledge to repeat what he saw.

In the sixteen years since that first effort, Van Kouwenhoven's instruments have been acquired and are presently being played by top soloists in major orchestras from New York to Moscow. More importantly, Van Kouwenhoven has managed to support his family doing it, something not always possible for a performer.

He designs his instruments to fit the performer, which he says is a bit unusual, even in a field as rare as quality violin making. "I'm told that I have infinite patience, good ears, and I can bring out the sound people want," he said. "Musicians usually can't articulate what they want. What might frustrate other instrument makers motivates me."

Van Kouwenhoven said he looks for what kind of sound fits with each performer, and designs the instrument to fit the performer's style of play.

"Some have a breezy style with the bow, others have a heavy style," he said. "Every great artist has a color palette of sound; they paint with sound."

An instrument can be made to be more resistant or less, to feel as solid as iron or as breezy as air.

"As a trained musician, I start with a knowledge of sound. I fine-tune the voice," Van Kouwenhoven said. "I listen to the play, get to know what they play, sometimes I even play a duet with them, that person on the violin, while I'm on the viola, and I see what kind of personal style they have and what color they need."

His design is a loose copy of the Italian style. He makes as many as twelve instruments a year, a process that he claims is more sculpture than craft, even when the pattern is repeated again and again.

"But it is a tool, too, and one that people make a living from," he said. "When someone uses one of my instruments in a competition, I get a wonderful feeling knowing I've made it for them."

Van Kouwenhoven said he is still learning, but now it is more than merely the learning of a craft.

"During the early years I was obsessed by wood and the process itself," he said. "I'm that type of person. But you can get too much of anything, even process. Now I'm struck by the idea of what I'm doing in society, and that's more important to me. I'm trying to encourage other people to appreciate the nondisposable."

This was part of his reason for his trip to Europe. He wanted to seek out the roots of his instruments, the flavor of the music, and the different rhythms of daily life.

"We needed to break away from island America," he said. "But Europe doesn't have everything. In some ways it can put you to sleep if you're not careful. Coming back, you learn to appreciate the great things about this country and all the things you give up when you leave it. You can create a dream here and it is more easily realized. We have a lot of freedom here. For all Europe has, it is closed there, each country has a club mentality."

Van Kouwenhoven is now speaking out for the need for Americans to begin rebuilding community, and said that he sees in Hoboken the very thing he'd been searching for.

"Hoboken has what it takes to become a thriving, creative cultural center with the unique position of retaining the desirable small-town feeling and yet the great advantage of immediate accessibility to international-caliber culture just across the Hudson River in New York City," he said. "I want to share my passion for culture and make it clear just how important creativity is in our highly competitive and commercial world."

Educating the public, he said, is one of the keys for creating community.

"I feel the need to emphasize the creation of nondisposable things," he said, "Things with value, things that people will cherish and pass on. The world is too comfortable with the disposable. There is a need for more permanence. We've moved up from tossing away Styrofoam cups to tossing away people, making people seem to be cartoon people like Dick Tracy or Fly Face."

As a violinmaker, Van Kouwenhoven has a particular insight into the nondisposable, since his instruments are designed to last a long time.

"Maybe even hundreds of years," he said, "if they're taken care of."

From *The Hudson Current,* Hudson Reporter Associates, 1995.

A Walk through Hell

In September 1997, I was standing on a road through the Kearny swamp taking a photograph for the *Secaucus Reporter* of a train that derailed on the way to Secaucus Transfer Station. A few feet away, bent over a camera and tripod, was a small Asian man with his lenses pointed toward the train as well. He was among the many who had come to witnesses the carnage across the swamp from us. I did not know until the next day, when his picture appeared on the front page of the *New York Times,* that this small man was Dith Pran, someone who had suffered through one of the more horrible moments in human history, and about whom the 1984 movie *The Killing Fields* was made.

Pran has been working as a photographer for the *New York Times* since 1980 and currently covers the Metro New Jersey area. In an appearance at a Georgia high school last year, he said, "I work five days a week like everyone else,"

This week, Dith Pran returned to Secaucus, not as an exceptional photojournalist but as a witness to the slaughter of millions of people in Cambodia during the 1970s. His crusade has taken him across the United States, from high school auditoriums to the studios of MSNBC.

At the age of fifty-five, Pran has become a spokesperson for children around the world who are threatened and hurt by war and brutality. He tours the nation to talk about what he saw during a four-year walk through hell, when the Khmer Rouge allegedly killed two million people.

Pran was born on September 27, 1942, in Angkor Wath, and worked as a French- and English-speaking guide for tourists visiting the area's historic temples, until the war spilled over from Vietnam; after that he worked as a correspondent for Sydney Schanberg of the *New York Times*.

After helping Schanberg cover the Communist takeover of Cambodia in April 1975, Pran was left behind, staying on to cover the story of the battle-scarred country under the control of the Khmer Rouge and its leader, Pol Pot.

Eight days after the takeover and the evacuation of foreign nationals, Dith Pran was forced, with hundreds of thousands of other Cambodians, to march from Phnom Penh to the countryside. There, he was to endure almost four years of unremitting horrors, during which one-quarter of the eight million people of the New Jersey–sized nation died through starvation, disease, hard labor, and execution.

"Because the Vietnam War spilled over into Cambodia, it turned Cambodia upside down in 1970. The war began, bombardment, war getting bigger and bigger until 1975," Pran said in an interview with Brian Williams on MSNBC in Secaucus last year. "The Communists took over all the Indochina and that area, and the Khmer Rouge came to power. And we thought that the Khmer Rouge would allow all of us to work together and rebuild the new Cambodia. But our dream didn't come true. When they came to power, they want something different. They want to empty the city. They force people to work fourteen to sixteen hours a day, and they treat people worse than animals and they killed a lot of people."

To students at Madison High School last summer, Pran said, "I came from a real hell. We were scared to death of the Khmer Rouge. One of their slogans was 'to destroy you is no loss, to keep you is no gain.' Your life was not important. They sought to destroy the individual, build up the community. So there was no thinking for yourself. Anything you did—the crops you grew—was not for yourself, but for community. Your parents were not your parents. The government was. And any people who did not follow their commands was killed or tortured.

"It comes back when you witness the killing and the torture of what they did, especially when you see them stab the children. I'm saying children as young as five, six years old, because they just don't care. I cannot believe why they did this to the children also. Even some journalists, they keep reporting; they say, 'Oh they only kill the intellectual.' It's not only the intellectual, it just go whatever they feel, it's like you kill an insect. Whatever is in front of them, they just wipe out. And that's what they did during the killing field."

During those years, Pran said his father starved to death, three brothers were executed, his sister was murdered along with her husband and her two children. In all, he lost more than fifty relatives, including nieces and nephews, as well as many of his neighbors, friends, colleagues.

"All of my generation, completely wiped out," he said in a 1998 interview by the Internet publication *The Site*.

In a 1989 article he wrote for the *New York Times*, Pran said, "Under Pol Pot, little rice or food was given to the people because the Khmer Rouge wanted us to become so weak we would not have the strength to rise up against them. But even then I believe rice was plentiful."

When he appeared at Elizabethtown College last year, he said, "If you're hungry, you will eat anything. A grain of raw rice keeps you alive maybe a minute. Eat a worm, you survive several more minutes. You might find more termites than me because I'm older,"

A student Madison High School during Pran's visit there last year asked how he had survived.

"I played stupid. Khmer Rouge did not like smart people. So you did the opposite of what you would normally do. You don't wake up clean. You wake up dirty. You don't show you love your parents. You don't show you have any faith or any religion," Pran said, claiming he retained hope the nightmare would end by telling himself that throughout history "evil never stays forever."

On October 3, 1979, Dith Pran crossed the border into Thailand.

Pran compared the slaughter to the Jewish Holocaust, something he has to tell people about so it will not be forgotten. Pran believes his destiny was to survive and speak for those who did not.

During his return trip to Cambodia many years after the fall of the Khmer Rouge, Pran still found trenches filled with human bones where people had been forced to dig their own graves. A museum has been made out of the high school where nearly twenty thousand people were tortured and killed.

Pran has also compiled a collection of personal essays by survivors of the killing fields, published in a book that is helping to fund his Holocaust Awareness Project, which teaches American high school students about what happened in Cambodia.

"I have to tell the world because I don't want history to repeat itself," he said during the *Site* interview. "I've come to talk about it; if we don't talk about it, people will forget, and it can happen again."

From *The Secaucus Reporter,* Hudson Reporter Associates, 1999.

A Breakfast
to Remember

"Do you remember when Tracy [name deleted] actually went through a whole day wearing two different shoes?"

The question is asked by Secaucus High School Activities Coordinator Robert Hesterfer from the stage of the school's cafetorium.

Although the last name has been omitted here to prevent the social humiliation so typical in high school life, all kids at the senior breakfast howl with laughter, vividly recalling their classmate's stroll through the halls of Secaucus High, not only utterly out of fashion but utterly unaware of her faux pas.

Yet the question is not Hesterfer's, but one of the many collected from the kids themselves as part of the day-long preparation for graduation in June, a day that starts with what school administrators traditionally call Senior Breakfast.

Reminiscing is part of a ritual that every senior class goes through in September, a look back upon themselves, to mock, laugh, and sometimes smile tenderly over what makes this graduating class different from all those that have come before.

But behind the humor, behind the bemused gazes of the laughing seniors, mixed emotions emerge, as they come to understand just how much their lives will change 170 school days from now when they graduate.

"Do you remember when Kathy [name deleted] introduced herself three times in one night to the same boy?" Hesterfer reads on, sending his audience into another frenzy of laughter.

The Senior Breakfast is the first of a string of events scheduled throughout the year, rituals that will mark out the final passage of these students from high school into the real world. This day's event includes not only jokes—and plenty of them—but also speeches, a pep rally, measurements for cap and gown, as well as the taking of the class picture.

"Nicky [name deleted] never tells stories," Hesterfer reads, as heads roll back with the sheer audacity of the remark. Nicky, apparently, is well known for his tall tales.

No one is out of control, but the music rising from the stereo in the corner has the shuffled backbeat of modern rap, the filtered white-boy version of rap so popular in suburban schools. Many heads bob to the rhythms, though only a few have their total attention on it as kids around the two dozen tables chatter over chocolate milk and eggs, with one or two containers of apple juice thrown in.

Hesterfer, who seems to be enjoying the day as much as many of the seniors, says these ritual days are an effort to reinforce a sense of community among the kids, drawing them together into a life raft of hope; school officials trust that the relationship will carry even the driftwood through graduation.

A group of young actors climbs up onto the stage as Hesterfer leaves, lining up in an imitation of the Broadway classic *A Chorus Line*. Students step out one at a time to deliver short comic speeches. Each speech is a parody of the habits, relationships, ego trips, gestures, vocal styles, quirks, and personalities of some of the best-known members of the graduating class. Hoots and hollers answer each sketch as the student audience identifies each character.

"That's him!" one student yells, slamming his hand down on the tabletop after one sketch. One girl, after another sketch, turns up her nose as students near her jab her with their elbows.

Around the roaring crowd, the walls are covered with slogans marking this particular class, banners drooping a little as the Scotch tape gives out. The slogans are as varied as the class. "Unlock your future," one banner said. "Seniors rule '95," says another. A third simply touts the greatness of seniors in general.

As in every class preparing to graduate, certain names rise out of the crowd, achievers who will leave their individual marks on the history of Secaucus High School. Names like Danielle Winters, Laurie Nuendorf, Amanda Rushing, Mike Clancy, Jeremy Fojas will be recalled years from now when someone mentions the class of 1995. Sandy Echeverri, a possible contender for the scholar-athlete prize, looks a little perplexed when asked if she's glad to be back at school after the long summer. With volleyball, indoor and outdoor track, as well as her academics, her schedule is stuffed. She grins a little, shrugs and says, "Yeah."

But not all is fun and games. Principal William Koenig says this class stands out a little from other classes for its seriousness.

"These kids are pretty serious," says Koenig. "A lot of the kids in this class are dedicated to the entire program, not just to their own ends. That's what makes them different."

By the time Hesterfer climbs back onto the stage, the laughter has largely exhausted itself. Hesterfer, a tall man with sandy hair and a rugged face, seems a little sadder than he had been as he gazes toward the assembled faces of the 1995 graduating class. Even as he squints to make out those most familiar, he seems to understand that not all of them will make it.

A jigsaw puzzle of the American flag has been put up at one corner of the stage. Across its face is written "The Class of 1995." Before the students leave the cafetorium, each will take a piece. It is hoped that by the end of the year they can fit the pieces back and have no gaps. In the twenty years that Hesterfer has been here, there has never been a class that has succeeded in completing the puzzle.

"The block is a symbol, it invites each student to take a part of the class," Hesterfer says. "It might sound a little hokey. But these are the kinds of things kids remember years from now."

More than 100 students make up this year's graduating class, a figure between 110 and 120 depending on whom you ask. In October, no on can predict for certain who will pass. Students also come and go throughout the year. One girl came this week from Forest Hills, New York, though she was originally from Beijing, China.

Many of the students appear to grow restless with Hesterfer's reappearance, as if sensing his sudden seriousness. After his speech, the group will sit through an inspirational film called *Hold onto the Moment,* a montage of graduations from throughout the country meant to rouse the desire in these kids to graduate.

"I have the lucky job at graduation," Hesterfer tells them. "As doorkeeper and ticket taker, I get to see the parents as they come in, and see their bewildered faces as they come to witness the great change in their children. They don't know what to expect. They just know something is different and they don't have control over it. When it's over, there's not a dry eye in the house."

Hesterfer tells the kids that in twenty years, not one senior class has graduated in its entirety.

"Something always gets in the way. Kids tell us they've got problems. But that's why we're here. Problems don't have to be negative. They are just lack of ideas," he says.

There is no joking now. While some kids squirm in their seats, most stare straight up at the stage and at the serious and concerned face of Hesterfer still staring out at them.

"People tell you that high school is the greatest time of your life," Hesterfer says. "But it isn't. Most kids aren't happy, and if they think this is the best, what's the point of going on? If high school happens to be good, that's great; it will keep on getting better."

But he says high school is often the time of the greatest change in people's lives. All the things the student actors mocked from the stage as funny are the things that traumatize kids. He says people keep putting off the idea of getting involved in life, saying they will get involved in college, or after they leave college, or later when they retire, and then find they've wasted their lives.

"But if you start right here, then you can say 'oh, yeah!' to high school, 'oh, yeah!' when you get married, 'oh, yeah!' when you have your first child, 'oh, yeah!' when you look back thirty years from now in your yearbook. Then when your grandchildren come along, you say 'oh, yeah, wow, not bad!'" Hester-fer says. "Too many people have no 'oh, yeahs' in their lives. You've got to give yourself some 'oh, yeahs,' that's what we're all about. This is one of those very important moments in your life, one you will want to remember."

Then with almost perfect orchestration, Hesterfer steps off the stage and the lights grow dim and the film starts, revealing an image of caps and gowns. But the darkness also hides many of the perplexed and thoughtful expressions of kids who twenty minutes earlier than been nearly rolling in the aisles in laughter.

From *The Secaucus Reporter,* Hudson Reporter Associates, 1994.

Shooting for the Moon

More than three decades after the first landing on the moon, Dennis May-cher thinks about his dream of going there, too. He mentions the dream in passing after a school board meeting in July, no doubt reminded by all the hoopla centered around the twentieth anniversary of Neil Armstrong's first step on the dusty lunar surface. Although Maycher was reappointed school board counsel for his ninth consecutive year, his face bears that "what if" look people get when thinking back and wondering about the past.

Maycher has an alarming way of switching sharply from a philosophic mood to a very practical one, a skill obviously helpful in his private legal practice, where his range of services extends from business to criminal law. Yet his man-ner seems old-fashioned, more a Perry Mason than one of the slick lawyers seen on shows like *The Practice.* He even has a philosophical approach to con-flict on the board, after several members tried to hold up his pay increase as a matter of holding the line on rising budgets.

"I'm not bothered by the fact people voted against my pay raise," he says. "I know it's nothing personal."

At most board meetings, Maycher seems invisible against the backdrop of distinctly boisterous school board members, coming into focus only when he is called upon for legal advice; even then, he often retires to a back room with resolutions or contracts to study the fine print.

"Time is money," he says. "If I can render a decision quickly, then the board can act. Sometimes, especially in the bidding process, money can be saved if the board can act right away."

This is a sample of his practical side, as he stares up with a stern look and says he needs to present a "fair and honest opinion" and be able to justify his position under the rule of law.

"Tonight, for instance, the board wanted to purchase several school buses," he says. "They had to know which bid was lowest and which met the letter of the specification. If they had to wait to make a decision, then the school board might have had to rent buses before getting the new ones. It was in their best interest to provide them with an immediate answer so they could decide what to do."

Although he seems to exude law with every breath, law was not his first love, the moon was. He had this idea in his youth—when the space program was still on track for landing people on other planets—that he might become the hundredth man on the moon.

Maycher learned to fly in the army, where he was scheduled to go to Vietnam just before the war began to wind down. When he couldn't get into the astronaut program he changed direction, studying law at Rutgers University, from whose law school he graduated in 1971—the Kent State shootings were a recent memory. He seems annoyed by the radical element he found prominent in the colleges at the time.

He wanted to go on beyond law, taking up a rare and study-intensive path toward medicine and law. But again, he got sidetracked by reality.

"My wife told me it was time to get out and start earning a living," he says with a wry smile—and that same disappointed look in his eyes, as if he could envision himself as a combination doctor-lawyer, the way he had as an astronaut.

Now at age forty-six and the moon program as much ancient history as Christopher Columbus's crossing the Atlantic, Maycher takes solace in those things he has achieved, noting that his attachment to the Secaucus Board of Education was only a small part of a much wider career path. Even coming here, however, he had to fill the shoes of a well-loved board of education lawyer who had died.

But Maycher said there have been no disappointments in his life. He set new standards as significant to his career as a trip to the moon and lived up to them, although there have been setbacks.

Recently, his Wallington-based legal firm reorganized after several years of hard times. Business boomed in the 1980s, then came crashing down when the economy did. The firm now has four lawyers and a ten-person support staff. In the glorious 1980s it had as many as eight lawyers and a seventeen-person support staff. Early in the 1990s, he found himself with one partner and four helpers, so things are looking up.

Yet all the goals he thought so out of reach, he's already achieved. When starting out, he said he wanted to take a case to the U.S. Supreme Court, wanted to win a million-dollar civil settlement, and be involved in a murder trial.

With still a significant part of his legal career ahead of him, Maycher has already achieved those goals. As an aide to a U.S. congressman, Maycher was involved in the controversial drug-testing program in the East Rutherford school system, a case that went to the Supreme Court. Several years ago, Maycher won a million-dollar settlement for one of his clients. Most recently, Maycher took up the defense in a murder trial in Clifton, where he is defending a battered wife who reportedly killed her husband.

Maycher's legal experience is a mixture of civil and criminal cases, letting him see the full spectrum of the law. Not only has he served in the political arena with a U.S. congressman, he has also been a municipal prosecutor in East Rutherford, served as counsel to several boards, and maintains his private practice in Wallington.

Although he's made no trips to the moon or even to the edges of the atmospheric envelope, Maycher says he likes pushing life to the edge. He has clocked over four hundred hours as a pilot and has delved deeply into the sport of scuba diving—with a trip planned in October to the South Pacific. He also likes hang gliding.

"Life's an adventure," he says. "I want to get a slice of it, and if I like it, maybe get the whole pie."

But like most people, he says he's looking for a balanced life in which family, profession, and interests lead to happiness.

"The triangle is the most stable geometric configuration," he says. "If I find the right balance between those three parts of my life, somewhere in the middle of it, there is spiritual satisfaction."

From *The Secaucus Reporter,* Hudson Reporter Associates, 1994.

Granting a Wish

Paul Iacono can do anything.

At least, that's what people closest to the nine-year-old boy seem to think.

Family members have always known he was special, a fact first noted when the boy was three and the family listened to a Frank Sinatra song on the car radio. When the song ended, Paul continued, belting out the song as if it were his own.

By age four, Paul had already begun a musical performance career, playing Tiny Tim in the Park Theater production of *A Christmas Carol*. In the years since, he has rolled up performance credits that include *The Rosie O'Donnell Show*, the memorial dedication for Frank Sinatra in Hoboken, two performances at a New York City nightclub, and a performance before eighteen thousand screaming Net fans at the Meadowlands. He even appeared with numerous other personalities at the unveiling of the Nets' logo earlier this year, at which time he received a letter of recognition from Vice President Al Gore. He has become one of the official radio voices for Radio Aaahs, doing commentary for the New Jersey MetroStars soccer team, will sing with the Duprees, and perform in *Children of Eden* at the Paper Mill Playhouse in November. He's even done commercials for the Parker Brothers game Sorry.

So in November 1996, when Paul told his father, Anthony Iacono, that he wanted to run in the New York Marathon someday, Iacono thought, of course he can.

"We were watching the marathon on TV together," Iacono said. "We were both amazed at the massive turnout, thousands of runners making their way through Central Park. That's when Paul said, 'I would like to do that someday,' and I said, 'Sure, why not?'"

It is a moment Iacono can't get out of his mind, a moment in time that haunted Iacono the following January when Paul came down with swollen glands and a sore throat, which should have been just another cold, yet prompted the family physician, Dr. Azzam Baker, to ask for additional tests.

These showed Paul's blood had a low white count, and further tests taken at Tomorrow's Children Institute in Hackensack showed an even greater loss. The doctor called on January 31, 1997, and said Paul had leukemia.

"It was the most shocking news of our lives," Iacono said.

Paul's fame caused his tragic diagnosis to touch many people's lives. On

Anthony Iacono and his son, Paul, have become quite a team. Paul has starred in venues from the Paper Mill Playhouse to numerous theaters on Broadway, sharing the stage with theater veterans such as Mickey Rooney. More importantly, Paul has made a full recovery. Anthony in 1999 was recognized for raising more money than any other single individual in the nation that year to fight leukemia.

the marquee of the Park Theater in Union City, a few simple words said it all: "Get Well, Good Luck Paul." But for the family, the impact was nearly indescribable.

"Our whole world came crashing down. We knew this could be the worst part of our lives," Iacono said. "As a parent, you feel totally helpless and you want to exchange places with him. But, of course, you can't do that, which makes it feel worse."

But of all the family members, Paul seemed to handle the news best, refusing to act sick, taking the disease and its treatments in stride. While he was scared at first, he has slowly become the anchor of the family, saying that the leukemia didn't affect him at all. Although he was tutored during the initial treatments, he is now back at school and running to become class representative at Clarendon Elementary School in Secaucus, promising classmates field trips and doughnuts every other Monday if he wins.

Iacono said the first six months of their lives after the illness have been challenging.

"It's like he's writing the screenplay where he is the star of the show and at the end of the play he has a heroic recovery," he said.

When he began treatment at the Hackensack Hospital Medical Center, Paul even sang for the nurses. At the time of his diagnosis, Paul had been preparing for the lead role in Oliver! at the Park Theater in Union City, and the only time he missed rehearsal was when admitted into the hospital for treatments. Paul has already undergone eight months of treatment. Fortunately, these treatments have changed now that Paul's cancer has gone into remission. Now he gets a blood test and a shot once a week and a spinal tap every eight weeks.

Iacono said his son has a 73 percent chance of completely recovering after two and a half years of treatment.

"We try not to think of the 27 percent—we try to think of the 73," Iacono said.

Leukemia is the number-one killer of children, though the results of years of research can now save seven out of ten children.

"We would want to save ten out of ten," Iacono said.

While Paul sees this as a challenge, and he and the family over the first eight months have received a great deal of support from the Leukemia Society, Iacono can't forget that moment before the diagnosis was made, when he and Paul sat together unaware of the danger ahead, watched the marathon. Because of that moment, Iacono intends to run the New York Marathon himself to raise money for the Leukemia Society of America, and so far, he has secured more than ten thousand dollars in pledges.

"I recently got involved with Team Training, an organization that raises money for the Leukemia Society through marathons," he said, noting that the pledges have poured in from all over the country. While he had started asking people on his Christmas mailing lists, responses have expanded into the hundreds, and Iacono wants more.

"From the moment I heard Paul was ill, I wanted to do something," he said. "Then I heard about Team Training. While it wasn't exactly what I had in mind, it was the best that I could do. It is something I can do to make sure that other kids like Paul will be able to survive."

While he's never run the New York Marathon before, Iacono has run in the New Jersey Shore Marathon.

"That was eight years ago, I've been working up for this for about six months," he said. "But I promise I'm going to finish this one. Paul always wanted to run in the New York Marathon. While he has a 73 percent chance of recovery, I want to make sure he'll get his wish. I'm going to run twenty-six miles and for the last two-tenths of a mile, I'm going to run with him on my shoulders."

When talking about this, Iacono fingers a two-inch piece of plastic that hangs from a chain around his neck. It is a piece of plastic tube that was inside Paul during the initial treatments, a symbol of the pain and doubt the family felt during the first few months after diagnosis.

"I wear it always," Iacono said. "I will wear it the rest of my life."

From *The Secaucus Reporter,* Hudson Reporter Associates, 1997.

A Drive through Secaucus's Past

When Anthony Just arrived back in Hudson County in 1952, he had spent almost two years away from home. While the military bus was supposed to let him off in Manhattan, he talked the driver into dropping him off on Manhattan Avenue in Jersey City, where he could catch the number 2 bus for Secaucus. While looking out the window of the number 2 bus, he noticed something odd—cars seemed to be driving along the railroad tracks. He realized that it wasn't the tracks he saw, but the New Jersey Turnpike, which had been constructed while he was away in the army.

Although he didn't know it at the time, Just was witnessing a dramatic change in the nature of his town, something that forever ended the era of farms and meadows and made Secaucus into a whole different place to live.

Now, driving through the south end of town nearly fifty years later, the former mayor is seventy-two years old, yet he remembers nearly every feature of the landscape in which he grew up. Just lived through two of the most significant moments in the history of Secaucus: the arrival of the New Jersey Turnpike in 1952, which ended the town's reign as a farm community, and the arrival of Hartz Mountain Industries in 1969, which turned Secaucus into a capital of retail and commercial development.

Just moved to Secaucus from Jersey City in 1932 when he was six years old. His father was a longshoreman until the Great Depression stole his job, and for the next eighteen years the family had to scratch out a living on a small

Former mayor Anthony Just is truly a man of the people. Although no longer in office, he still finds time to share old stories and sage advice. Here he is talking to volunteers from Integrity House.

farm off County Avenue, near where the Duck Pond is today.

"My father worked very hard, and my mother raised ten of the twelve children she bore," Just said recently. "Two of them died as infants. It was a tough life for a woman."

Just's mother died in 1949, a year before he got news he had to go into the army.

Driving south on County Avenue, Just slows his car to point between several houses to the Turnpike rest area that now occupies the place where his family's farm had been.

"My house was where the gasoline pumps are now," he says with a slight sadness in his voice.

During World War II, Secaucus served as one of the country's food resources, raising two hundred thousand hogs per year, translating into fifty million pounds of pork. Much of it went overseas to the military. Just remembered as a boy traveling around the area collecting leftover food from factories and restaurants to feed the pigs.

"We had no grain. The pigs fed off day-old Silvercup bread and Drake's cakes, or swill from restaurants," Just says. "Now seagulls feed on that stuff after it's dumped in landfills."

As he drives, Just names the owners of the farms, though now in their place there are a car wash, a pizzeria, a cafe, and warehouses. Near Secaucus Road and County Avenue were vegetable and fruit farms, with a patch across from the current UPS building where the county raised its own tomatoes.

The south end of Secaucus was known as the back end. It was the most rural part of town, and the last to let go of its farms. Kids later came to call the area the "airport" because Curtis Wright, the manufacturer of aircraft engines, had a facility here.

The meadows around what is now the Duck Pond were Just's playground, a wonderland of wide open spaces through which hunters used to roam in search of starlings—common birds now found living in the eaves of business buildings in places like Jersey City and Paterson, but then a food staple for poor families. Just remembers having meals of starling and spaghetti.

"Hunters used to come here carrying double-barreled shotguns to shoot at the flocks of starlings," he said.

The hunters rarely found all the birds they shot, but Just and other kids did, and brought them home for meals.

Years later, in 1969, Hartz Mountain purchased 750 acres from a man named James Colt, the son of a Chicago transportation tycoon who had once had great hopes for the area but had never cashed in on them.

"After Hartz took over, people worried about the Duck Pond and what might come of it," Just said. The town later forged an agreement with Hartz that allowed the pond to be used as a park. Now thousands of ducks live or stop over at the place. "We managed to get a three-hundred-year lease," Just says.

Bumping over the potholes of Castle Road where warehouses line the sides of the former Colt property, Just talks about how Hartz went about filling the land in order to build on it, shipping in tons of sand from Sandy Hook, pumping it into the swamps, and later leveling it off with bulldozers.

Farther west on Castle Road, Just passes the former railroad property over which he wandered during his childhood on his way to the Hackensack River to fish or swim. He and his friends walked along the Jersey City Waterworks pipeline that still crosses the south end of Secaucus today.

Just recalls railroad debris along one section and how the roundhouse, constructed to allowed trains to turn around, had stood here when he was a kid. The Lackawanna train track was on one side, and the fast track—the line for passenger trains—was on the other. Some of the freight trains had more than a hundred cars, he says, something that has come full circle with the arrival of container freight at nearby Croxton Yards.

A large portion of Castle Road back then had been a dirt track designed to service one of the railroad bridges over the Hackensack River. Although now invisible after all the filling of meadows here, this part of Secaucus was once called Sauer Island, and in the late 1800s housed the Sauer Island Iron Foundry, where steel was smelted. Trainloads of ore were used to feed the furious furnace. As a kid, Just often stumbled into reminders of that era, bits of slag hardened into rusting chunks of what looked like stone. One huge chunk has been preserved, sitting like a statue among the warehouses near Seaview Drive.

As he drives, Just points to the now-abandoned Hartz Mountain sewage plant on the shores of the Hackensack River, south of Harmon Cove Towers. This is property the town took over long ago. Just passes Harmon Cove's twenty-five-story towers and the townhouses that line the west side of the Meadowlands Parkway, with outlets and Panasonic headquarters on the other side. Meadowlands Hospital, the Crowne Plaza Hotel, and studios for WWOR-TV run along this road, testimony to the massive changes that overtook Secaucus in the 1980s.

As Just turns the car onto Route 3 East and steers through the Plaza section, he leaves the area he wandered as a kid. But he remembers Brinkman's farm and Tonne's farm and the fine housing built upon in the first residential breakthrough.

"There was as building boom in the north end during the 1960s and 1970s," he says.

As he travels, he points to buildings he had once considered in his plans for the town library and other uses, saying that much could be done with them even today. He talks about the time the west side of Paterson Plank Road was largely a trash dump. But it has since become one of the principal residential neighborhoods of the town.

The car passes near where the Aratusa was once docked; the boat restaurant burned and sank in the late 1980s. Then he drives passes Schmidt's Woods, named after a well-known farmer who owned most of the land in this part of town, while the family of another man of a similar name, Jacob Schmidt, a former mayor and tavern owner, still owns and operates a concrete firm in the north end near Trolley Park.

Finally, as he makes the circle back toward the center of town, he passes the sewage plant constructed in the 1950s during the term of then-Mayor James Moore. He shakes his head a little as if not quite believing the changes he's seen, yet he's still as much in love with Secaucus as he was as a boy.

"This is a good town with fine people and a wonderful history," Just says. "I don't know what the future will be, but I know it will be different, just as it was different for me when I lived through it."

From *The Secaucus Reporter,* Hudson Reporter Associates, 2000.

Not Just Luck

Evelyn Ronell looks more like a poet than an opera singer. While her height—four feet eleven inches— has allowed her to convincingly play the role of a young boy with Jerome Hines, many people simply can't figure out how such a big sound comes out of woman so small. Many of her neighbors in the Harmon Cove section of Secaucus have heard her high soprano voice practicing in the morning, but they have almost always mistaken the taller woman downstairs for the opera singer. Even people who have seen Ronell perform on stage don't always believe it is she who makes the sound. Following one stage performance, audience members congratulated Ronell's best friend by mistake even though they had just seen Ronell perform.

While Ronell is hardly a household name—even among operagoers— her career has all the magic of a Hollywood film, a romantic rise-to-fame story filled with hard work, determination, and a little bit of intrigue—all this setting the stage for a September comeback performance at Carnegie Hall.

"I've lived a full nine lives," Ronell says in describing herself, claiming to have been born with remarkable luck—luck that allowed her and her family to escape Berlin on the eve of World War II, luck that allowed her to immigrate to Israel from Switzerland when the war ended.

Before this small woman took up music, she served in the Israeli Air Force, and later she was part of the diplomatic mission to Prague, tiny slivers of her past that she says seem more impressive than they were.

"I counted cans as a clerk in the air force," she says, "and I was an executive secretary to the [Israeli] ambassador in Prague."

Yet, oddly enough, this same sense of luck started her musical career while she was employed at the Israeli embassy. While music had always been a vital part of her life—her mother was a pianist in Berlin before the war and had hosted famous pianists in the family's home—Ronell had not taken any formal training until the Israeli ambassador insisted upon it.

"He had a girlfriend who studied at the conservatory," Ronell said. "The school wouldn't give her a diploma because she had not passed the political exam. The ambassador said she should give me lessons, saying she needed money, and a standing, in order to stay in Prague."

This training would eventually lead Ronell to Carnegie Hall, though she could not have known it at the time. She simply felt the urge to pursue music. Once back in Israel, she found a conductor and opera singer to help her while she worked, before politics and fear of violence brought her family to America.

In New York, she tried to continue her musical career, seeking out a now-famous pianist whom her mother had helped in prewar Berlin. Ignored by this pianist, Ronell sought out others, writing to all the assistant conductors at the Metropolitan Opera. Most of those also turned her away.

"They were polite, but they said they were too busy," she said. "But one of them saw me as a challenge and took me on. He told me I was his hobby. He said I could grasp things in one or two lessons that took other people weeks to learn. He said he enjoyed giving me lessons."

Ronell says she had a much more practical reason for learning so quickly.

"I was so poor that I had to concentrate and get everything I could out of each lesson," she says. "The others could afford to come back every day. But I could only come once a week."

Besides, by this time, she had two children, and had to work full time to keep them clothed. She says she'd seen too many other careers come up empty ever to depend upon music for her bread and butter. Yet, through persistence, auditions, and additional training, she made the climb up. At the height of her career in the 1960s, Ronell made regular appearances in venues from Manhattan's Benjamin Franklin High School to Carnegie Hall, studying or performing with many of opera's notables.

In the 1970s, she stopped. She had problems with her voice, made a recovery, and then grew weary of the whole scene, especially the pressure of auditions and the off-stage intrigue. She decided to sing at home for pleasure, and, for over a decade, did just that; her husband, a pianist she had met in Israel, served as her accompanist. Then, in 1991, her husband died, devastating her more than losing her career had done. She started to make out her own will. She even picked out and recorded music for her own funeral. Friends, concerned over these things, urged her to pick up her music again.

In this comeback, Ronell met another displaced Israeli pianist, who became her new coach and accompanist and is now helping her prepare to return to Carnegie Hall. Although she has played there before, this marks her first performance since the 1960s and could mean success or failure for her revitalized career. Ronell says she's not looking for superstardom—though she doesn't rule out anything luck might bring her. She would be willing to settle for a career in small venues, and with that aim, has invited managers from many of the smaller venues to see her September performance.

"Maybe if they like what they see, they'll invite me to perform in their places, too," she says.

September seems to be a lucky month for Ronell. Many of her more memorable past performances have been held in that month, at Carnegie Hall and elsewhere. But she's still nervous, and says that's good.

"If I wasn't nervous before a performance, I would fall on my face," she says. "You can't be overconfident, though I am looking for some middle ground."

Part of her nervousness comes from the importance of the occasion. Over the years she's come to realize just how important music is to her.

"I love music, music is the only thing that has never disappointment me in my life," she says. "People are moody, but music has been my only friend at times. I can live without almost anything else."

From *The Secaucus Reporter*, Hudson Reporter Associates, 1995.

Behind the Veil

Even without her veils, finger cymbals, slippers, and exotic costume, Amira Mor draws attention. In a half-hour at the Plaza Diner in Secaucus, one man tripped, one man walked into a counter, two men, seated on either side of her, forgot to eat their lunches, and two women, seated at the booths, stared enviously.

Mor's flowing, dark—almost black—hair, sumptuous dark brown eyes, and shapely face exude a sense of the Middle East. She sits and talks with a sense of foreign intrigue that draws people's gazes, interrupts people's talk, and causes many men to gawk without manners or mercy.

While few would guess that she was a belly dancer, no one would deny that she has an almost mystical appeal. She describes herself as a friendly person who loves people; but she is not unaware of her own beauty, nor of the reaction she gets from men around her. She receives their admiration with the graceful acceptance of someone long used to accolades.

Her résumé reads like a biography of success. She has toured the world, performed with stars like Robert Plant and John Cougar Mellencamp, and is still a regular performer at clubs in Las Vegas and Atlantic City. She has choreographed dances, designed her own advertisements, and performed in some of the poshest nightspots from New York to the Middle East. Locally, she performs weekly at the Club Aladdin, an Arabian hot spot in Hasbrouck Heights. She also teaches belly dancing at the Adult School in Secaucus, where she makes her home.

Now thirty-one, Mor came to belly dancing relatively late. Although she was born and raised in Jerusalem, she didn't study belly dancing until she came to the United States thirteen years ago. "I was trained in ballet and jazz dance," she says. "When I came here I saw someone belly dance and knew that's what I wanted to do."

She says she felt a longing to keep contact with her Middle Eastern heritage, though there are dozens of explanations as to why her students come to learn her art. While she teaches more advanced students in Manhattan, women from every walk of life—young girls and old women, nurses and housewives, librarians and salespeople—come to her beginner classes at the Adult School in Secaucus. Some come for the exercise. Some are drawn by the exotic nature of the dance. Still others come just to see what it's all about.

"This is my third semester teaching belly dancing [at Secaucus Adult School]," Mor says. "Some of the women have been with me since the beginning. They keep coming back. We're like a family."

Why is she teaching?

"You want me to be honest?" she asks. "I really do enjoy performing much more than teaching. But teaching gives me a title. Here I'm a teacher, not a belly dancer. It also makes me pay more attention to what I'm doing. I break each movement into parts. Sometimes dancers do things naturally without thinking about them. This makes me aware of what I'm doing.

"It's very hard work, and the techniques are much more difficult than they seem to the eye," she says. "Unlike jazz or ballet, belly dancing is more emotional." Ballet is formal and stiff, she says. Jazz is structured. "But belly dancing is liquid. It's much softer than ballet."

Only a few times does she slip into the more technical aspects of the art, revealing a little of the mechanics hidden behind the veil and the swirling motions of her dance. Curing the public's ignorance about her art seems to be one of her chief missions, but at times, she takes on a puzzled look as if she is unsure of how much she can reveal or how much people will understand. She slips back into the more personal aspects of the dance, of how it makes her feel when she does it, and how fervently she wants to keep on doing it.

"The technique is very complicated," she says. "The movement of hips, the use of the veil and the finger cymbals all involve a lot of study. There are over one hundred hip movements alone."

She smiles at this juncture, and a devious light comes into her eyes.

"I love to dance with the sword in my hand," she says in a lowered voice that none of the men at the counter can hear.

People mistake the nature of belly dancing, she says, equating it with more vulgar dancing done in bars. She struggles to find the right words, but she seems unable to draw in the English language the distinction between sexual and sensual. Her dance, she says, is often suggestive, but with a sense of intrigue, not vulgarity.

"Yes, men love to look at me," she says. "But when I perform I find more women looking at me. Each takes what she wants from the dance, depending on her point of view. It feels natural. That's why it's attractive."

She says she avoids places where the connotation is too sexual.

"I don't perform in singles places or pick-up bars," she says. "I dance at weddings or family-oriented places. The private parties I do are the family kind."

She says it is an art of deception, an entertainment that does not deal with revealing the body, but in the suggestive nature of what might be revealed.

"We're not go-go dancers," she says. "Ballet dancers show more leg than we do."

Mor says vulgar sexual impressions of belly dancing come out of the art form's history.

"Belly dancing has been around for thousands of years," she says. "But in Arab countries it was done only for the kings."

A turn toward religious fundamentalism pushed the dancers onto the street, where they had to dance to survive. The art devolved and people confused the artist with untrained erotic dancers who cropped up in cheap imitation. Mor says it is this persistent misperception that has kept belly dancing from serious consideration as art by the public.

"People relate us to go-go dancers," Mor said. "We're a million light years away from go-go dancing, and when people see us perform, they know it, too."

Mor says she is obsessed with dance.

"This gets into your blood," she says. "It's more than an addiction. You can get over an addiction. I can't get over this any more than I can get over breathing."

Mor, who has two children, a boy, four, and a girl, seven, says she danced through both her pregnancies even though doctors warned her against it.

"I performed until I was six months pregnant," she said, "and then again two weeks after the delivery."

Even when she stopped performing, she never stopped dancing, spending the hours at home instead, keeping her art sharp.

"Being an artist is nonstop," she says.

From *The Hudson Current,* Hudson Reporter Associates, 1994.

A Dual Identity

Nancy Trauppner stops uptown traffic better than any traffic light. As the hot-dog lady on the corner of Fourteenth and Washington Streets in Hoboken, she has become one of the in-transit crowd's most popular lunchtime stops, a tanned blonde to whom everyone from truck drivers to businessmen flock in their hurried journey in and out of town. During an interview last week, she drew hoots and hollers from passing road workers and men driving pickup trucks, even though few if any of them know of her secret life as a rock-and-roll singer for the band Centerfold.

"I get that all day long," Trauppner says, standing under the shade the yellow-and-blue Sabrett hot-dog vendor's umbrella, which she set up on the corner near the Hudson United Bank here in April 1995 and has brought back to that spot on every warm, sunny day since. "I have to admit most of my customers are men, and I love it."

The hotdog part of her dual identity started in 1986, when she started helping her mother sell from a cart at Eleventh Street and Washington, and her move up to Fourteenth Street in April 1995 was an expansion of that business. But she doesn't come out in the rain or the cold. In winter, she does secretarial work for a lawyer, but she says she hates sitting behind the desk. A lover of sunshine, she'll even sneak out in the middle of the winter if the weather's warm enough, and last year, she stayed out late into the fall as the fair weather lingered.

In her shorts, with her tanned face and blonde hair, Trauppner, for many, is one of the Uptown attractions, rapidly becoming part of the subculture that helps define the texture of Hoboken street life. She loves making her living from the hustle and bustle of the city. Indeed, Trauppner considers herself part of old Hoboken.

She was born and raised in Hoboken. "I've been here for all thirty-four years of my life," she said.. "I've seen it all happen here."

Trauppner says she's seen Hoboken change from one of the East Coast capitals of blue-collar workers to the capital of young urban professionals, and that she was here when the artists came, and the musicians, and Hoboken became what some have called the West West Village. In fact, over the last fifteen years, she's been part of that music scene, living with the dual role of part-time secretary and hot-dog lady, and the nighttime throbbing voice for her band Centerfold. She loves rock and roll nearly as much as she does the sunshine, getting out into the nightclub scene as much as once a week, in Hudson County and elsewhere across the state, playing keyboards as well as singing for the four-piece band.

Singing and performing is the love of her life, though, oddly enough, she amazes her daytime customers when they come to see her perform. During the day, she actually has a carefree attitude, jawing with people who come up for lunch as if they were old friends, laughing as her portable radio hums with classic rock tunes. But at night, on the stage, she's all business, performing what she calls alternative rock, bordering on what others call Corporate Rock. Although she has been singing since she was five years old and has toured Hoboken and northern New Jersey performing anywhere people want from block parties to private parties, from club scene to picnics, she treats it with remarkable seriousness.

"I'm all business," she says. "People come to see me and they get freaked out. But I'm not there to socialize. I get up and sing, and then I go home. I'm really like Dr. Jekyll and Mr. Hyde. Customers come back after hearing me and they think I'm a totally different person."

While she really has a good time performing (and says she wouldn't know what she would do without live music in her life), she doesn't think she'll ever make money from it, says she shouldn't expect to, and doesn't think she'd like it half as much as she does if she thought she'd wanted to make it big. She just likes having a good time and making good music. She also likes doing benefits, and helping others, like a local volunteer ambulance corps or other groups that ask her to help.

"I've got an outgoing personality. I like people and like to talk to people," she says. "My father says I'm the only one in the family with an outgoing personality. I like to talk to everybody."

Trauppner likes being in the middle of things, both as a hot-dog vendor and on the stage, though Fourteenth and Washington has become her home and office for both, the beeper on her belt and the convenient public phone acting as her communication center. Her voice has that deep, husky sound of a seasoned singer, the kind of voice Janis Joplin had, bluesy and powerful. But her heroes are Cher and Bon Jovi. And her admiration for Cher makes sense. Trauppner has a similar air of confidence that makes people want to be around her and want to talk to her. But Bon Jovi has her heart, and she says she dreams of the day when she can actually meet him.

Centerfold plays a lot in northwest New Jersey, and not so much locally, because like many people in today's complex world, she feels a little funny about the conflict of roles.

"Too many people know me here," she says with a laugh, though plenty of her customers come to see her perform. It's sort of an inside joke, one buzzing around her during the interview as customers order hot dogs and comment on her rock-and-roll status. She laughs as she hands them hot dogs with mustard and sauerkraut, her beret, with its Harley-Davidson logo, advertising her next local gig down at the MC Motorcycle Club beach party or a Hoboken block party in August.

Oddly enough, she doesn't define herself as a rock-and-roll performer or as the hot-dog lady of Fourteenth Street, but as the happily divorced mother of three, who likes to bake cookies and cakes. She is drug-free, doesn't drink, and, like old Hoboken itself, is family-oriented.

"That's who I really am," she says.

But on a bright summer morning or late summer afternoon, you might see her rolling her hot-dog wagon along Washington Street, just another part of Hoboken's diversity.

From *The Hudson Current*, Hudson Reporter Associates, 1996.

All the World Loves Ollie

There is no mistaking Oliver Garfunkel when he comes to work, especially if he is wearing his official gear. For many performances, especially with the two-year-old audience, he doesn't dress up until he arrives, giving the kids the thrill of seeing what it's like to put on all those little things that make a clown a clown.

For a recent photo session at Barnes and Noble in Hoboken, Garfunkel comes with face already made up, drawing stares from the store's salespeople as he comes through the door.

Their looks say they've seen everything now. Kids attending story hour in the children's section turn immediately upon his approach, as does the head of every other kid in the store. Even before he removes his coat, their

*Oliver Garfunkel plays Ollie the Clown
before kids at the local bookstore. As Ollie,
Garfunkel is now in Nevada.*

eyes are alive and their attention is focused on him. In this brief introduc-
tion to the store's regular story hour, Ollie the Clown greets the kids with enthusiasm and with the ease of someone who's done this many times before. He
asks their names. He asks about books. He asks if they know what kind of store
Barnes and Noble is.

Then, he begins to fill out his outfit, drawing out of his bag an old campaign hat with a red, white, and blue band. He also removes his snow boots
and replaces them with clown shoes. With this done, he takes a book on
dinosaurs from the shelf and begins to ask questions. What kind of sound do
the kids think dinosaurs made? Did they have claws and teeth? To each
question there is an enthusiastic and varied response.

Garfunkel's shows vary depending on the age group. For kids as young as
two or three, his performance is pure entertainment without the more
sophisticated educational message contained in shows designed for older children. For the very young, he usually arrives without makeup and goes
through the process in front of the kids.

"I put the paint on in front of them to show how it is done," he says.

While he always has his puppets on hand, he does not try to get the very
young kids involved in a story. For audiences aged four to eleven, however,

the puppets and their story, along with numerous other elements—like an imaginary junket to a far-off place, an adventure, a magic train, and music—are vital components of the performance. In some of these tales, Ollie the Clown brings kids to Africa, where they visit the world of nature, taking all the same precautions that they would if they were really to visit an African plain or jungle.

"We all put on imaginary sunblock. We all take pictures with our imaginary cameras. We do all the things that we would have to do if we were actually there," Garfunkel says.

His stories are often centered around the site of his performance. At the Barnes and Noble, for instance, his stories involve books and copyrights. In another setting, kids might play shopkeeper with him, learning to barter, learning the value and denominations of money. During their nature journey through Africa, kids learn about environmental issues like poaching and the illegal use of rhino tusks as ornaments.

"Every lesson is one about the vast experiences of life," Garfunkel says.

For these stories, Garfunkel has developed a full set of characters, each with a background history he keeps in his head.

Cassandra, for instance, is the Queen of Ollieland. She originally came from the Upper East Side of Manhattan, but, according to Garfunkel, was not very successful there.

"So she immigrated to Ollieland, and the minute she stepped off the plane, she drew attention," Garfunkel says. "As she was walking through the mall people saw her and immediately made her queen."

As queen, Cassandra married Mervin, an accountant. Now the palace books are finally in order.

Other Garfunkel characters include Rudi Rabbit, Freddi Fox, and Bad News Balzebub, who is constantly wreaking havoc on Ollieland. For the Barnes and Noble shows, kids will write a story with Ollie the Clown and Bad News Balzebub will steal it.

"This is a lesson about copyright," Garfunkel says, noting that he tries to incorporate lessons on life and the world with each performance.

Yet everything is full of music, singing, and performances by the clown—and of course, stories.

"I want to bring back the magic flavor of story telling," Garfunkel says. "It's the kind of thing you don't see any more. You know the magic feeling of *The Wizard of Oz* or of Hans Christian Andersen's tales. Beautiful magic that brings out the fantastic world for children."

In Ollieland, imagination rules. Yet whatever takes place during a story, all the issues are resolved by the end.

"I know it's not like that in the real world, but I want kids to see that problems can be resolved," Garfunkel says. "If they see resolution in these stories they might have a chance to find resolutions to problems in their lives."

Garfunkel has a degree in clinical and industrial psychology, has worked as an education counselor, and has performed internationally for over eighteen years. At twenty-seven, he is already an international star on the children's circuit, although he is just now making noise in the United States.

Garfunkel started performing when he was eight years old and living in South Africa. One of his relatives caught a performance when he was using socks over his hands for puppets. The show was so captivating that the relative saw it as a good investment and bought Garfunkel everything he needed to start his own puppet theater. Even from the beginning, it proved a thriving business, though Garfunkel only charged a dollar for a two-hour show. Over the ensuing eighteen years, he has performed before millions of kids live and on TV and radio. One of the highlights of his career was a stadium gig before seven thousand young fans.

Garfunkel, who claims Afrikaner ancestry, performed throughout South Africa at the height of apartheid; his tours took him to black townships as well as white areas.

"I went all over South Africa," he says. "I tried to rise above the conflict. The sincere smile of a clown took me through all those situations."

During those years, he went to homes, hospitals, and wherever children waited to see him. Now, seeking the kind of success only America can bring, he has come here at the urging of his Union City–based agent, Best Entertainment Around.

Sitting at a table in the Barnes and Noble Cafe, Garfunkel grins at the curious face of the tiny tot a few tables away. He wiggles his fingers as the child's eyes widen, the clown makeup so attractive that the youngster lifts his small hand as if to touch it.

As Ollie the Clown, Garfunkel is currently doing some volunteer programs at New York Hospital for kids with HIV and sickle-cell anemia. He frowns when asked if he's had any other ambitions.

"You mean be something else besides a clown? No way. This is my career," he says. "I intend to do this until the day I die. I love my work. I think about it all the time, when I'm eating, when I doing other things. I think of stories, think of visuals for the programs and the issues. I try to figure out what the trends are so I can tie my stories to them."

From *The Hudson Current*, Hudson Reporter Associates, 1995.

A Familiar Setting

The literary landscape of New Jersey has been changing lately. It used to be you could count on one hand the number of writers who dared set their stories in the Garden State, and you'd always come back to the works of writers like Philip Roth. Robert Ludlum started his best-seller career with a CIA plot in a loosely disguised Paramus as part of *The Osterman Weekend*, then quickly abandoned it for more exotic localities. For years, New Jersey has been largely the subject of abuse, with the state serving as the birthplace of some of fiction's more ludicrous characters. This has changed over the years, with writers like Janet Evanovich, Valerie Wesley Wilson, and Jon Katz helping to shape New Jersey into a more fashionable locale for mystery novels.

In 1995, Harlan Coben helped give New Jersey's fictional real estate values a boost with the release of *Deal Breaker*, in which not only is the main character from New Jersey, but many of the scenes take place in such familiar settings as Secaucus, the Meadowlands, Hoboken, Union City, and Weehawken, as well as New Jersey's rich sister, New York City. Coben even came to Hoboken's Barnes and Noble bookstore recently to promote the book.

"A lot of the scenes in the novel take place in northern New Jersey," Coben said, not so much of a coincidence since Coben himself was born, raised and still lives there.

Although the action of the novel centers around the Meadowlands Sports Complex in East Rutherford and the football Giants (renamed the Titans for legal reasons), the novel's characters wander throughout the state.

"In the novel, Myron is scouting out the uptown post office in Hoboken," Coben said. "He goes there waiting for someone to pick up a package."

Local readers who travel in and out of New York City will recognize many scenes in the book, including a well-known sign for the York Hotel hanging along the highway winding up from the Lincoln Tunnel.

"I tried to give something to my New Jersey readers, though it isn't just aimed at them," Coben said.

Most serious detective fiction has a gimmick, some device off which the author can work, like the melody of a familiar pop tune in jazz. In *Deal Breaker*, the trick is less New Jersey than it is Myron Bolitar, a wisecracking detective-turned-sports agent.

Coben said he was looking for a particular flavor to his character that was slightly offbeat yet not so strange that it would seem out of touch with average America. Oddly enough, he was struck by a name he heard while watching a dog show on TV. He twisted it around a little and came up with something strange enough that even the character questions where it came from.

"Myron Bolitar," reads one passage. "He still couldn't believe someone would name a kid Myron. When his family first moved to New Jersey, he had told everyone in his new high school that his name was Mike. Nope, no dice. Then he tried to nickname himself Mickey. Unh-unh. Everyone reverted to Myron. The name was like a horror-movie monster that would not die. To answer the obvious question: No, he never forgave his parents."

Don't expect Shakespeare, or even a detective as deep as Sherlock Holmes. This is airport reading, the fast-paced, breeze-through stuff you pick up in New York and put down again when you reach L.A., but the attitude and edge of suspense keep you turning its pages through the whole flight.

The plot basically centers around a huge sports deal. Myron has latched onto a second-round draft pick for the New York Titans. But Myron's client has a ghost in his closet: authorities suspect the biggest football prospect since Joe Namath of murdering his girlfriend, who has been missing for two years. Then, in the middle of negotiations, someone anonymously drops off a skin magazine with what appears to be her photograph in it.

As in most classic detective novels, *Deal Breaker* has its sidekick, a less than stable Dr. Watson who defies many of the role's conventions. This sidekick is, well, a little dangerous.

Coben said he didn't want to copy the now old-hat style of having a street-smart sidekick, and decided to install a blond whose name is nearly as ridiculous as Myron's: Windsor Horne Lockwood III—or Win for short. Coben said he had to type this manuscript and wasn't about to go through all the drudgery each time Win's name came up. But, in short, Coben said in describing this character, "Win is a psychopath."

Deal Breaker, Coben said, is written in the style of a classic whodunit, designed to keep a reader turning the pages.

"I used to write suspense novels, which are pure plot," he said. "But I wanted to add a little character."

Mysteries range from hard-boiled to cozies, according to Coben, who describes cozies as two old ladies sitting around trying to figure out who the killer is.

"I wasn't about to write that kind of fiction," he said. "I wanted my book to have some action."

Although *Deal Breaker* is light reading, it has attitude, leaping from one wisecrack to the next while unfolding its mystery and later its resolution as its characters chase each other from Giants Stadium to Atlantic City.

This novel is the first in a series using the same cast of characters. The second, *Drop Shot,* is about a killing at the food court at the U.S. Tennis Open. As full of wisecracks as his main character, Coben said that since between their low quality and high prices mall foods are practically killing people anyway, he figured he literally stage his murder there. [Since this novel was published, food courts have improved their fare if not their prices.]

While developing a series is good for sales—readers like to see the same main characters again—Coben said he would like to use the series to allow his characters to change and develop, altering the plot, aging the characters, creating personal problems to interweave with the plots.

Coben has published two other novels: *Play Dead* and *Miracle Cure.*

Miracle Cure got national attention because it was published just before Magic Johnson announced his retirement due to AIDS.

"There were a number of similarities between Magic Johnson and my character," Coben said. "Both became rookie of the year, both wives were pregnant, both started playing basketball the same year."

Coben was born in Newark, raised in Livingston, and now lives in Ridgewood. Although *Deal Breaker* and his other novels involve professional sports, Coben never played football beyond college.

"I wasn't very good," he admits. "But I was an All-American. But then, I was picked All-American by the *Jewish Post* of Indianapolis. So I don't know how much that counts."

Coben got into novel writing more or less by accident.

"I worked for a travel club," he said. "While I was in Spain I wondered what it would be like to write about an American on vacation."

While that idea didn't pan out, he did get the writing bug and liked mysteries.

"So it went on from there," Coben said.

He sold his first book in 1990 and is now working on his fifth novel, with the settings of all but one centered in the New York metropolitan area. He said he thought about placing his characters in the faraway places he'd visited during his travels, but somehow managed to put them right here in New Jersey.

"I tried an exotic setting in one book," he said. "Now I'm writing about the post office in Hoboken. Isn't that strange?" Stranger still is the fact that his book has the unofficial backing of YooHoo chocolate drink. A distributor found out that Coben's main character liked drinking YooHoo and gave Coben cases of the drink as well as several display coolers to bring with him on his book tour. Now readers can meet the author, buy an autographed copy of his book, and get a free YooHoo to boot.

Coben has been doing the rounds at Barnes and Noble and other bookstores throughout the state. At one stop, he sold thirty-five copies of his book. He likes personalizing his books, and left in the Hoboken Barnes and Noble a number of signed copies with such messages as: "You're too cool," "You're the best" or "You're too sexy."

"I used to bring my baby daughter on tour with me," Coben said. "She used to have a sign: 'Buy a book; feed the baby.' "

But the sales are better now, and the YooHoo seems to be enough.

From *The Hudson Current*, Hudson Reporter Associates, 1995.

Chapter and Verse

Long before Joel Lewis came to Hoboken, he had been dubbed the poet laureate of Hudson County. Even during the years at William Paterson College, rumors of his local touch floated among the literati, often as a subject of abuse. Who did Joel Lewis think he was: William Carlos Williams? In the smug literary world of the early 1980s, it wasn't fashionable to write about such mundane things as the Hoboken ferry or wandering around North Bergen, Weehawken, or Jersey City.

Yet Lewis had the fortitude to maintain his standards, to build the first significant literary map of New Jersey since Williams, Allen Ginsberg, and Jack Kerouac. Lewis seemed to understand something important about the function of poetry that many of his contemporaries only learned later, that in order for people to like poetry it must have some relevance to their lives.

Many of the literary elite of that time have finally come around to Lewis's thinking, yet few have managed to paint better pictures of a changing Hoboken and Hudson County than Lewis has. In a way, Lewis's poetry has drawn on his experiences growing up here as a comparison to what this part of the state has become.

Although Lewis is a Hoboken resident, his reputation has always been greater outside Hudson County, where he is accepted as one of the premier New Jersey poets. *Bluestones and Salt Hay*—an anthology of New Jersey poets he edited for Rutgers University Press in 1990—is considered by many in the literary field as the work that best defines contemporary New Jersey poetry.

But Lewis's *House Rent Boogie* and *Palookas of the Ozone* are books that

*Poet Joel Lewis just published his fourth book.
Since 1995, he has taught creative writing at
Rutgers University, Newark, and the history of
the 1960s at New York University. He is also fully
engaged in social work.*

define him, and in them, Lewis has managed to convey what it means to grow
up and live here along the south edge of the Palisades.

Many of the poems he's written about this place have been published
throughout the country in small presses and various anthologies, and over
the years Lewis has received gradual accolades from local and national literary
societies. In 1990, his manuscript won a prestigious Ed Berrigan award,
resulting in the publication of *House Rent Boogie*. In New Jersey his efforts have
gotten him a grant from the New Jersey Council on the Arts.

Although he has received degrees from William Paterson College and the
City College of New York, Lewis cites his study with Allen Ginsberg at
Naropa in Boulder, Colorado, as one of the most significant times in his
literary life.

Lewis says his writing is about the experience of experience, about the sense
of being around.

"It is about walking around the town, about little things like a friend losing his jacket at the Brass Rail, about the interior things that are the experience, anything from Carlo's Bakery to a description of City Hall," says

Lewis. "Even seemingly mundane experiences have their value. There is a fabulousness about everything.

"I consider myself a political person," he adds, "not in the civic sense but the greater political sense, living in an era of late capitalism. I want people 150 or 200 years from now to understand what it is like to have lived in Hoboken during this period of change."

What many people in the new literary scene now reemerging in Hoboken may not know is that Lewis reintroduced poetry to Hoboken after a long, long hiatus. While Allen Ginsberg, Jack Kerouac, and Hershel Silverman used to make regular visits to Hoboken's Clam Broth House during the early 1950s, the real literary scene here did not start until the late 1970s.

During that period northern New Jersey underwent a renaissance, thanks to federal Comprehensive Employment and Training (CETA) money. In Paterson, the Silk City Poets formed. In Passaic, another literary group formed around its library. The Bergen Poets solidified the scene from Fort Lee to Fair Lawn. Here in Hudson County, Lewis began readings at Lady Jane's Café, which was then in North Bergen. Later, he and other Hudson County poets started regular readings at the now defunct Beat'n Path on Washington Street in Hoboken.

"That was the summer of 1979," Lewis says. "At the time it was a homey sign in Hoboken's new community. John Vitell owned the place. He had a back room. We said if we could hold readings we might bring in some customers on his slow nights. And it worked."

Some of the biggest names in contemporary poetry came: Amiri Baraka, Joseph Ceravalo, Max Greenberg, Ted Berrigan, Alice Notley, and Jim Brody as well as many of the less established poets.

"We wanted to match up local poets with some of the better-[known] poets," Lewis says. "This was a learning experience. It was a chance for local poets to associate with people who had made a name for themselves."

In these early years, the poets would wander over to the Brass Rail, where they would discuss their art over a few glasses of beer.

"That was when the place was still an old guy's bar," says Lewis. "We used to hang out there."

Audiences were pretty large. Many writers active in the New York literary scene lived in Hoboken because it was cheap. This was all before the real estate boom, when artists could actually afford to live here.

"A lot of the writers lived in basements for a hundred dollars a month rent," Lewis recalls. "I knew one writer whose rent was fifty-five dollars. His landlord hadn't raised the rent since World War II."

By the 1980s, the mantle of local poetry passed onto others. The poetry moved up to Maxwell's, where it continued for another ten or eleven years.

Recently, Maxwell's revived its regular reading series, although poetry plays second fiddle to the music scene.

Lewis also ran a poetry series at the Unicorn Bookstore in 1982—where the Café Roma is today. This was a precursor to the Barnes and Noble concept, where bookstore, café and art gallery were combined.

"We always introduced local people to the best writers," Lewis says. "It helped make that scene work."

New York people flocked here, taking advantage of the thirty-cent PATH fare.

"Ted Berrigan said at the time that if you wanted to see what New York looked like in the 1950s, you should come to Hoboken," Lewis says. "All that, of course, changed when Hoboken started to convert into what it is now."

But the early poetry scene here, Lewis says, drew attention. During the changeover, numerous profiles were done on the readings; people came and filmed the readings.

"We got a lot of attention," he says. "They wanted to show that Hoboken still had culture. Yet development put the kibosh on the cultural scene. Even with the artists' tours it's not the same. Many of the writers here now are not as serious as the group of people we had ten years ago. The poetry scene has not come together the way as it should have."

One big difference is the approach to art. The younger crowd is more interested in its own work, looking to get heard and to publish, but not to listen to what others are doing, Lewis says.

"It's hard to develop community if you don't care about other people's work," he says. "You have to care about the art form and helping it survive."

Lewis does not make a living writing poetry. In today's society such an arrangement is rare. He calls himself a "working writer," one who has published poetry, reviews, and other forms of narrative regularly since the late 1970s. But he is a social worker by trade, part of a modern tradition of men who, like William Carlos Williams, must work at one trade while keeping up his career as a writer. Yet, he says, it takes the strain off his art.

"A painter has to start making money right away just to cover the cost of materials and a studio," Lewis says. "And any musician with a full-time day job is hardly taken seriously, especially in the jazz world. But a writer can work a job and still work as a writer if he has self-discipline."

He says what makes it difficult to be a creative person in the 1990s is finding the inner resources from which to draw.

"I'm not just talking about making a living as an artist," Lewis says. "But so many people are career-minded today that they don't take time to learn anything that might bring them joy later. For a while, they leap into their careers, then later, after they've settled into their jobs, they find there is something missing in their lives. They never bothered to learn about other things, like poetry, when they were in school. So they go from one fad to another, expecting to fill that emptiness. Most people don't understand that you have to cultivate culture inside yourself, learning things when you're young that you can draw on later like poetry, music, or art."

This is a big part of his writing, a cultivation of that other side of life inside himself.

"I go out and work with families as a social worker," he says. "Then, when I'm home I can draw on this other side. I share this side with friends from all over the country. I write letters. I share my poetry and discuss other interests and read and discuss other people's work."

He says one of the most dangerous messages in modern culture is the demand for conformity and careerism.

"I'm often reluctant to identify myself as a writer because I'm not taken seriously," he says. "People question how I can be interested in something where I don't make any money. Things without that kind of money value are seen as suspect—'Why are you doing this?'"

From *The Hudson Current,* Hudson Reporter Associates, 1995.

Poetry in the Woods

Twenty-five years from now, it is unlikely your children or grandchildren will ask if you attended the 1996 Geraldine R. Dodge Poetry Festival the way kids today ask their parents about Woodstock. Yet pulling into the parking lot and walking up the wide paths from the road to the festival site at Waterloo Village, the feeling was largely the same—though this was a four-day festival and the rain didn't start until it was nearly over.

Maybe the lines weren't quite as long for the telephone booths, though Barbara Stewart of the *New York Times* did complain about the line outside the women's room. The food was better, too, veggie burgers and health snacks, with cases of bottled water. Woodstock didn't have pizza, either, and the announcements from the main tent dealt mostly with mis-parked cars or headlights left on.

*Poets Danny Shot, Laura Boss, and Hershel Silverman
paid tribute to Allen Ginsberg at a special memorial
near Paterson's Great Falls in 1997, a few months
after Ginsberg died.*

Borders Books, which opened its first Manhattan store in the World Trade
Center early in September 1996, had its own tent, selling the books of the
poets who were to appear at the festival. They sold remarkable numbers of
books; vendors selling T-shirts and posters also did well, and despite the rain
on the last day of the festival, more than ten thousand people attended the
four-day event, making this the largest event of its kind in the United States.
The 1994 edition of this every-two-year event was featured in the Bill Moyers PBS series *The Language of Life.* The show had been credited for increasing attendance.

While hardly the household names that performers like Jimi Hendrix and
Janis Joplin became after Woodstock, some of the most important names in
poetry came to this year's festival, including Allen Ginsberg, Philip Levine,
Galway Kinnell, Lucille Clifton, Maxine Kumin, Carolyn Kizer, and Donald
Hall. Although the ninety-year-old Stanley Kunitz was also scheduled to
appear, he caught cold a week earlier and chose not to come.

Also included were the twenty-nine winners of the New Jersey High School
Student Poetry Contest and countless other poets and would-be poets, who
spread across the setting with impromptu performances of their own. In fact,

people came from up and down the East Coast, with a few poets coming from as far as California. Waterloo Village, with its eighteenth- and nineteenth-century buildings, working gristmill, sawmill, church, general story, tavern, blacksmith, apothecary, and re-created Lenape Indian Village, made a perfect backdrop.

Hudson County had its share of representatives. Guttenberg's Dodge Poet Laura Boss, who has received two Geraldine Dodge Foundation fellowships, was there. So were Hoboken poet and publisher Danny Shot and Hudson County's unofficial poet laureate Joel Lewis. In fact, more than four thousand students, teachers, and poetry fans showed up on Thursday and Friday, with many more coming over the weekend despite the rain on Sunday.

In a way, this was a tribute to the power of New Jersey in the growing poetry scene, with cheers going up repeatedly in the big tent every time New Jersey was mentioned or a poet claimed residence here. In fact, poets and writers from *Riff* magazine, a new literary magazine from Edgewater, took over one of the open reading sessions, the way they had invaded a reading at the Hoboken Barnes and Noble a month earlier. Poets proffered their prolific poems to the gurgling waters of the Musconetcong River, talking about trains, planes, and heartaches.

Although Ginsberg stole the show, Pulitzer Prize–winning Philip Levine filled the 1700s-era church with his talk about the nature of poetry and was the top act at the big tent closing Friday night. As a professor of literature at New York University, Levine said he is constantly confronted with parents who have an apparently more practical future in mind for their children. He said he remembered one student's parents calling him up saying their son wanted to be a poet.

"They wanted me to talk him out of it," Levine said. "I told them the boy would have to make up his own mind."

In the course of the conversation that ensued, the parents protested, saying they wanted their son to become a doctor.

"They said they were a professional family. I told them poetry is an ancient and honorable profession," Levine said. "Later, their son became a fairly successful poet. They seemed to have forgotten where the phrase came from when they proudly told me that poetry was an ancient and honorable profession."

For the first few days, people kept asking "When's Allen Ginsberg coming?" and mistaking other older men they saw on Thursday and Friday, although he was not scheduled to appear until Saturday afternoon. He did a benefit reading at Columbia University on Friday, celebrating also the release of his new book, *Selected Poems*. When he climbed out of the car people of all ages swarmed around him, treating him like a superstar.

Ginsberg was a discovery of William Carlos Williams, among the greatest twentieth-century American poets. Ginsberg went to Williams to show his poetry the way many of the kids at this festival came to him to show him theirs. Williams shook his head, saying it wasn't good enough, and then Ginsberg showed Williams some journal entries he'd made during trips across the country with Jack Kerouac, entries written in powerful and intense jazz-like language that began a revolution in writing. Williams told Ginsberg these journal entries were his poetry.

Ginsberg had grown up in and around Paterson, gleaning lessons from that historic city and from the thriving sense of life that still exists there. I got drunk with him (though he would not remember) at his fifty-fourth birthday party in Paterson, after a Great Falls Festival in 1980. But in 1985, a friend and I cornered Ginsberg during an interview he held at William Paterson College. Ginsberg's *Collected Poems* had just been published by Harper & Row, the first time his work had been accepted and published by a national publisher. We thought he had sold out, and we told him so. Now, a decade later, he proved us wrong. Success had not ruined the seventy-year-old poet, but had deepened his commitment to poetry, so that above all others at the festival, he was the grandfather of poetry, the wise old man who had come to teach the children the rituals of the muse.

James Haba, coordinator of the festival, called Ginsberg one of the "absolutely great literary figures of our century."

It was a small man with a loud voice who sat down before the waiting crowd of thousands, his music box on his lap, his eyeglasses slightly askew, yet he managed to sound larger than life. This is the man who crossed America with Kerouac in 1949, the man who set the poetry world into shock when he read "Howl" in San Francisco in 1956, the man who was carried out of the Chicago Eight Trial in 1969. He was the man who had breached the Iron Curtain in 1968, and returned when the Iron Curtain lifted in 1990.

Above all others at this year's festival, Ginsberg made poetry sound like fun. He sang it. He cursed with it. He chanted it. He protested through it, and under the big tent he kept people riveted in their seats, none daring to blink for fear of missing something. Over the years, Ginsberg has grown weaker with various diseases, some of which he listed jokingly during his protest song against smoking. He may not be with us much longer, yet, for one sparkling moment, at one great occasion in the woods, we met him again and he shone, receiving the kind of accolade as a poet of which Plato would have been proud.

From *The Secaucus Reporter,* Hudson Reporter Associates, 1996.

Final Chapter

Last summer, during a trip to San Francisco, Elena Skye met a wealthy entre-preneur who offered to give her the money to open a bookstore along the coast. While tempted by the offer, Skye, one of the principal owners of BlackWater Books, turned him down. She decided she loved Hoboken too much to leave it, even though her own bookstore had been struggling to make ends meet for years.

"Somehow we've always managed to pull things together enough to keep the store going," she says. "Hoboken is a special, magical place and I couldn't just leave it because someone offered to let me run his bookstore."

On March 1, Skye and her partner, David Cogswell announced that Black-Water Books would be closing after nine years on Washington Street, an ironic twist that has Skye shaking her head.

For people in the artist community, BlackWater Books has been more than a bookstore over the last nine years. It has served as a hub around which they have learned to live their lives, coming and going with their daily visits, if not to buy a book or tape then just to say hello. And for many, the store has been a service center, something akin to the 1960s cultural centers like the Free Church in Berkeley or the Renaissance Switchboard in New York City.

"We've kept people's keys here, accepted their UPS deliveries, we've even lent people money," Skye says. "We keep the list of names under the regis-ter drawer of all the people who owe us money."

To the uninitiated the store actually has a cluttered look, with wall-to-wall art that has been stuffed into bookshelves and onto the walls, creating a mosaic of apparently contradictory images. Elvis Presley and Hank Williams grin down from walls that also hold posters of local rock-and-roll bands and paintings from several of Hoboken's cutting-edge artists. From the shelves and tables, the faces of William Burroughs, Allen Ginsberg, Jack Kerouac, William Faulkner, and James Joyce stare up like old friends, as comfortable here as the neighbor-hood artists. Perhaps the whole effect of the store over the last nine years is summed up by the rock advertisement taped across the inside of the door: "Artists are the bravest souls in the world."

Going out of business has brought out friends in batches, people showing their support for the institution that had been a part of their lives and regret at its passing.

*Since closing BlackWater Books in 1995,
David Cogswell and Elena Skye have moved
on to new careers. Cogswell has become a
travel writer, Skye a successful musician
who has received some national recognition.*

"I can't believe the number of people that are coming in," Skye says. "They're very supportive. For two and a half months we had no money coming in, and now we're selling everything. People are telling us to hang in there, and they're very encouraging."

People have been writing notes on the store's going-out-of-business signs, tiny messages of support that make closing that much more painful. Yet in determining the fate of the store, it is too little support coming way too late.

The closing has also drawn in numerous strangers, who in the past had avoided crossing the threshold of a place they saw as part of the town's subculture, people drawn in by the signs promising a discount. While Skye is talking, one broad-chested man meanders in. He has the bearing and face of an old-style Irish boxer and wears an expression of obvious distaste. While clearly drawn in by the chance of finding a bargain, he snarls routinely at the more artistic offerings, passing them over to purchase a package of greeting cards. While at the register, he asks if the store has any of Rush Limbaugh's books left.

For the many friends who come, Skye has brought in a borrowed video camera, recording their faces for posterity.

"We were here for a very cool period in Hoboken, and it is something we want to remember. It may soon be all gone," she says.

BlackWater books opened on Washington Street in 1986 under the name Rogers & Cogswell. Mark Rogers and David Cogswell, after running two very successful book kiosks for six years near Central Park and Bryant Park in Manhattan, decided they wanted a traditional bookstore.

"It's ironic," says David Cogswell. "We actually took over our New York businesses from Barnes and Noble, now Barnes and Noble is one of the reasons we're going out of business here."

Skye says while Rogers and Cogswell ran the book stalls she had always wanted to open a regular book store, and with a little searching found a place here on Washington Street in Hoboken.

"When we opened in 1986," she says, "the only other bookstore in town was the Literary Shop, which now sells comic books, but sold a lot of used books then as well as best-sellers. With our ideas for selling new books, we thought we had found a slot here."

When the partnership broke up in 1990, Cogswell renamed the store Black-Water Books, and judging by that first year's sales, Cogswell believed he had a good future.

"The store's best year was 1990," he says. "Even though we had a lot of debt when the partnership broke up and we didn't even have books to cover the backs of the shelves, we had some lucky breaks. We got a small loan and started doing events, and somehow we aroused the community to come support us."

But Hoboken and the world changed, and by the beginning of 1991, other bookstores moved into town.

"The market here got crowded," Cogswell says. "The worst part was the fact that the rents didn't correspond to the depressed economy.'"

Still the store stayed alive despite the competition.

"When you're back to the wall you develop talents you didn't know you had," Cogswell says. "The only really bad thing was that the cash flow tended to make doing anything else difficult. Sometimes we had a hard time stocking the store."

Life for Cogswell and Skye became a struggle to meet the monthly rent. But the final blow came just before Christmas when Barnes and Nobles opened its doors in Hoboken.

"We were absolutely affected by them. When they got into town, business dropped off," Cogswell says.

The precarious balancing act by which the store had survived for so long suddenly tilted. They fell behind on their monthly rent. The landlord asked them to leave.

"We pleaded with our landlord," Cogswell says. "We told him that the only kind of store than could pay two thousand dollars a month for this kind of space would be a restaurant. We tried to work him. He didn't want to hear it. He just wanted us out."

Cogswell says he is still looking at spaces where he can continue doing business.

"There's a good chance to come up with something, but it will mean a whole different kind of approach," he says. "For one thing we won't be on Washington Street anymore."

Skye says they are rethinking things, looking to change their focus.

"Whatever we do it will deal with the arts," she says, "and perhaps provide a real alternative, adding something like gay and lesbian literature. There is a strong gay community here. But whatever we do, we have to go out on the edge. We will continue to have some literature at discount, but we'll be more adventurous, too."

Cogswell says Hoboken still offers opportunities for the small business-person, but it means taking a chance.

"We definitely want books, want to be there," he says. "We won't want to be a big mainstream retailer, since that market is saturated. We're going to try and bring out a bookstore with a boutique edge, something off the main drag of Hoboken. We'll offer select books and music and boutique things—and events."

Cogswell says a new store will have to be small and adaptable in order to compete with Barnes and Noble.

"They have a huge capital investment, but that can have its disadvantages," he says. "They have to buy to suit the mass market; we can be more selective."

As they get ready to close the Washington Street store, both Cogswell and Skye say the experience has been tremendous.

"Being around people in this environment has been a rewarding experience and one that I'm never going to forget," Cogswell says. "We weren't just selling books here, we provided a place for people to come to discuss things like literature, a place where artists could gather and interesting people could generate some stimulating conversation."

The store, Cogswell says, had become a big part of his life, almost a second home.

"After our daughter was born, we used to keep her in a basket behind the cash register, so she would be near us all the time," he says. "She practically grew up here."

Cogswell says that while there are parts of the experience that he would like to forget, most of it was a labor of love, from which something better would eventually emerge.

"Over the last few years it has meant more to Elena than to me," Cogswell says. "It was her originally vision. I was more the businessperson, who figured out how to pay the bills. She loved what the store was, and loved being here. But neither one of us will ever forget the place or the people that came there. It has been an amazing and wonderful experience running this store."

From *The Hudson Current*, Hudson Reporter Associates, 1995.

By the Time I Got to Woodstock . . .

The first time I ever heard the name "Woodstock" was when my top sergeant yanked me from my bunk saying I'd volunteered for duty there. I was too busy overcoming my fear of helicopters to ask many questions, or point out the 1969 rock festival was actually held fifty miles southwest of the town.

I was part of one of the medical evacuation teams sent to the area to transport the ill and injured to area hospitals. But I kept my eyes closed for the greater part of the time in the air, much to the chagrin of the Vietnam-hardened pilot. On the ground I dragged people on or off under the swipe of the helicopter blades. My best friend was flown out with pneumonia by a crew from the New York National Guard. Reportedly he screamed the whole time that he wanted to wait and see Jimi Hendrix. It was only when my unit left that I opened my eyes and briefly glimpsed the magnitude of what has been called Woodstock Nation.

For years the town of Woodstock has been the place that people go seeking to recapture a bit of the old magic, and celebrated as a place where some of the 1960s ideals had been put into practice. I studiously avoided the place, having once been turned away from Alice's Restaurant of the Arlo Guthrie song for not having a reservation. The experience made me a cynic on 1960s myths. But as the twentieth anniversary of the concert neared I gave in to the urge to see just how much better the people of Woodstock were handling the crisis of the 1990s.

The site of the original Woodstock concert in Bethel, New York, was slated to become the site of a new arts center, although many people still wander there to pay homage to the historic musical event. Many people leave stones on this monument.

Strangely enough, I found the people of Woodstock struggling with many of same problems people in Hudson County faced: questions on development, how to attract tourism, and how small communities deal with nationally advertised events.

Hanging over Woodstock were not rumors of traffic woes caused by World Cup soccer, but much more acute concerns about the impact of this week-end's anniversary concert on what was normally a sleepy community. While Hudson County had the benefit of mass transportation and a variety of highways to help siphon off the invasion of cars, many of the roadways around Woodstock are narrow two-lane roads, never designed for high volumes of traffic. Like Hoboken with its recent bar-closing hysteria, Woodstock fears a major social impact, yet refuses to shut out the traffic entirely the way Secaucus has during the World Cup. The businesses of Woodstock look forward with mixed feelings to the concert, hoping it will revitalize their economy.

One essential difference you notice when turning off Route 375 into Woodstock is the lack of development. No condominiums. No chain stores. No office buildings of any kind. But along both sides of Tinker Street, there is store after store straight out of 1967, selling everything from beads to wind chimes

It is like stepping back in time, with many of the local residents dressed in period costumes, beads, and headbands, as conventional in that setting as suits and ties are in most places. White-haired hippies walk side by side with high school-age kids. Few but the tourists stare. At the local outdoor fruit café, a Janis Joplin lookalike lectures kids half her age about 1969 and that era's philosophy.

The name "Woodstock" is an obvious selling point, with nearly half the stores in town incorporating it into their own names. But plenty of other places opted for the usual 1960s hype, with names like the White Buffalo, the Warm Store, or Sunflower Natural Foods.

The smell of candle wax and incense inside the Candlestock brought it all back. The seven-foot-high collection of wax drippings might well have been started right after the Woodstock festival ended.

Although many people came here after the 1969 concert, Woodstock has a long history as a center of the arts, contrasting with Hoboken—where the gallery scene started after development began to transform the town. Ralph Whitehead, a utopian English philosopher, founded the Brydcliff Art and Crafts colony here in 1902. Woodstock became the summer home of the Art Students League, and in 1910 the Woodstock Artists Association was started. In 1940, the Woodstock Guild was formed to promote the development of arts and crafts and form the basis for the current Colony of Craft the Arts.

A variety of chamber music concerts began in 1916, and in 1937, the Woodstock Playhouse began theater and dance performances—for which Woodstock was initially famous. Famous writers, musicians, artists, and craftspeople are among those who live in the woods and hills around the village. Indeed, Woodstock is now known for some of the finest recording studios in the world.

While development in Hoboken and other parts of Hudson County has spurred the economy, here in Woodstock, there is a not-so-silent dread of developers. Development is strictly limited.

"The owner of one piece of property tried to put in a small strip mall, but it was voted down," said Roz, owner and operator of a small bookstore in the center of town.

Most of the local economy here runs on tourism, something Secaucus is now investigating as an antidote for shrinking ratables and its own rebellion against development. Yet Woodstock has taken much from the 1960s. Competition is not welcome here. While the 6,700 full-time residents endure the tourists, it does not open itself up to increasing business.

"This is not the kind of place where new faces are welcomed," Roz said. "We started our business here and they didn't want us. They said they already had a bookstore in town, they didn't want two. That's the way it is with everything here."

This vision of limited potential economic growth was common in the 1960s. Tourist trade—no matter how busy a year—may not be sufficient to support additional businesses

"The streets were so packed on a weekend in the summer you couldn't walk down them," Roz said. "Business is down. The recession has hurt us. People are staying away."

The burning down of the Woodstock Playhouse, one of the chief attractions of the town, in the early 1990s and the later laying off of workers by IBM left local residents with some hard choices for the future. Could they afford to maintain their previous way of life, or would they need to bring in some of the business attractions they had previously excluded?.

One answer to the slumping economy is nostalgia. Woodstock is world-famous for the 1969 concert that bears its name. A twentieth-anniversary concert planned next month for eight miles out of town has many people hopeful of a tourist revival. Indeed, the town is dripping nostalgia, taking its cue from the national event to re-create 1960s magic here and now.

This weekend, Woodstock was holding a festival of its own in a nearby field, featuring twenty bands and forty crafts concessions. The names of the bands were hardly the household variety of the original 1969 event. Many of these bands have copycat names typical of generic perfumes and video pornography. The Clearwater Singers, Pepe Santana, Ellis and Friend, and Chiapas Indian Peace Caravan were among those scheduled to play.

Even the local movie house has gotten in on the act, featuring a Cinema '69 series that includes *Yellow Submarine, Woodstock, Easy Rider, Alice's Restaurant, In the Year of the Pig, Gimme Shelter,* and other films, as well as guest speakers like Arlo Guthrie. The cost of admission to each performance is five dollars, half price if you come in period costume.

Lacking the highway and hotel infrastructure Hudson County had to handle additional people brought in by World Cup soccer in 1994, Woodstock struggled with more limited resources. In the weeks before and after the concert, Town Hall estimated that twenty-five thousand visitors descended upon the small community during the weeks before and after the concert. The volunteer rescue squad, already shorthanded, is out seeking more volunteers. The local soup kitchen, set up in 1993 to help feed people suffering as a result of the recession, closed its doors for the summer.

"We do not have the resources," said Victoria Langling, of Woodstock soup kitchen. "We did not have enough food and we did not have enough volunteers."

The soup kitchen had been feeding forty people a day until last month, when the numbers began to increase. Last count it was at seventy-five per day. The church out of which people are fed has a maximum capacity of eighty.

There have been burglaries, too. Over a three-day period at the beginning of July, police reported several break-ins to local restaurants. Over the July Fourth weekend, police made forty arrests, up from eighteen the year before. Many of the people arrested gave addresses in Texas, California, Idaho, and Florida.

"Several said they were in the spirit of Woodstock," Woodstock Police Chief Paul Ragonese said. "But these people can't just do their own thing."

The police have also found people camped out on private property around the area. This weekend, storeowners say, the local green has seen a significant increase in new faces. Many of those coming are in their early to mid-twenties.

Chief Ragonese said there are plans to bring in the auxiliary police and ask for volunteers. But this is largely to handle the expected traffic woes. For the most part, he said, people were well behaved.

"They made very little noise and didn't leave much litter behind," he said.

One of the clerks at a town jewelry store said many residents are worried about what kind of people the concert will bring in.

"The organizers initially wanted to bring in rap and other new bands," she said. "We don't need that kind of trouble around here. We pressed them to cut out most of that music. But there's still the heavy metal bands to worry about and the kind of kids that music attracts."

Members of the Family of Woodstock, a local social organization, said they have noticed an influx of people, too. There have been reports of panhandling, trespassing, and other minor illegal activities. On my brief tour of town, I saw several girls hitchhiking. Although they were dressed like hippies, down to the almost obligatory backpack, they were barely twenty years old.

An umbrella organization called Woodstock Ambassadors met in order to deal with the incoming crowds associated with the festival. Their agenda included festival hours, drugs, noise, trespassing, pay phones, directions for local roads, lost and found, free food, transportation, festival information, parking, trash recycling, baby sitting, and auto repair.

In the typical Woodstock tone, a spokesperson for one of the participating organizations said the idea was to show care and concern.

"We want to show them the real Woodstock in all its variety," said Eric Glass of Woodstock Youth Center. "We want to offer reassurance and a deep sense of community good will."

Although ticket sales for Woodstock are not moving as quickly as first expected, organizers from Polygram Records say they will pick up. As of July

5, 128,000 tickets were sold. It is estimated that the event will draw 250,000.

Will the festival bring back the postrecession business of the 1980s? Some business people like Roz from the bookstore think not. Roz said her business is solid, based less on tourists than on local residents. But many are not so lucky. At the Sunflower Natural Food store, women walk around in full regalia, straight out of photographs from Haight-Ashbury, yet inside, an elder hippie and his son are paying for their natural food drinks with food stamps.

From *The Secaucus Reporter,* Hudson Reporter Associates, 1994.

Index

Addeo, Felix, 164–166
AIDS (acquired immune deficiency syndrome), 13–14, 15, 217
Alcoholics Anonymous, 14, 15, 92
Alexander, Dorothy, xv
Ali, Muhammad, 96
Allied Junction (Secaucus), 135
American Littoral Society, 128
American Merchant Marine Academy Museum, 45
American Revolution, 151, 174
Amico, Paul, 132–136, 139, 180
animals, nature, 114–120, 123–132
Antonovich, Bernard, 121–122
Argow, Sam, 72, 73
art, 96–100. *See also specific performing arts*
Austin, Ruth, 16–18
Australia, 49, 53–56

Barnes & Noble (Hoboken), 187, 214, 218, 224, 227, 231–232
Baykeepers (American Littoral Society), 128
Bellis, George, 74
Bergen Poets, 223
Bergmanson, Carl, 122
Better Homes and Gardens, 58
Bianco, Thomas, 76–77
Bluestones & Salt Hay (Lewis), 222
Borders Books, 226
Bosnia, 3–7

Boss, Laura, 226, 227
Bourne, Midge, 29–31
Boyle, Robert, 130
Brady, Richard, 114–116
Brady-Danzig, Patricia, 65–67
Britains (toy soldier manufacturer), 41
British Ship Journal, 45
Broke Heart Blues (Oates), 94
Buccino, Anthony, xiv

Caldwell College (Caldwell), 66
Cambodia, 191–193
Canfield Home (West Caldwell), 17
Cardone, Ron, 80–83
Carnegie Hall (New York City), 66, 207–208
Carson, Rachel, 130
Ceglie, Rachel, 5–6
CETA. *See* Comprehensive Employment and Training Act
Chigrupati, Ester, 51–53
Church of Our Saviour (Secaucus), 6, 60–65
Ciccone, Sam, 10–11
Civil War, 169
Clarendon School (Secaucus), 170–175
Clark's Pond (Bloomfield), 125–128
clowning, 214–217
Coben, Harlen, 218–221
Coccuci, Pat, 165

Cogswell, David, 229–233
Colt, James, 205
Comprehensive Employment and
    Training Act (CETA), 223
Conk, Judith, 105, 107
Constitution (ship), 45
Crecco, Marion, 10
Croatia, 3

Dachau concentration camp, 32
dance, 209–211
DARE. *See* Drug Abuse Resistance
    Education
Dealbreaker (Coben), 219
Deiner, Richard and Jo Ann, 34–36
D'Elia, Anthony, 170–175
Delson, James, 40–43
DePice, Doug, 183–187
Dodge Foundation. *See* Geraldine R.
    Dodge Foundation
Drug Abuse Resistance Education
    (DARE), 79
Duck Pond (Secaucus), 123–125,
    204–205
Dundon, Lewis J., 29–31

Edison, Thomas, 18; factory in West
    Orange, 18
education, 105–108, 157–180,
    183–187, 194–197
Elwell, Howie, 182
emergency services, 71–80
England, 54
Environmental Protection Agency
    (EPA), 121–122
EPA. *See* Environmental Protection
    Agency
Essex County Bee Society, 109
Essex County Police Academy, 78

Finland, 49–51
firefighters. *See* emergency services
Flanagan, Robert, 33–34
Florida Game and Fresh Water Fish
    Commission, 119
Fontana, Joe, 57–60

Garfunkel, Oliver, 214–217
Gehm, Michael, 167–170

Geraldine R. Dodge Foundation, 186,
    227; Poetry Festival, 225–228
Germany, 29–31, 38–40, 66, 207
Ginsberg, Allen, 221–222, 226–228
Glen Ridge, 29–31; rape (1989),
    105–108
Glen Ridge Volunteer Ambulance
    Squad, 71–73
Gonnelli, Michael, 6
Gore, Al, 200
Graziolli, Margaret, 142–147
Great Depression, 11, 17, 35, 36, 94,
    203
Grecco, Claire, 150
Green, Ralph, 85–88
Guild of Master Sweeps, 54

Hackensack Meadowlands
    Development Commission
    (HMDC), 129, 148, 181
Hackensack River, 128–132
Hague, Frank, 138–139
Hamilo, Esko T., 49–51
Hansen, Joe, 108–110
Harmon Cove (Secaucus), 63,
    206–207
Hartz Mountain Industries, 15, 146,
    203, 206
Hayes, Robert, 71–73
health care, medicine, 12–16, 80–83,
    88–93, 110–113, 200–203. *See also*
    specific institutions
Hesterfer, Robert, 194–197
HMDC. *See* Hackensack Meadowlands
    Development Commission
hobbies, 36–47
Hoboken Volunteer Ambulance
    Corps, 91, 93
Holland, Fran, 137–141
homeless people, homelessness, 8, 9,
    10–12, 88–93
Hospital Center of Orange, 17
Howard Stern Chat Club (Prodigy),
    101–105
Huber Street School (Secaucus),
    165–166
Hudson County Correctional Facility,
    84–88
Hudson Dispatch, 49

Hudson Reporter Associates, xiv
Hudson River: A Natural and Unnatural History, The (Boyle), 130

Iacono, Paul and Anthony, 200–203
Immaculate Conception Church (Secaucus) 65
immigrants. *See specific countries*
Impreveduto, Anthony, 5, 32–34, 151–154
Impreveduto, Patrick, 33, 170
Impreveduto, Rocco, 31–34, 154
Independence (ship), 45
Independent Press of Bloomfield, 157
India, 51
Integrity House (Meadowview Hospital, Secaucus), 14, 80–83
Interfaith Council of Churches, 5
Intrepid Air and Sea Museum (New York City), 38
Ireland, 47–48, 66
Israel, 207–208

Jackson, Herb, xiii, xiv
Jersey City State College, 137
Jersey Journal, 143
Job Haines Home (Bloomfield), 16–18
Jones, Erin, 19–23
Just, Anthony, 60, 146, 182, 203–206

Kaplan, Harmon, 36–40
Kearny High School, 162–164
Kelip, John, 74
Kerr, David, 80, 106–108
Kessler Institute for Rehabilitation (East Orange), 79
Khmer Rouge, 191–193
Kieffer, Phil, 150
Knox, Bill, 117–120
Koenemund, William "Bo," 74
Koenig, William, 158–161, 195
Koeppen, Richard, 123–125
Korean War, 35

Language of Life, The (TV series), 226
Leukemia Society of America, 202
Leviathan (ship), 45
Lewis, Joel, 221–224, 227

Lewis, the Reverend Mark, 6, 60–65
Lincoln, Thomas, 105–108
Living Theater, 138
Lynch, Robert, 157–158

Mall at Mill Creek (Secaucus), 15
Manente, Sal, 146
Manney, Richard, 15
Markisello, Louis, 26–29
Mauritania (ship), 45
Maxwell, Kimberly, 84
Maxwell's (tavern, Hoboken), 223–224
Maycher, Dennis, 197–199
McClure, Al, 110–113, 114
McEnroe, Maryann, 3–4
McGrath, Terence, 78–80
McNiff, Jack, 79
Meadowlands Hospital (Secaucus), 14–15, 74
Meadowview Hospital (Secaucus), 57, 80, 206. *See also* Integrity House
Metropolitan Opera (New York City), 208
Mexico, 66
Miller, Bill, 43–47
Moore, James, 183
Mor, Amira, 209
Mother Teresa, 12
Mountainside Hospital (Glen Ridge), 71
Moyers, Bill, 226
municipal government, services, 24–25, 121–122, 132–141, 147–154, 180–183, 203–206. *See also* social services
Murray, Catherine, 6, 63
music, 65–67, 187–191, 207–209

NASA, 162–163, 197
National Association of Housing and Redevelopment Authority, 23
nature. *See* animals, nature
Netherlands, 24–25, 29–31
New Amsterdam (ship), 45
New Jersey Historical Miniature Association, 36
New Jersey MetroStars (soccer team), 200

New Jersey Nets (basketball team), 200
New Jersey Shore Marathon, 202
New Jersey Society of Certified Public Accountants, 165
New Jersey Supreme Court, 140
New Jersey Turnpike, 203
Newman, Andy, xv
New York Marathon, 202
New York University (New York City), 38
North Hudson Community Action Corporation, 15
Norton, James, 76–77

Oates, Joyce Carol, 93–96
O'Hara, John, 162–164
On the Waterfront (film), 94

Paine Webber (brokerage house), 9
Panasonic, 146, 206
Paper Mill Playhouse (Millburn), 200
Park Theater (Union City), 200–201
Pascrell, Bill, 121
Patterson, Floyd, 96
Peace Corps, 35
Pearl Harbor, 26–29
Pizzino, Angel, 79
Plate, Steve, 122
police. *See* emergency services
Pope, Dennis, 180–183
Port Authority of New York and New Jersey, 45
Pran, Dith, 191–193
Princeton University (Princeton), 94
Pumill, Dr. Rick, 75

Ravitch, Diane, 175
refugees. *See* Cambodia; Bosnia
Reilly, John, 74
Richardson, Michael, xiv
Rolnick, Diane, 97–100
Romania, 66
Ronell, Evelyn, 207–209
Rosenbaum, Karyn, 4–7
Rosenberg, Tracy, 12–16
Rosenblum & Rosenblum (law firm), 137
Rosie O'Donnell Show (TV show), 200

Ross, Lois, 125–128
Rubberbaby (pseud.), 101–105
Russia/Soviet Union, 35, 36, 42, 46, 50
Rutgers University Constitutional Law Clinic, 139
Ryan, Beere, 47–48

Saint Mary's Hospital (Hoboken), 88, 91, 93
Saint Thomas the Apostle Church (Bloomfield), 76
Sarajevo, Bosnia, 3
Scott, Willa, 7–10
Sears, Roebuck mail order, 68, 108
Secaucus Animal Hospital, 114–116
Secaucus Housing Authority (SHA) 5, 6, 19–23, 33
Secaucus Public Library, 142–147
Secaucus Community School, 65
Secaucus Middle School, 33, 170
Secaucus High School, 158–161, 195
See, Ellen, 72. 73
Seton Hall University (South Orange), 139
Sheehan, Bill, 128–132
Shot, Danny, 226, 227
Silent Spring (Carson), 130
Silk City Poets, 223
Silverman, Hershel, 223, 226
Simpson, Ron, 53–56
Skye, Elena, 229–233
Snyder, William, 6, 19–20
social services, 3–7, 10–12, 19–23. *See also* health care, medicine
South Africa, 217
Spalding, Alan, 91
Stern, Howard, 101–105
Stewart, Barbara, 225
Steinberg, Lisa, 97–100
Sullivan, Tom, 49–51

Tagliani, Joe, 74
tax assessor, Secaucus, 147–151
ten Velde, Nick, 24–25
Terhune, Jim, 147–151
Texas A&M University (College Station, Tex.), 115
Thoreau, Henry, 34

Titanic (ship), 17
Tomorrow's Children Institute
    (Hackensack), 200
Toy Soldier Company (Jersey City),
    40–43
Trauppner, Nancy, 212–214
Troubled Crusade, The (Ravitch), 175
Troyer, Tom, 183
Tufts University (Medford, Mass.),
    52
Twain, Mark, 96

United Nations, 49
United States Air Force, 30
United States Army, 26, 31, 41
United States Navy, 34, 35, 38, 109,
    167, 168
University of Medicine and Dentistry
    of New Jersey (Newark), 38
University of the South (Sewanee,
    Tenn.), 62
University of West Virginia
    (Morgantown), 109

Van Kouwenhoven, Jon, 176–180,
    187–191
Van Kouwenhoven, Nathan, 176–180
Veterans Administration, 14
Veterans of Foreign Wars, 32

Vietnam War, 38, 40 89, 91, 192
Virginia Theological Seminary
    (Alexandria, Va.), 62
Voyages (Miller), 46

Walden (Thoreau), 94
Waller, Mary, 152
Washington, George, 151
West, Ronald Jr., 12–16
Westinghouse, 35
Whitman, Christine Todd, 80
Wiecorneck, Martha, 56–57
Williams, William Carlos, 221
Woodstock (N.Y.), 233–238
World Cup soccer, 234
World Ship Society, 45
World War One, 17, 174
World War Two, 94, 175, 204, 207,
    223; downed pilot, 29–31;
    internment in Japanese concen-
    tration camp, 24; liberation of
    Dachau concentration camp,
    31–32; models, 38–40; Pearl
    Harbor, 26–29
Worrall Community Newspapers, xiv
writers and writing, 93–96, 218–228;
    bookstore, 229–233; libraries,
    142–147
WWOR-TV, 206

About the Author

Al Sullivan grew up in and around Paterson, New Jersey, and currently lives in Jersey City. After a troubled youth, he settled into a variety of professions that included truck driver, cook, baker, and salesman. He started writing in the early 1970s, publishing short stories and poems in various literary magazines. In 1982, he was co-founder or an underground New Jersey literary newspaper called *Scrap Paper Review*. In 1985, he worked briefly for the *Paterson News* as a stringer and, in 1988, for Today Newspapers in Butler. Since then, he has worked as a staff writer for the Hudson Reporter Associates and the Worrall Community Newspapers where he has won numerous awards from the New Jersey Society of Professional Journalists and the New Jersey Press Association. He is currently senior staff writer with the Hudson Reporter Associates.